MICHEL FOUCAULT'S

ARCHAEOLOGY OF

WESTERN CULTURE

Michel Foucault's Archæology of Western Culture Toward a New Science of History Pamela Major-Poetzl

The Harvester Press

First published in Great Britain in 1983 by
THE HARVESTER PRESS LIMITED
Publisher: John Spiers
16 Ship Street, Brighton, Sussex

© 1983 The University of North Carolina Press

ISBN 0-7108-0484-9

To my parents
Muriel and Stephen Major

CONTENTS

PREFACE

When I began to study his works ten years ago, Michel Foucault was recognized as a major thinker in France, but was still largely ignored in the United States. By the time this study was completed in 1979, American interest in Foucault had increased considerably, due in part to the publication of *Discipline and Punish: The Birth of the Prison* (1975) and the introductory volume of *The History of Sexuality* (1976). These two works, as well as Foucault's earlier study *Madness and Civilization: A History of Insanity in the Age of Reason* (1961), have appealed largely because they offer new perspectives on fundamental problems in our society. Yet Foucault's major work to date, *The Order of Things: An Archaeology of the Human Sciences* (1966), has had little impact outside France, and the significance of Foucault's "archaeological" method for historical studies is still a relatively unexplored issue.

Since I am primarily concerned with Foucault's methodology, I have examined his "archaeological" studies in order to discover the categories he establishes. The structure of Foucault's analyses attracted me because, despite his unusual terminology and extraordinary style, I sensed something strangely familiar in his works. Foucault's effort to dissolve the objects of thought and to view the knowing subject in terms of varying functions within a spatiotemporal field struck me as a vision of "the order of things" almost identical to that which modern physics presents to our imagination. Foucault himself does not claim to be adapting relativity theory to the study of cultural phenomena, and he would probably oppose the effort to reduce his "archaeological" studies to a form of field theory. Nonetheless, it is the similarity between archaeology and field theory that has made me wonder if Foucault's abstract and seemingly artificial constructions might actually be the first step in the formation of a new science of history independent of the nineteenth-century model of evolutionary biology.

Foucault's method and the substance of his arguments are inter-related, since he has collapsed the distinctions between form and content; as a result, meanings emerge from the structure of his analyses. A general discussion of Foucault's "archaeological" methodology and the principal issues he addresses are the topics of the first half of this work (chapters 1 through 3). Chapter 1 attempts to locate archaeology between the established disciplines of history and philosophy and draws primarily on Foucault's methodological study *The Archaeology of Knowledge* (1969). Chapter 2 examines a number of Foucault's published articles and interviews in order to present Foucault's own explanation of his purposes, his interpretation of major cultural figures (Nietzsche, Marx, and Freud), and his assessment of the relationship between power and knowledge. Chapter 3 summarizes the history of field-theory physics and isolates those concepts similar to concepts Foucault employs in his archaeologies. This chapter also discusses Gaston Bachelard's historical epistemology and Georges Canguilhem's history of science, since these studies have been significant influences on Foucault and since both Bachelard and Canguilhem dealt explicitly with the relation between modern science and epistemology. Finally, chapter 3 concludes with a brief discussion of Kuhn's concept of paradigms, Saussure's theory of linguistics, and Foucault's literary essays in an effort to suggest that Foucault's work is part of a larger cultural paradigm which spans contemporary scientific, social, and literary thought.

The second half of this work (chapters 4 and 5) deals specifically with four of Foucault's early publications. Since these writings vary considerably, I have had to approach them in different ways. Foucault's first work, *Mental Illness and Psychology* (1954), is short and relatively straightforward, and I have limited myself to a summary of those issues that suggest the direction of his subsequent studies. *Madness and Civilization* (1961) is a more complicated work which I have cut through at four levels: the metaphysical level encompassing the relation between Reason and Unreason; the general cultural perception of madness; the specific medical perception of madness; and the historical conditions that contributed to the confinement of the mad. *The Birth of the Clinic* (1963), Foucault's first archaeology, presented special problems because it has almost no narrative line and imposes itself as a nearly impenetrable bloc of overlapping and irregularly shifting perceptual structures. I tried to separate these structures and to construct a narrative line, a procedure that distorted Foucault's text but hopefully also rendered it more accessible.

The Order of Things (1966) posed very different problems. There is both a historical (temporal) and a structural (spatial) dimension to this work, so there was no need to superimpose a temporal order. The main difficulties were comprehension and selection. Like other speculative philosophies of history, this work is virtually inexhaustible in its richness and originality. I have extracted what I believe to be the principal organizing categories, and the result is a radical simplification in two major parts: a general overview of the entire work and an examination of the specific "shape" of knowledge in each of Foucault's four epistemological structures (epistemes).

Among the many controversies that *The Order of Things* has provoked, two issues have predominated. One is the problem raised by the seemingly inexplicable gaps separating Foucault's archaeological "strata," which has resulted in charges that his work cannot account for change and is therefore antihistorical. The other more passionately argued issue arises from Foucault's assertion that the study of man as both a knowing subject and a knowable object is a recent phenomenon in Western thought and that the Age of Man is coming to an end. As a result, Foucault has been accused of antihumanism. Less attention has been given in the critical literature to the more basic question of the meaning of Foucault's conception of order. In this study Foucault's archaeology, like modern physics, is seen as an abstract and highly formalized system of knowledge that imposes order on a more fundamental experience of disorder and throws into doubt the traditional categories of scientific and social thought.

Although this book does not examine Foucault's postarchaeological publications, a brief discussion of these works is included in the epilogue. After the French uprising in 1968, Foucault turned to a more explicit analysis of power—a concern reflected in his subsequent studies of the French penal system and the history of Western sexuality. Despite the thematic continuity between these two works and Foucault's earlier publications, there is a distinct methodological break between Foucault's last archaeology, *The Archaeology of Knowledge* (1969), and *Discipline and Punish* (1975). Foucault refers to his latest studies as "genealogies" and plans to publish an additional five volumes on the genealogy of Western sexuality. Until this series is completed, it will be difficult to assess the relationship between

Foucault's "archaeological" and "genealogical" works. Alan Sheridan has begun to explore this issue in a recent book entitled *Michel Foucault: The Will to Truth*. Sheridan's study, as well as several recent articles, are included in the bibliography, although they appeared after this manuscript was completed. With the literature on and by Foucault growing rapidly, this bibliography cannot claim to be exhaustive.

I have not included in the text a discussion of my own methods, although it must be quite obvious that my methods are those used in the history of ideas and consist largely of assumptions Foucault has rejected. I have assumed, for example, that there is a continuity within and between Foucault's early works and have consequently minimized the discontinuities that no doubt exist. I have also suggested that Foucault could be located by placing his work between supposedly coherent disciplines such as history and philosophy, and that "archaeology" could be made familiar (and thus less original) by invoking cultural traditions (such as Cartesian, Kantian, and Hegelian philosophy) and specific influences (such as Bachelard and Canguilhem). I recognize, however, that disciplines, traditions, and influences do not really explain Foucault's thought and that "archaeology" may be part of an unconscious perceptual structure which determines what can be thought and what will be believed in our time. If there is a "deep structure" to contemporary thought, language may determine its form but modern physics must be its major expression, since without the prestige and power of this form of knowledge much of contemporary thought would be either unthinkable or unbelievable.

The research and writing of this book would have been much more difficult without the assistance of many people to whom I am indebted. I would like to thank, first, the reference librarians at Mount Holyoke College, particularly Nancy Devine, who made important and nearly inaccessible materials available to me. I am also grateful to Thomas S. Szasz of the SUNY Upstate Medical Center, Linda Klafter of the University of Rochester, Joyce Berkman and Norman Simonson of the University of Massachusetts, R. Jackson Wilson of Smith College, and Stanley Goldberg of Hampshire College, who have given me new perspectives and needed encouragement. I owe a special debt to Charles Rearick of the University of Massachusetts, whose patience, kindness, and gentle criticism allowed me the freedom to follow my own interests at my own pace while protecting me from many errors.

My deepest gratitude goes to my parents and to my husband, although I can express here only a small portion of my debt to them. My father, Stephen Major, not only read and corrected my manuscript with loving care, but translated several Italian articles that greatly assisted my research. My mother, Muriel Major, proofread both the Italian and French translations and provided, in her superb manner, a continuing source of encouragement and assistance. Finally, I would like to thank by husband, Herbert Poetzl, for aiding me in my research, listening to my ideas, and carefully editing and proofreading the entire manuscript.

Pamela Major-Poetzl
Binghamton, New York, 1982

MICHEL FOUCAULT'S

ARCHAEOLOGY OF

WESTERN CULTURE

A NEW SCIENCE BETWEEN

PHILOSOPHY AND HISTORY

A Model from Physics

A new concept appears in physics, the most important
invention since Newton's time: the field. It needed great
scientific imagination to realize that it is not the charges nor
the particles but the field in the space between the charges
and particles which is essential for the description of physical phenomena. . . . Could we not reject the concept of
matter and build a pure field physics?
Albert Einstein and Leopold Infeld, *The Evolution of Physics*

We must rid ourselves of a whole mass of notions, each of
which, in its own way, diversifies the theme of continuity.
. . . We must recognize that they may not, in the last resort,
be what they seem at first sight. In short, that they require a
theory, and that this theory cannot be constructed unless the
field of the facts of discourse on the basis of which those
facts are built up appears in its non-synthetic purity. And I,
in turn, will do no more than this.
Michel Foucault, *The Archaeology of Knowledge*

The first statement, made by Einstein and Infeld, indicates
the arrival of a new theoretical model, a model that had already
established itself when these words were written in 1938 and has
since dominated all reflection on the nature of physical phenomena.
The second statement, made by Foucault in 1969, refers to a point of
departure from traditional forms of philosophical reflection and indicates the need to formulate a new model for the analysis of cultural
phenomena. Both Einstein and Foucault have expressed profoundly

3

new ways of thinking, ways that violate the evidence of our senses and the assumptions of our culture. For both thinkers this has involved a fundamental reordering of previous forms of classifying phenomena and a fundamental redefinition of major concepts. And for both Einstein and Foucault, the new organizing principle is the concept of the "field."

Einstein's field theory has shifted attention from things (particles) and abstract forces (charges and gravity) onto the structure of space itself. Although Einstein was not able to eliminate things (matter) entirely and to develop a theory of pure relations, he was able to equate matter and energy and to formulate laws describing matter-energy fields. These descriptions, however, had two remarkable peculiarities. First, they were not constant but varied with the spatiotemporal position of the observer. Second, they revealed a fundamental discontinuity: matter-energy fields (as was demonstrated for electrons and photons) change by a series of quantum jumps rather than in a continuous fashion. These characteristics of modern field theory, as well as other aspects of relativity theory and quantum mechanics, have had dramatic consequences. The technological power of science has been enormously expanded, but at the same time the conceptual basis of science has become more abstract and more tentative. Simultaneously, traditional philosophical as well as scientific concepts of time, space, objects (substances), subjects (observers), and change (causality) have been radically altered.

Michel Foucault, a contemporary French thinker whose formal training has been in philosophy and psychology,[1] is concerned with precisely these concepts, and he has developed a theory of cultural systems very similar to field theory in modern physics. But, rather than remain within the confines of epistemology or the philosophy of science, Foucault has sought to combine theory and practice in a new discipline that he calls "archaeology." His archaeology deals with many of the same issues which have traditionally been the province of history and philosophy, but is based on a different mode of analysis and a different set of concepts. Indeed, one of the first tasks of this archaeology is to distinguish itself from the conceptual structure of both history and philosophy and to question those "notions" which assume that change is a continuous process. Among these notions are many of the concepts historians have invoked to explain change —the notions of "tradition," "influence," "development," and "evolution." Other concepts that function for both philosophers and historians to ensure continuity are the ideas of a "spirit of an age" and of the inherent unity of the "books" and "collected works" of an "author."[2]

Foucault's archaeology, by contrast, treats discontinuous change and different "strata" of the past. It is concerned with description rather than interpretation and questions those abstract forces (Reason, History, Libido) used to explain phenomena in terms of something else. And archaeology is suspicious of objects. It aims "to dispense with 'things' " and seeks to examine "the space in which various objects emerge and are transformed" and to describe "*systems of dispersion.*"[3] Most radical, however, is the intention of archaeology to dispense with the subject and thus to reject all speculation based on the continuity of consciousness or the universality of human nature. The subject becomes merely "an empty function," a "vacant place that may in fact be filled by different individuals . . . [but] this place varies."[4] Thus archaeology, like field theory, has shifted attention from things (objects) and abstract forces (ideas) to the structure of "discourses" (organized bodies of knowledge and practice, such as clinical medicine) in their specific spatiotemporal articulations. Although Foucault, like Einstein, has not been able to eliminate the concept of things entirely and build a theory of pure relations, he has been able to relativize "words" and "things" and to formulate rules describing epistemological fields ("epistemes"). But his descriptions of these fields, like Einstein's descriptions of physical fields, reveal two disturbing peculiarities: they reduce the role of subjects to variable functions in time and space, and they involve fundamental discontinuities in the conception of cultural change.

These are strange ideas. They are in fact so strange as to be, like Einstein's, practically unthinkable. However, while Einstein's theories rest on a firm basis of mathematical proof in addition to extensive experimental verification, Foucault has no such mathematical language at his disposal. He is forced to use words, words that he must first wrench from their accustomed meanings and put into a new series of relationships. This task has involved a complex dialogue in which he is continually discussing, in an endless series of variations, both what he is and what he is not saying. Yet Foucault's efforts to challenge both the concepts and the limits of established fields of knowledge have already shown impressive results. His "archaeological" analyses have enabled him to penetrate into the past—into what is no longer thought but may once have been thought—and to examine the present as well as the past in terms of what has been excluded as unthinkable. Foucault's studies of madness, medicine, crime, and sexuality portray a series of abruptly changing perceptions of rationality, health, and normalcy from the Renaissance to the present.[5] These studies, furthermore, have revealed the systematic nature of the exclusion of people classified as mad, sick, criminal, or deviant, and have illuminated the intimate relationship between power and knowledge.

Foucault has also written a penetrating study of similar perceptions, of what it was possible to know in a group of related discourses within specific "epistemic" periods between the Renaissance and the modern period. *The Order of Things*[6] is an examination of various discourses on life (natural history, biology, psychology), labor (analyses of wealth, political economy, sociology), and language (general grammar, philology, literature). But rather than studying how the earlier discourses "progressed" into subsequent discourses, Foucault has described the formations and transformations specific to each discourse and the interrelations of discourses within the same epistemological field. However, before a further discussion of the nature of Foucault's cultural field theory or the basic features of field theory in physics, it may be useful to briefly examine Foucault's relationship to philosophy and history in order to understand where he intends to locate his own archaeological discourse.

The Limits of Philosophy

"It seems to me that philosophy today no longer exists—not that it has disappeared but that it is dispersed in a large number of diverse activities: thus the activity of the axiomatician, the linguist, the ethnologist, the historian, the revolutionary, the politician can be forms of philosophical activity."[7] The dispersion of philosophy discussed by Foucault is made visible by the fact that many contemporary French philosophers have moved into other disciplines. It is perhaps also the reason why academic philosophy in France is presently viewed as bankrupt.[8] Tensions within the discipline, however, have been evident for some time. According to Emile Bréhier,[9] philosophy had already split into two major tendencies in the 1930s. The first was a tendency toward concreteness in which "structures and forms appear as a datum which cannot be constructed by the mind but is simply reported or described."[10] This tendency was represented by men such as Jean Laporte, who offered a critique of the concept of abstract categories of mind, and by two philosophers of science, Gaston Bachelard and Stéphane Lupasco, who attempted to assess the significance of new concepts from modern physics for philosophy. Bachelard recognized that certain fundamental concepts in physics, such as mass, could not be abstracted from the conditions under which they are experienced (since, for example, mass alters with velocity) and that it was incumbent upon philosophy as well as physics to seek a new precision "at the level of principles and concepts."[11] Stéphane Lupasco, influenced by new discoveries in quantum physics, especially by Heisenberg's uncertainty principle, attempted to formulate a new logic based on the concept of "dynamic contradiction" in which determinism and indeterminism coexist.[12] A similar idea was developed in the philosophy of values by Eugène Dupréel, for whom a "concept . . . summons up the corrective of its *anticoncept*. This word does not mean its contrary but its complement."[13] Other representatives of this tendency toward concreteness include Étienne Souriau, who set out to discover "universal laws of philosophy" through a process of opposition that involved a "law of destruction,"[14] and Raymond Ruyer, whose *Outline of a Philosophy of Structure* (1930) attempted to establish a nonmaterialistic mechanism which would reveal that each "form had its own reality, patterns of behavior and laws."[15] Although these philosophers were still working within established schools of thought, they dealt with many of the issues that concern contemporary structuralists (among whom Foucault is often classified): an interest in structure itself, the relevance of science for other disciplines, the need for a new form of conceptualization, and an interest in systems of opposition (a dialectic without a synthesis).

And yet it was not this current of thinking which dominated the 1940s and 1950s; that role fell to what Bréhier identified as the second tendency of philosophy during the 1930s, namely, the subjectivist tendency, which was represented primarily by Husserl and Heidegger. With the coming of the second world war and the birth of the French resistance movement, the meaning of "existence" and the role of "subjects" became vital concerns, and the subjectivist tendency became predominant. It took two main forms: existentialism and phenomenology. Existentialism, particularly as developed by Sartre, stressed individuality, consciousness, and free choice. Phenomenology in France was represented mainly by Merleau-Ponty, who applied Husserl's method to a study of perception. Both Sartre and Merleau-Ponty attempted to accommodate their subjectivist philosophies to Marxism, which resulted in uneasy alliances between philosophies rooted in individual freedom and a theory based on economic determinism. During this same period, and stimulated by a similar concern with Marxism, there was a French revival of interest in Hegel. Jean Hyppolite, through his translations of Hegel's works and his years of teaching at the Sorbonne, the Collège de France, and the École normale supérieur (an elite school that has produced most of France's intellectuals, including Foucault), was the dominant figure in this revival.[16] Foucault, who was born in 1926, reached adulthood during these years, and his early philosophical interests centered on Husserl, Hegel, and Marx.

But by the 1960s philosophical concerns in France had changed. The publication of Sartre's *Critique of Dialectical Reason* in 1960 failed to produce a revival of existentialism and instead "marked the end of its reign in France."[17] Interest in phenomenology also declined, although Husserl (more than Merleau-Ponty) continued to be studied seriously.[18] Hegelian studies too decreased during the sixties, but Marxist studies continued unabated and a radical new interpretation was given to Marx's writings by the philosopher Louis Althusser (one of Foucault's teachers). The philosophy of science enjoyed a resurgence in the 1960s, and despite the fact that Bachelard's publications in the 1950s were largely psychoanalytic and literary, his earlier studies in epistemology and philosophy of science exerted a continuous influence throughout the 1950s and 1960s—an influence that is still strong, particularly among the "groupe d'épistémologie" at the École normale supérieur.[19] Another important development in the 1960s was the belated acceptance of Freudian studies, which displaced attention from traditional French philosophies of consciousness to an investigation of unconscious phenomena. Modern linguistics, particularly Saussure's and Chomsky's works, have also been extremely influential in France since the 1960s.[20]

These changed philosophic interests are reflected in the new "structuralist" studies that have dominated French thought since 1960.[21] Their differences notwithstanding, "structuralists" share a common interest in the nature of language and in the structure of nonconscious forms of thought and expression. More remarkably, they share a deep distrust for metaphysics and a sense that philosophy can no longer be contained within a single discipline. Consequently, Jacques Lacan is a psychoanalyst, Jacques Derrida a linguist, Claude Lévi-Strauss an ethnologist, and Michel Foucault an "archaeologist"—representatives of the four human sciences that threaten to replace philosophy as the focus of speculative thought.

Foucault's own archaeological studies, then, represent not so much a rejection of philosophical interests as a conviction that comprehensive synthetic philosophies are no longer possible and that theoretical work must take place within more concrete and limited areas. In this sense Foucault has continued that tendency toward concreteness discussed above, but has moved from the reflective posture of philosophy of science to an application of such a philosophy. However, Foucault has rejected all forms of subjectivist philosophy, the philosophy which dominated his own education in the late 1940s. In recounting his cultural formation, he recalled that:

> As all of my generation, I was . . . formed by the school of phenomenology . . . [and] by the problem of the relationship between . . . phenomenological method and Marxist method. And I believe that, as for all of those in my generation, between 1950 and 1955 I experienced a kind of conversion that at the beginning seemed nothing, but that in reality has deeply differentiated us. . . . In other words, we re-examined the Husserlian idea that there is meaning everywhere. . . . And from 1955 we dedicated ourselves mainly to the analyses of the formal conditions of the appearance of meaning.[22]

Analyzing the "formal conditions of the appearance of meaning" meant that Foucault has studied patterns of perception that are largely unconscious and deterministic. This required a rejection of all philosophies from Descartes to Sartre that are based on consciousness. It also led Foucault to examine Kant's relation to subjectivist philosophy and in 1964 to publish a translation of what is perhaps Kant's most subjectivist work, *Anthropology from a Pragmatic Point of View*.[23] Moreover, in spite of his admiration for Jean Hyppolite, Foucault broke with Hegelianism.[24] Before 1968, however, he had not rejected Marxism, despite his hostility toward dialectics.

Foucault's denial of transcendentalism, the primacy of the subject, and the Marxian notion of historical change has brought him into conflict with existentialism, a conflict that the French press frequently reduces to a confrontation between Sartre and Foucault. Foucault's

1966 interview with Madeleine Chapsal, given after the appearance of his controversial *Order of Things*, intensified this debate. In discussing the reorientation of philosophical thought since the 1950s, Foucault commented that:

> We have experienced Sartre's generation as a generation certainly courageous and generous, which had a passion for life, politics, existence. . . . But we, we have discovered something else, another passion: the passion for concepts and for what I will call "system." . . . By system it is necessary to understand an ensemble of relations which maintain themselves and transform themselves independently of the things they connect . . . an anonymous system without subjects. . . . The "I" has exploded (look at modern literature).[25]

It is this explosion of the "I" which, according to Foucault, has made existentialism untenable. But Sartre, in a special issue of *L'Arc* entitled *Sartre Today*, responded primarily to the political implication of the new structuralist studies. According to Sartre, "Foucault gives the people what they needed: an eclectic synthesis in which Robbe-Grillet, structuralism, linguistics, Lacan, and *Tel Quel* are systematically utilized to demonstrate the impossibility of historical reflection. . . . The task is to come up with a new ideology: the latest barrier that the bourgeoisie once again can erect against Marx."[26] For Sartre the "disappearance, or as Lacan says, the 'decentration' of the subject, is needed just to discredit history."[27] Sartre's concern is not to deny cognitive or historical structures (he does not deny them), but to return to what he considers essential, and this is "not that man is made, but *that he makes that which made him*."[28]

Foucault's response to these statements was published (without his permission) in an article in *La Quinzaine littéraire* in 1968.[29] He defined the purpose of his own work as an effort to discover the unconscious rules that govern knowledge, including scientific knowledge. He assumed that these rules would be as systematic as those governing the individual unconscious, and he clearly did not feel that an analysis of the individual's conscious control of the social forces that "made" him was the essential issue. Nor did he feel that his position made historical reflection impossible. What it did do was to destroy the philosopher's myth of History, that is, history viewed as a "type of grand and vast continuity." Foucault further denied that he represented a bourgeois defense against Marx; he noted, in fact, that during his previous (and brief) involvement with the Communist party Sartre himself was viewed by the Communists as "the last bulwark of bourgeois imperialism."[30]

The real issue in this debate, however, was not the relative purity of Sartre's or Foucault's Marxism, but the status of a humanistic philosophy that Sartre defended and Foucault rejected. As Foucault made clear in his "archaeological" works (particularly in *The Order of Things*), the concept of man upon which modern humanism is based was developed in the nineteenth century and is rapidly disintegrating in the twentieth century. Moreover, Foucault is pleased at the prospect of its imminent demise, for he views humanism as the "prostitute" of all postwar culture. He maintains that this humanism, which "justified both Stalinism and the Christian-Democratic hegemony, . . . is the same humanism found in Camus or in Sartre's existentialism."[31] And it is this humanism, Foucault insists, that is "cut off from the scientific and technical world which is our real world."[32] In opposition to a decaying humanism, Foucault defends

> the attempt made by those of our generation, which is not to assert man *against* knowledge and *against* technology, but is precisely to show that our life, our way of being, even our daily habits, are a part of the same systematic organization and are thus dependent on the *same* categories as the scientific and technological world. It is the "human heart" which is abstract and it is our research, which wishes to tie man to his science, to his discoveries, to his world, which is concrete.[33]

Such concrete studies, however, are often written in a language so dense as to be practically impenetrable. And they combine, at least for Foucault, two sources of philosophical inspiration that at first sight appear contradictory. On the one hand, Foucault has welcomed a number of philosophical formalisms: theories derived from the philosophy of language and logic, from mathematics, and from philosophy of science in general. On the other hand, Foucault claims as his true intellectual mentor that most unsystematic of all philosophers: Nietzsche. And he counts among the most profound of modern thinkers a series of antirationalists from Sade to Artaud and Bataille.

These two seemingly divergent interests really reflect, once again, a single concern—the elimination of the Subject. Formalism displaces philosophical inquiry from the subject to the system; Nietzsche explodes the subject from within. And Nietzsche reveals, according to Foucault, the limits of philosophy. Philosophy can no longer aspire to synthesis; its proper function is criticism, diagnosis, demythologizing. And for this one needs to philosophize with a hammer.

The Limits of History

"History, in its traditional form, undertook to 'memorize' the *monuments* of the past, [to] transform them into *documents* . . . in our time, history is that which transforms *documents* into *monuments*. . . . There was a time when archaeology, as a discipline devoted to silent monuments, . . . aspired to the condition of history . . . in our time history aspires to the condition of archaeology, to the intrinsic description of the monument."[34] Traditionally history has sought to seize the artifacts of the past, to remove them from the field in which they were located, and to erase those features that testified to their fundamental strangeness. It has sought to render the unfamiliar familiar (to transform "monuments" into "documents"), and to do so it imposed on these artifacts "interpretations" which blurred the differences between past and present. Such interpretations assumed that the past was either an embryonic form of the present or a variation on a set of constant human themes, retrievable because of the unchanging and universal nature of a collective consciousness. Conventional archaeology, on the other hand, describes artifacts as they appear and as they are found in relation to other artifacts in the same archaeological layer. It does not attempt to erase the uniqueness of the artifact nor to blur the borders separating different archaeological layers. It seeks, rather, to make differences visible.

Foucault's "archaeological" analysis is also concerned with description, field relationships, and discontinuous change. But it must first get rid of those notions upon which the concept of continuity is based. One such notion is the belief that a book is an independent whole. According to Foucault, however, "the frontiers of a book are never clear-cut . . . beyond its internal configuration and its autonomous form, it is caught up in a system of references to other books, other texts, other sentences: it is a node within a network . . . its unity is variable and relative. . . . As soon as one questions that unity, it loses its self-evidence; it indicates itself, constructs itself, only on the basis of a complex field of discourse."[35] Like the book, the oeuvre of an author represents a questionable unity, based as it is on the assumption that certain writings are significant and that others, which have been excluded from the collected works, are not. But the process of selection itself "presupposes a number of choices that are difficult to justify or even to formulate." What status, Foucault inquires, "should be given to letters, notes, reported conversations . . . in short to that vast mass of verbal traces left by an individual at his death? . . . In fact, if one speaks . . . of an author's *oeuvre*, it is because one imagines it to be defined by a certain expressive function. . . . But it is at once apparent that such a unity, far from being given immediately, is the result of an operation; that this operation is interpretive."[36] Beyond the oeuvre, Foucault questions those more encompassing unities called disciplines, which establish the independence of major forms of knowledge. He doubts that one can accept the distinctions between science, philosophy, history, and literature, for example.

We are not even sure of ourselves when we use these distinctions in our own world of discourse . . . but neither literature, nor politics, nor philosophy and the sciences articulated the field of discourse, in the seventeenth and eighteenth century, as they did in the nineteenth century. In any case, these divisions . . . are always themselves reflexive categories, principles of classification, normative rules, institutionalized types . . . they are not intrinsic, autochthonous, and universally recognizable characteristics.[37]

On an even larger scale, Foucault challenges the idea of "forces" that unite such tenuous entities as books, oeuvres, and disciplines within the same time period or between different periods. Thus he regards with suspicion the notion of tradition, which reduces differences by referring disparate phenomena to a common origin. Tradition, Foucault believes, "makes it possible to rethink the dispersion of history in the form of the same; it allows a reduction of the difference proper to every beginning, in order to pursue without discontinuity the endless search for the origin; tradition enables us to isolate the new against a background of permanence, and to transfer its merit to originality, to genius, to the decisions proper to individuals."[38] Even more pernicious and indefensible than tradition is the notion of influence. Foucault describes the effects of this concept in much the same way that modern scientists criticize the Newtonian concept of gravity and the belief in "ether." The idea of influence,

Foucault claims, "provides a support—of too magical a kind to be very amenable to analysis—for the facts of transmission and communication; which . . . links, at a distance and through time—as if through the mediation of a medium of propagation—such defined unities as individuals, *oeuvres*, notions, or theories."[39] And this brings Foucault to a consideration and rejection of the entrenched concepts of development and evolution, concepts that "make it possible to group a succession of dispersed events, to link them to one and the same organizing principle . . . to discover, already at work in each beginning, a principle of coherence and the outline of a future unity."[40] Finally, there is the notion of spirit, world view, or "climate of opinion," which is frequently invoked to characterize an ensemble of relations that are not themselves analyzed. For Foucault, the concept of spirit "enables us to establish between the simultaneous or successive phenomena of a given period a community of meanings, symbolic links, an interplay of resemblance and reflexion, or which allows the sovereignty of collective consciousness to emerge as the principle of unity and explanation."[41]

None of these concepts, according to Foucault, are valid as explanatory constructs. They are, rather, specific modes of classification with their place and function in an epistemological structure that enforces similarities and minimizes differences. The task for archaeology is to question the self-evidence of such classifications, to reveal differences, to locate these differences within a field, and to recognize multiple forms of discontinuous change. In this task archaeology is assisted by recent developments within the discipline of history itself. On the one hand, "history proper" (political, social, economic, and cultural history), at least in France, has substantially altered the concept of historical time and has introduced new concepts of spatial relationships. On the other hand, histories of ideas (e.g., histories of philosophy, science, and literature) have introduced various concepts of discontinuity into their theory and practice. Consequently, history "in our time" is approaching archaeology and may eventually absorb it.

Both types of changes within the historical profession have been welcomed by Foucault. He has benefited particularly from theoretical developments in the histories of ideas, and mentions as especially significant the following concepts:

There are the *epistemological acts* and *thresholds* described by
Bachelard . . . they direct historical analysis away from the search
for silent beginnings . . . toward the search for a new type of
rationality. . . . There are the *displacements* and *transformations* of
concepts; the analyses of G. Canguilhem may serve as models;
they show that a history of a concept is not wholly and entirely
that of its progressive refinement . . . but that of its various fields
of constitution and validity. . . . [There are] *recurrent redistributions* [which] reveal several pasts . . . for one and the same science,
as its present undergoes change . . . (in the field of mathematics,
M. Serres has provided the theory of this phenomenon). There
are *architectonic unities* of systems of the kind analyzed by
M. Guéroult, which are concerned not with the description of
cultural influences, traditions, and continuities, but with internal
coherences.[42]

These concepts of threshold, displacement, redistribution, and transformation are all concerned with the structure of a field and with the
process of restructuring which produces discontinuous change—
change marked by sudden shifts and jumps, by ruptures and systematic rearrangements. This is a concept of change far removed from
the evolutionary model of Darwinian biology but very similar to the
concept of quantum jumps in contemporary physics. It also shares
certain similarities with concepts of change found in other twentieth-
century sciences, mutation in biology and plate tectonics in geology,
for example.

Foucault's relation to "history proper" is somewhat more ambivalent, although he admires the innovations introduced by the *Annales*
school and is respected by many of the theorists of the "new history"
of the 1960s and 1970s. Since the *Annales* school has been the
dominant school of historical scholarship in France for the last thirty
years, it may be worthwhile to summarize briefly the characteristics
of what Traian Stoianovich has called its "functional-structural" paradigm.[43] According to Fernand Braudel, a leading figure in the *Annales* group, this paradigm was formed in the 1930s and implemented
in the following decades.[44] It was inspired in part by the efforts of
Henri Berr to "construct a scientific philosophy of history"[45] in the
early decades of this century. Berr's *Revue de synthèse historique*, which
articulated his project for a synthetic and scientific history, challenged
historians' preoccupation with political events and sought to unite

history and sociology. This project attracted young scholars, particularly Marc Bloch and Lucien Febvre, the founders of the journal *Annales d'histoire économique et sociale*, who wished to broaden history even further by incorporating economics and geography. Subsequent generations of *Annales* historians have drawn upon ever more diverse areas of inquiry, among them psychology, linguistics, and anthropology. They have also been increasingly critical of narrative history and have been prepared to view change "not as progress, regular development or continuity, but in terms of a need for other functions, or as part of a process of structuring, destructuring, and restructuring."[46]

During the 1950s, under the impact of Braudel's leadership and the example of his monumental *La Méditerranée* (1949), *Annales* scholars investigated the "dialectical tension between space and time."[47] Braudel combined geography and history into a "geohistory" that considered both the distribution of phenomena in space and the interaction of several different types of historical time. This interest in spatial relationships has made the *Annales* school receptive to studies such as those charting the outbreak of revolutionary panics, the spread of contagious diseases, and the relationship between climate and demography.[48] It has also led to the incorporation of contemporary spatial models such as communication theory from linguistics and theories of exchange from anthropology.

Just as important as this interest in spatial configurations was the sophistication with which Braudel analyzed temporal changes. He distinguished three main varieties of historical time: *temps géographique*, in which "change is almost imperceptible and consists of extremely slow cyclic regularities"; *temps social*, which deals with "shifts in economic and social structures to produce *une histoire lentement rythmée*"; and *temps individuel*, which consists of "transitory, disjointed daily events."[49] The combination of Braudel's interest in extensive geographical areas, long periods of time, and shifts in structures has been the effort to create a total, or global, history—what Braudel calls "une impossible science globale de l'homme."[50] According to Traian Stoianovich, this global science of man represents the merging of three older traditions:

> The extension to history of a tendency manifest in epistemology, biology, field-theory physics, and Gestalt, or configurationist, psychology, during the 1920s and 1930s to replace "the earlier

purposive view with that of wholeness." . . . total history derives
also from Marx's conception of the "total man" and "total society."
. . . A third tradition comes from the anthropology of Marcel
Mauss, which maintains that a "total social fact" is expressed
socially, psychologically, and historically, and that the observer is
included in each observation, just as the symbolic system of the
unconscious is contained in each fact observed.[51]

All of these traditions represent an interest in structured "wholes,"
and have encouraged *Annales* historians to seek such structures in
previously neglected areas and to consider unconscious as well as
conscious structures. This has led to the "demasculinization of history" and to histories "of women, of youth, of childhood, of oral
cultures, of voluntary associations, [and] of non-Western civiliza-
tions."[52] It has prepared historians to "look at a text not only for
what it says but for its silence as well," to focus on repetition (as
manifested in festivals and folklore) rather than on evolution, and
to look more closely at the recurrent drama of life and death.[53] It
has also encouraged some French historians to welcome Foucault's
archaeologies as a stimulus for further expansion of their own research.[54]

Besides the structural dimension of the *Annales* paradigm, there
is also a functional dimension, which stresses localized subsystems
of relations and is critical of the attempt to write "total" histories.
Stoianovich sees Foucault's interest in archaeological strata and the
relationships within epistemological fields of separate strata as an example of functionalism. He is concerned that such functional studies
will result in an antihistorical posture that rejects all temporal relationships. Moreover, he is alarmed by Foucault's efforts to "remove
subjective factors . . . to summon man and society only to the extent
necessary to identify the epistemes, or ordering codes, underlying
the functions of human discourse."[55] This concern is shared by other
French historians, although some, particularly those who advocate a
"new history" (what Pierre Nora calls *une histoire autre*), view Foucault's archaeologies as models for the study of contemporary history.[56] This latter group fears that contemporary history is rapidly
being displaced by the mass media, which eliminate all but the most
trivial events.[57] They believe that contemporary historians need a
different kind of history, one which allows them to step "out of their
own time into 'another time'" in order to see "the present through

the prism and strangeness of the past."[58] And this, they think, is what Foucault's histories of madness, disease, crime, sexuality, and the human sciences (literature, psychology, and sociology) have done.

Foucault's works have also appealed to theoretically minded historians specializing in areas other than contemporary history. Paul Veyne, for example, who teaches the history of Rome at the Collège de France, is interested in reexamining fundamental historical concepts and questions, not merely the notion of linear time but also the nature of historical objects. Events, he feels, cannot be viewed as fixed objects of historical discourse, nor as symbols of something other than themselves. They do not have a natural unity but exist, rather, in an "eventmental field" in which they form "intrigues" that vary in time and space.[59] Veyne's model is similar to Foucault's own method of examining "the space in which discursive events are deployed" and his own depiction of events as a form of massless matter, what he calls "incorporeal materialism."[60] Like the concept of facts, the role of events (particularly political events) has been a long-standing issue in historical thought. Foucault has recently commented that, although contemporary history stresses structures rather than events, "history as it is practiced today does not turn its back on events; on the contrary, it is continually enlarging the field of events, constantly discovering new layers . . . in order to establish those diverse, converging, and sometimes divergent, but never autonomous series that enable us to circumscribe the 'locus' of an event, the limits to its fluidity and the conditions of its emergence."[61]

The controversy over the meaning of historical events is only one of a number of issues in which Foucault has become involved. After the publication of *The Order of Things* in 1966 and the resulting flood of accusations that this work was antihistorical, Foucault discussed his complicated relationship to history in a series of articles and interviews.[62] He then published a lengthy explanation of his methodology and terminology in a work entitled *The Archaeology of Knowledge* (1969). Although Foucault has made clear his rejection of all views based on evolutionary or dialectical change and on the narration of discrete events, he has been far more ambivalent toward the "very important mutation of historical knowledge" since the 1940s.[63] Despite his differences with Braudel and Althusser, Foucault has welcomed their examination of complex types of periodization, various forms of discontinuity, and the integration of history and the human sciences.[64]

These conceptual innovations are similar to Foucault's own efforts in *The Order of Things* to describe the formation of a specific discourse (such as natural history in the seventeenth and eighteenth centuries) and its relationship to other discourses (general grammar and the analysis of wealth in the same period) rather than to explain the development of natural history into nineteenth-century biology and psychology and twentieth-century psychoanalysis, or the development of general grammar into nineteenth-century philology and literature and twentieth-century linguistics, or the development of the analysis of wealth into nineteenth-century political economy and sociology and twentieth-century ethnology. He does not see the systems of discourse specific to one period as developing into anything. Rather, he sees a shift in fields and the formation of new discourses occupying part of the same ground ("space") as the previous ones but fundamentally different in their internal configuration and in their choice of objects. He does not, however, feel that it is yet possible to determine the rules responsible for such shifts, and consequently he is skeptical of the possibility of global, or total, history, although he thinks it may be possible to develop a "general history." General history will attempt to "determine what form of relation may be legitimately described between . . . different series . . . what 'tables' it is possible to draw up. A total description draws all phenomena around a single center—a principle, a meaning, a spirit, a world-view, an overall shape; a general history, on the contrary, would deploy the space of a dispersion."[65] Moreover, according to Foucault's own methodological principles, one could describe a number of fields different from those he himself has described but equally systematic. Thus, for example, a study of historical consciousness would locate Marx at a juncture between archaeological "layers," whereas Foucault's own analysis of political economy locates Ricardo, not Marx, at the focal point.[66]

Foucault recognizes that, according to this relativistic view, his own work can, indeed must, be regarded as part of the epistemological field of the modern period and not as an act of free creation. In referring to *The Order of Things*, he asserted that "my book is a pure and simple 'fiction': it is a novel, but it is not I who invented it; it is the relation of our epoch and its epistemological configuration to a whole mass of utterances. So although the subject is in effect present in the totality of the book, it is an anonymous 'someone' who speaks today in everything which is said."[67] Although Foucault's concern here is with the effacement of the subject, and consequently of the author, one cannot help noting the paradox of regarding his methodologically rigorous works as fiction. Yet historians have experienced the same paradox. In a recent symposium on the meaning of "new history," the participants seemed united in their belief that historical scholarship is scientific, yet aware of the many similarities between history and fiction. Thus, Michel de Certeau adopted the expression "science fiction" as descriptive of historical analyses, and Paul Veyne commented on the metaphorical nature of the constructs used by modern physicists.[68]

Despite Foucault's contention that his work is "a pure and simple fiction," the influence of scientific models is obvious. The fundamental concepts of formation, threshold, transformation, and redistribution come largely from the natural sciences and from the history of science. Foucault has, in fact, even wondered whether he is not really a historian of ideas who wanted "to achieve a rigor so many other, similar descriptions have recently acquired; but who, unable to . . . cross the threshold of scientificity . . . declares that he had been doing, and wanted to do, something quite different. . . . I cannot be satisfied until I have cut myself off from 'the history of ideas,' until I have shown in what way archaeological analysis differs from the description of the history of ideas."[69] Archaeological analysis differs from the history of ideas both in its more scientific aspirations and in its rejection of the fundamental historical themes of genesis, continuity, and totalization.[70] But even beyond the limitations inherent in historical concepts of objects and change, Foucault believes that history, like philosophy, is fragmented and that a new discipline is needed to establish coherence in the study of both thought and action. This seems to be the meaning of a comment he made in 1966 when he mentioned that he was shocked by the existence of a multitude of subphilosophies (histories of ideas); their existence revealed the inability of our culture to come to terms with "the history of its own thought. That is why I have tried to write, in a style evidently a little unusual, the history not of thought in general, but of everything which 'contains thought' in a culture, of everything in which there is thought. Because there is thought in philosophy, but also in a novel, in jurisprudence, in law, even in an administrative system, in a prison."[71]

A Space for Archæology

By the late 1950s, Foucault had separated himself from traditional forms of philosophy and history by rejecting the notion of a unified subject of knowledge, the belief in fixed objects, and the concept of linear change. He had turned instead to an examination of the space that determined, if not the existence of discourses, at least the possible forms in which configurations of knowledge and practice could emerge. Rather than focusing on *what* was known (history) or *why* knowledge is possible (epistemology), he investigated *how* fields of knowledge are structured (archaeology). Foucault assumed that these fields are ordered according to rules in much the same way that physical phenomena, linguistic behavior, and unconscious phenomena such as dreams and myths are ordered. This suggests that archaeology is a science, an assumption Foucault called his "initial hypothesis" when he explained that,

in France at least, the history of science and thought give pride of place to mathematics, cosmology, and physics . . . rigorous sciences . . . all close to philosophy. . . . The other disciplines, however—those, for example, that concern living beings, languages, or economic facts—are considered too tinged with empirical thought . . . [to] be anything other than irregular. . . . But what if empirical knowledge, at a given time and in a given culture, *did* possess a well-defined regularity. . . . [What if it] obeyed, at a given moment, the laws of a certain code of knowledge? If, in short, the history of non-formal knowledge had itself a system.[72]

Although empirical knowledge may be systematic, as Foucault implies, there is some doubt that systematic knowledge is necessarily scientific. Foucault himself has been ambivalent on this point, stating at different times that archaeology is a science, that it is not a science, and that it is neither scientific nor nonscientific.[73] This confusion rests less on the nature of archaeology than on the various uses of the term *science*. Foucault has not made clear his definition of science, although he has suggested that the difference between scientific and empirical knowledge is not primarily one of kind but one of degree. Thus, the field of empirical knowledge is characterized by systematic relations, as is that of scientific knowledge, but the latter field is denser and the network of relations tighter. Still, differences do exist, and these differences are marked by "thresholds" which indicate various levels of systematicity. At the lowest level, that marking the threshold of positivity, the field is structured enough to form a specific discourse which has a positive existence. The next threshold is that of epistemologization, which is reached "when some of the units of discourse start to organize themselves coherently and start acting as standards for the corresponding forms of knowledge."[74] Thus, the existence of parallel discourses within the same period (for example, general grammar, analysis of wealth, and natural history in the eighteenth century) indicates the existence of a more intricate set of relations known as an "episteme."

The discourses that Foucault has studied come primarily from these two levels of systematicity. There are, however, two further levels, one marked by the threshold of scientificity and the other by the threshold of formalization. A discourse crosses the threshold of scientificity "when its statements comply not only with archaeological rules of formation, but also with certain laws for the construction of propositions";[75] that is, when the relations established are logically consistent as well as regularly patterned. Discourses at the threshold of scientificity have been investigated by Gaston Bachelard and Georges Canguilhem, who examined how concepts were purified and how "a science was established over and against a pre-scientific level."[76] To cross the threshold of formalization, a discourse must "define the axioms necessary to it, the elements that it uses, the propositional structures that are legitimate to it, and the transformations that it accepts."[77] The model for this form of discourse is mathematics. The history of a discourse is largely the history of its transitions from one level to another, although not all discourses make these transitions and those that do change levels do not necessarily move uniformly from the lowest to the highest level. They may jump across levels in either direction, cross several thresholds simultaneously, split up and form new discourses which disperse at various levels, or interact with other discourses. As an example of one series of transitions, Foucault cites the case of economics:

> In the seventeenth century, one can recognize a threshold
> of positivity: it almost coincides with the practice and theory of
> mercantilism; but its epistemologization did not occur until later,
> at the very end of the century, or at the beginning of the next

century, with Locke and Cantillon. However, the nineteenth
century, with Ricardo, marks both a new type of positivity, [and] a
new form of epistemologization, which were later to be modified
in turn by Cournot and Jevons, at the very time that Marx was to
reveal an entirely new discursive practice on the basis of political
economy.[78]

Foucault's conception of discourse as a fundamental unit in a spatiotemporal field which alters position by crossing thresholds and
occupying various levels is a conception very close to the contemporary model of atomic structure. This analogy is not quite exact,
however, since Foucault's discourses appear to have the characteristics of both atoms (that is, a limited variety of distinct formations
incorporating more elementary particles) and electrons (mass-energy
fields that reach thresholds, occupy various specific levels, and interact in complex ways with a number of other fields). But since discourses are composed of even more elementary units which more
nearly approximate the concept of "electrons," it may be easier to
visualize discourses as atoms despite the rather forced nature of the
comparison. In any case, it is obvious that Foucault's entire conceptualization is spatial in nature, a fact that has attracted considerable
attention. Although most commentators view this space as flat and
immobile, and thus describe Foucault's archaeology in terms of cartography, topography, or geology, a few reviewers recognize that
Foucault's conception of space is three-dimensional. Thus the mathematician Michel Serres has commented on Foucault's "geometry"[79]
and the philosopher Gilles Deleuze has noted that, like the musician
Anton Webern, Foucault has "created a new dimension . . . [a] di-
agonal dimension . . . no longer in a plane but rather in space."[80] The
reference to atonal music suggests (although Deleuze did not develop this point) that archaeology involves a fourth dimension, a
temporal dimension, which takes Foucault beyond geometry into
field theory.

The terms *discourse* and *episteme* are frequently regarded as idiosyncratic expressions for the more common terms *discipline* and *world
view*. Foucault stresses, however, that his terms refer to a different
classificatory scheme (a different "order of things") and thus to a
different modality of knowledge. Because he is no longer dealing
with objects (facts or events), disciplines (groups of objects), abstract

forces (unifiers of objects), or subjects (creators of objects), the new units Foucault identifies cannot be regarded as "things." They must instead be viewed as functions. This makes them difficult to identify in isolation, for, strictly speaking, they do not exist in isolation. Yet they do exist, and their existence is determined by complex rules of formation and transformation. The problem here is similar to that confronted by physicists and linguists in defining the fundamental units of their models. Neither atomic particles nor language elements have a meaning independent of the field (or syntax) in which they are embedded. A description of such units must, as Bachelard recognized, involve a new precision "at the level of principles and concepts." For Bachelard these principles and concepts are derived from relativity theory and quantum mechanics, whereas for contemporary linguists they are derived from Saussure's theory of language. Both the physical and the linguistic models are relevant for Foucault, but, since he deals with cultural phenomena, the linguistic model is the more obvious if not necessarily the more significant one.

Besides discourse and episteme, Foucault identifies a more fundamental unit that he refers to as the statement or the enunciative function. Although he recognizes the similarity of statements and linguistic signs (that is, relations between sounds and concepts), Foucault nevertheless does not equate signs and statements. Yet statements are not symbols either; they do not have another meaning that requires interpretation. Statements, then, are neither pure form nor buried meaning and do not fall within either semiology or hermeneutics. Rather, they are both form and substance; like events (which are a type of statement), they are incorporeal and material. Consequently, they are "neither visible nor hidden."[81] And like electrons, which appear as both waves and particles, statements do not indicate " 'things', 'facts', 'realities' or 'beings', but . . . laws of possibility, rules of existence." One cannot, Foucault claims, "find structural criteria of unity for the statement . . . because it is not in itself a unit, but a function that cuts across a domain of structures and possible unities, and which reveals them, with concrete contents, in time and space."[82] A statement, then, can only be described as a function "in its actual practice, its conditions, the rules that govern it, and the field in which it operates."[83] Thus, although a phrase can be a statement, two identical phrases in different fields are not identical statements. For example, the statement "species evolve" formulated in the field of eighteenth-century natural history is not identical to the statement "species evolve" formulated in the field of nineteenth-century biology.[84] The difference between these two statements is not simply that the words *species* and *evolution* had different meanings in different periods. Rather, these statements differ because their functions in the discourses of natural history and biology differed.

Groups of statements having a regular pattern and meeting specific criteria constitute "discourses." Unlike disciplines, discourses do not necessarily refer to a body of logically consistent theories or to a body of irregular practices, but to patterned forms of thought and action that include both compatible and contradictory elements. Archaeology, which is itself a "discourse about discourses,"[85] allows Foucault to treat "on the same plane and according to their isomorphisms, practices, institutions and theories. . . . I seek the common knowledge which made them possible, the historical and constituent layer of knowledge. Rather than seeking to explain this knowledge from the point of view of the *practico-inerte* I seek to formulate an analysis of what one could call the *'théorico-actif'*."[86] This analysis makes it possible for Foucault to examine discursive formations (the different levels of formalized coherence of a discourse) as well as discursive practices. It also permits an examination of the nondiscursive "space" surrounding the discursive field. This space is made up of institutional, political, economic, and social constraints. It is a "filled" space impinging on discursive fields and marking their borders and may itself have a structure visible to an observer situated elsewhere.

What, then, are examples of Foucault's discursive "atoms," and what are the criteria used to identify them? Foucault himself asks rhetorically: "When one speaks of *psychiatry*, or of *medicine*, or of *grammar*, or of *biology*, or of *economics*, what is one speaking of? What are these curious entities? . . . There are units which . . . undergo such radical mutations that one would have difficulty in considering them as identical to themselves (how can one maintain that economics remains the same, uninterrupted, from the physiocrats to Keynes?)."[87] These "curious entities" are neither pure theories nor mere activities; they are patterns of ideas and practices specific to certain periods and places. Therefore Foucault does not "explain" them by seeking their hidden origins in an ever-receding past or by referring to a magical moment of creation in the mind of a founding father. Instead, he examines the rules that delimit the types of forms discourses may assume, the series of transformations they may undergo, and the types of relations they may establish with other discourses and with the nondiscursive environment. Still, these rules do not indicate which specific forms and relationships must emerge, they only indicate a range of possibilities. As Foucault himself admits, rather "than *founding* a theory—and perhaps before being able to do so (I do not deny that I regret not yet having succeeded in doing so) —my present concern is to *establish* a possibility."[88]

Foucault specifies three groups of criteria for identifying the possible emergence of discourse. The first is the criterion of formation, which refers to the rules governing the dispersion of objects, the distribution of subjective positions, and the choice of concepts and theories characteristic of each discourse. Thus, what permits one

> to individualize a discourse such as political economy or general grammar is not the unity of an object; it is not a formal structure; nor is it a conceptual coherent architecture; it is not a fundamental philosophical choice, it is rather the existence of rules of formation for all its objects (however scattered they may be), for all its operations (which often can neither be superimposed nor linked together in succession), for all its concepts (which may very well be incompatible), for all its theoretical options (which are often mutually exclusive).[89]

The second criterion, that of transformation, includes those rules controlling the appearance, modifications, and disappearance of a discourse. For example, one can identify natural history as a discourse if one can "define the conditions which must have been brought together at a very precise moment of time, in order that its objects, its operations, its concepts and its theoretical options could be formed; if [one] can define what internal modifications it was capable of . . . [and] from what threshold of transformations new rules have been brought into play."[90] Transformation, however, does not mean continual or homogeneous change. On the contrary, it refers to many types of discontinuous change. There are, for example, "derivations," which refer to transformations within a discursive formation. Foucault cites as an illustration changes in the concept of the verb within the discourse of general grammar. Then there are "mutations," which affect the entire discourse. An example of this would be the displacement of the boundaries that define the field of possible objects, which in fact occurred in the nineteenth century when medicine turned from surface classification to anatomy and the "three dimensional space of the body."[91] A further transformation involves "redistributions," which affect several discourses simultaneously. This might take the form of a shift in the hierarchical order of discourses such as occurred in the early nineteenth century when biology replaced the analysis of language as the dominant model.[92]

The third criterion defining a discourse is that of correlation, which includes the rules governing relations among discourses and relations between discourses and nondiscursive conditions. For example, clinical medicine can be said to comprise an autonomous discourse if one can establish "the whole of the relations which define it and situate it among the other types of discourse (as biology, chemistry, political theory or the analysis of society) and in the non-discursive context in which it functions (institutions, social relations, economic and political circumstances)."[93] These three criteria, particularly the criterion of correlation, make it possible to describe the episteme of a period. Neither a world view, nor a form of knowledge, nor a type of rationality, an episteme is, rather, "the total set of relations that unite, at a given period, the discursive practices that give rise to epistemological figures, sciences, and possibly formalized systems."[94] It is, moreover, "a constantly moving set of articulations";[95] it must not be regarded as "a sort of grand underlying theory" but as "a space of dispersion . . . an *open field of relationships and no doubt indefinitely describable.*"[96]

In Foucault's major work, *The Order of Things*, he attempted to describe large epistemological fields. Consequently, much attention was devoted to the rules correlating various discourses within each episteme. Considerable space was also allotted to articulating the rules of formation and transformation specific to each discourse. Little attention was given to the relation between discourses and the nondiscursive environment, which has led some commentators to suspect that Foucault's discourses are formal systems isolated from the realities of social and political power. Yet Foucault insists that he selected discourses in the human sciences precisely because they are intimately related to the exercise of power. He even sees a definite relationship between the role of various discourses on life (especially biology and psychology) and the establishment of hospitals and asylums. A similar relationship obtains between certain discourses on labor (political economy and sociology) and the existence of factories, prisons, and barracks. Likewise, the discourses on language are intimately tied to the organization of the school system.

The relation between discourses and the nondiscursive environment was made more explicit in Foucault's earlier study of madness and asylums as well as in his investigation of clinical medicine and hospitals. After the publication of *The Order of Things* and *The Archaeology of Knowledge*, Foucault turned once again to an analysis of specific discursive fields and to a closer examination of their relationship to nondiscursive conditions. His recent works on the prison system and on sexuality indicate this more explicit concern with the relation between knowledge and power. In his inaugural lecture at the Collège de France in 1970, Foucault made clear his intention to study this relation, which had become a pressing issue for French intellectuals after the uprisings of May 1968. In this lecture, which outlined the direction of his subsequent research, Foucault explained that "in every society the production of discourse is at once controlled, selected, organized and redistributed according to a certain number of procedures, whose role is to avert its powers and dangers."[97] Foucault summarized these procedures, whose function is to control the formation of discourses and to limit the use of discursive knowledge in the nondiscursive environment.

The first of these systems of constraint deals with external controls on discourse and involves several types of exclusion, the most obvious being the prohibition of certain areas of expression. Foucault maintains that in our time prohibitions concentrate on limiting expressions of desire and power and thus focus on sexuality and politics. A second type of exclusion is not an overt prohibition but a "division and a rejection," for example, the creation of oppositions like reason and madness and the subsequent isolation of those persons a society rejects as mad. A third form of exclusion, one more complicated than the previous two, is based on the "opposition between true and false" that has been central to Western thought and that has resulted in what Foucault calls the "will to truth." This will to truth excludes all nonverifiable knowledge and forms the basis for modern technological civilization. While prohibition and division are forms of exclusion which appear to be weakening, the will to truth is becoming ever more dangerous.[98] Consequently, Foucault regards as "signposts for all our future work" such figures as Nietzsche, who clearly perceived the relation between the will to truth and the will to power, and Artaud and Bataille, who, like Nietzsche, "have attempted to remold this will to truth and to turn it against truth."[99] He does not, however, mention thinkers like Max Weber, whose similar view of the destructive rationalization of the modern period has greatly influenced young French historians.

In addition to external controls, there are also internal rules that force various forms of continuity on discourse. First is the role of commentary, the unceasing effort to relate thought to an original "true" text and to deny the possibility of discourse expressing anything that has not already been said. A second type of internal control refers to rules determining the position of the author, a position that prevents statements from revealing fundamental differences by referring them back to the unity of a creating consciousness. A third type of internal control regulates the classification of discourse by creating distinctions between disciplines which limit the "theoretical field" and exclude certain vital questions from consideration (thus nineteenth-century biology was incapable of incorporating Mendelian genetics).[100]

A third system of control refers to the use of discourse rather than to the limits imposed on the production of discourse. This sort of control restricts the access of knowledge to certain groups under certain conditions. Thus there are rules regulating rituals of initiation which enforce specific forms of thought and behavior. These restrictions are maintained by the standards of a "fellowship" or closed community (such as the medical community) whose "function is to preserve or to reproduce discourse." There is also the restriction imposed by doctrinal adherence (be it religious, political, or philosophical) that "links individuals to certain types of utterances while consequently barring them from all others." And finally there is the educational system, which is a "political means of maintaining or modifying the appropriation of discourse with the knowledge and the powers it carries with it."[101]

Archaeology, then, like other contemporary human sciences (psychoanalysis, ethnology, and linguistics) reveals the nature of constraints on thought and behavior. Unlike these other sciences, however, archaeology is not itself tied to a specific discipline. It functions in the space between disciplines, exposing their limitations and challenging their exclusions. Foucault's archaeology is therefore a method as well as a discourse and, like much contemporary philosophy and history, its real aim is criticism. Its purpose is to unmask systems which produce and consume discourse and to reveal the tight network of relations between knowledge and power. Its "field" is that enormous, still uncharted space of contemporary thought whose boundaries have been marked by Marx, Nietzsche, and Freud and whose basic configuration has been defined by Einstein.

 *Two*

FOUCAULT ON KNOWLEDGE,

POWER, AND POLITICS

Although the works of Nietzsche, Marx, and Freud are central to Foucault's thought, he seldom specifies his relation to them. He believes that all modern social thought takes place within the space delimited by these figures and he uses them just as modern physicists use Einstein's theories, without feeling the need to cite the obvious reference.[1] The most explicit discussion of these and other theorists important to the development of Foucault's own ideas may be found in a variety of articles and interviews published since the mid-1960s. The earliest of these articles, on which the first section of this chapter is based, deals with Foucault's assessment of the forms of knowledge made possible by Marx, Nietzsche, and Freud. The second section is based on an article published in 1971 which reveals, through an examination of Nietzsche's *Genealogy of Morals*, the close relationship Foucault perceives between Nietzsche's genealogy and his own archaeology. The remaining sections of this chapter are based on articles and interviews that appeared between 1968 and 1975 and that discuss Foucault's conception of power, his political activities, and the connection between his theoretical works and his political positions.

Interpretive Techniques: Nietzsche, Marx, Freud

In French the terms *savoir* (knowledge) and *pouvoir* (power) have an obvious superficial relation based on the verb *voir* (to see). According to Foucault, they also have an actual profound relation that has rarely been investigated. Studies of power, he claims, have usually been anecdotal narratives of the actions of political leaders or histories of economic processes and social institutions. Power as a fine network of strategies and mechanisms and the relation between knowledge (including scientific knowledge) and power have seldom been closely examined. Yet Foucault believes that there is a "perpetual articulation of power on knowledge and of knowledge on power."[2] This relation was partially recognized by Marx, who held that ideas as well as objects are products of specific economic systems. It was also partially analyzed by Freud, who saw the relation between desire and knowledge. But for Foucault the major philosopher of power was Nietzsche, who understood the psychological as well as the material nature of power and who could describe power without imposing a political or psychological theory. In doing so, Nietzsche exposed all systems of thought and value as expressions of the will to power, thereby undermining any possibility for neutral knowledge.

At a philosophical colloquium on Nietzsche in 1964, Foucault presented a paper entitled "Nietzsche, Freud, Marx."[3] This presentation and the ensuing discussion foreshadowed many of the themes that appeared two years later in *The Order of Things*. One of Foucault's purposes in writing the latter work was "to reveal a *positive unconscious* of knowledge,"[4] a collective, constitutive unconscious similar to that described by Lévi-Strauss in his studies of "primitive" peoples.[5] But whereas Lévi-Strauss analyzed the myth-science of primitives and their largely unconscious systems of social classifications, Foucault analyzed the science-myths of Europeans and their systems of classifying words and things. Yet Foucault has gone even further than Lévi-Strauss in questioning the process of analysis itself. He has followed Nietzsche to the edge of language, to the point at which language either falls back on itself or disappears in madness. The limits of language, and thus the limits of knowledge, have defined the possibilities for modern hermeneutics, and this is the issue Foucault addressed in the 1964 colloquium.

Foucault opened his presentation with the reflection that it might be possible to compile an encyclopedia of interpretive techniques from the Greeks to the modern period. Such a compilation would reveal at least one constant: the suspicion that there is another reality behind language or apart from language altogether, namely, that language hides a "deeper" meaning and that other things such as nature, objects, and gestures also "speak."[6] What all these languages "mean" depends on the system used to interpret signs, and each culture has its own system of interpretation. In sixteenth-century Europe the interpretive system was based on resemblance. Everything belonged to a system of similarities divine in origin and one had only to recognize the specific type of resemblance in question. For this two kinds of knowledge were essential: *cognitio*, or knowledge of lateral resemblances, and *divinatio*, or knowledge of depth resemblances.

The Renaissance system of interpretation based on resemblances collapsed at the end of the sixteenth century and was replaced by another system during the seventeenth and eighteenth centuries, the period of French classicism. The Classical system of representation, which constitutes the core of Foucault's archaeological analysis in *The Order of Things*, was in turn replaced in the nineteenth century by new techniques of interpretation. These techniques differed from previous ones in that they did not interpret the world, they interpreted man. They provided a mirror for man, and it was this mirror, or rather these mirrors, which Foucault now proposed to turn back on Nietzsche, Marx, and Freud. Marx's *Capital*, Freud's *Interpretation of Dreams*, and Nietzsche's *Birth of Tragedy* and *Genealogy of Morals* constituted the third in a series of what Freud himself referred to as deep wounds in the narcissism of Western culture. The first of these wounds had been inflicted by Copernicus, the second by Darwin, and the third by the "decenterings" effected by Nietzsche, Marx, and Freud. The consequence of this last shock to Western narcissism was not to provide new meanings for things which had no meaning before, but to fundamentally alter the nature of signs and the way in which signs could be interpreted. From the new hermeneutics that emerged during the nineteenth century, Foucault isolated four characteristics which all derived at least in part from the interpretive strategies of Nietzsche, Marx, and Freud.

The first transformation involves the profound modification of "the space of distribution in which signs can be signs."[7] The sixteenth-century space of interpretation was homogeneous and signs were uniformly distributed in the system of resemblances. The nineteenth-century space of interpretation became a differential space with signs clustering around Man and Society. Morals, money, and symptoms were all signs suggesting the profundity of deep interpretive "spaces." But Nietzsche, Marx, and Freud exposed these interior spaces as folded surfaces concealing nothing profound but serving instead as mere mystifications of ordinary power conflicts. The illusion of profundity that they shattered was the illusion of the virtuous soul of man. Nietzsche revealed that the very concepts of good and evil were masks concealing the self-interest of dominant groups and the resentment and hypocrisy of the weak. Marx exposed the bourgeois concepts of value as camouflages for the platitudes of ordinary monetary values. And Freud uncovered symptoms of the "psychopathology of everyday life" in both the hidden and visible layers of the psyche.

The second characteristic of modern hermeneutics is that "interpretation has finally become an infinite task."[8] Whereas there were a limited number of signs in the sixteenth century, since the nineteenth century there has been an inexhaustible network of signs. Nietzsche, Marx, and Freud all reflected, in varying ways, this sense of the incompleteness of interpretation. All three, according to Foucault, refused to deal with origins, and Nietzsche and Freud (more than Marx) recognized the peril as well as the impossibility of this quest.[9] Freud withdrew from an analysis of infinite regression and Nietzsche distinguished between beginnings and origins in his genealogy. Both men, Foucault claimed, realized that "the further one proceeds in interpretation, the closer one approaches an absolutely dangerous region, where interpretation not only reaches a point of self-contradiction but where it will itself disappear as interpretation, followed perhaps by the disappearance of the interpreter himself."[10] The possibility that interpretation could end in madness or death was sensed most acutely by Nietzsche, who believed that "to perish through absolute knowledge may well form part of the foundation of being."[11]

A third characteristic of modern hermeneutics, and one closely tied to the theme of the essential incompleteness of interpretation, is the belief that there is nothing primary to interpret. Interpretation is infinite because signs are not objects passively waiting to be interpreted; they are themselves interpretations of other signs. Thus Marx interpreted the bourgeois interpretation of production, not production itself. Freud interpreted the patient's interpretation of dreams, not the dreams themselves; consequently, he discovered fantasies, not symptoms. And Nietzsche did not interpret the "real" meaning of words; he interpreted the interpretations words had previously been given. All of these interpretations are based on the belief that instead of existence preceding essence, as Sartre would have it, interpretation precedes sign. Since signs are themselves "interpretations which try to justify themselves,"[12] they have become suspect. In the sixteenth century signs were benevolent: they were simple resemblances ordained by God. In the nineteenth century signs became malevolent: "money," "symptoms," and "morals" were all masks. They concealed negative concepts; they included oppositions and contradictions.

The last characteristic of modern hermeneutics is that interpretation has become infinite self-interpretation. Consequently, one no longer asks what the sign signifies, one asks who is speaking; one interprets the interpreter. This is what Althusser is doing to Marx, Lacan to Freud, and Deleuze to Nietzsche. Another consequence of infinite self-interpretation is that whereas dialectics (despite appearances) is linear, interpretation is circular. There is an eternal return of interpretation as it constantly interprets itself, a cycle that could only be broken if signs cease to be interpretations and become independent objects.

> The death of interpretation is to believe that there are signs, signs which have a primary, original, real existence. . . . The life of interpretation, on the contrary, is to believe that there are only interpretations. It seems to me that it is necessary to understand something that too many of our contemporaries forget, that *hermeneutics and semiology are two fierce enemies.*[13]

Efforts to combine hermeneutics and semiology represent a return to the belief in the absolute existence of signs and a denial of interpretation as an infinite possibility of reinterpretations imposed violently on signs tied to other meanings. Such a denial has been the fate of Marxism after Marx, in that Marxism is deeply suspicious of language. A living hermeneutics must remain, as Nietzsche realized, within the realm of "madness and pure language."[14]

The questions raised after Foucault's paper dealt for the most part with Marx and with the role of Hegel, whom Foucault had not mentioned. In response Foucault acknowledged that his treatment of Marx was undeveloped. He maintained, however, that Marx had not presented his economic theory as a final interpretation. Despite the distinction Marx had drawn between interpreting the world and changing it, Marx had only criticized philosophical interpretation; he saw his own political economy as both an interpretation and an action. Foucault had omitted Hegel because he was not interested in the history of philosophy but in the archaeology of thought. Consequently, Foucault's analyses were concerned with signs and the interpretations that made meaning possible, not with meaning itself.

The modern techniques of interpretation that have made it possible to analyze the mystifications of consciousness owe more to specific changes in early nineteenth-century concepts of language, political economy, and natural history, Foucault argued, than they do to Hegelian philosophy. Foucault did agree, however, with the point made by one questioner, that Nietzsche, Marx, and Freud had all developed "therapeutic" techniques aimed at curing the individual (Freud), society (Marx), or humanity (Nietzsche). But there is some question whether Foucault himself believes in the possibility of such cures. While he frequently refers to archaeology as a "diagnostic" technique, he appears to be diagnosing the terminal condition of Western society. Moreover, Foucault did not explain (nor was he asked) on what grounds he justified his own attempt to escape from the endless cycle of interpretation and self-interpretation to achieve the privileged position of archaeological "description."

Genealogy and the Will to Knowledge

Although Foucault still regards Nietzsche as the main influence on his own thought, he has discussed Nietzsche less frequently in recent years. He regrets the "ambiguous, absolutely privileged, meta-historical" status that he gave Nietzsche in *The Order of Things*.[15] Moreover, he is anxious to distance himself from the growing number of "faithful" commentators on Nietzsche in order to use, even deform, Nietzsche's thought for his own purposes.[16] The clearest example of this use and abuse of Nietzsche is an article Foucault published in 1971, entitled "Nietzsche, Genealogy, History," in which he examined Nietzsche's genealogy in terms of his own archaeology.[17] In this reading, genealogy becomes not a study of origins but a disclosure of differences; values do not develop out of the past, they emerge in a field of forces; and history is no longer an antiquarian, heroic, or critical remembrance of the past but a dangerous countermemory that threatens the present.

Genealogy, Foucault began, is "gray, meticulous and patiently documentary. It operates on a field of entangled and confused parchments, on documents that have been scratched over and recopied many times."[18] It is, in other words, an interpretation of interpretations, constructed from a careful examination of the "archive"[19] and sensitive to the "singularity of events" that emerge from such unlikely places as sentiments, instincts, and conscience.[20] Genealogy studies the recurrence of these events, "not in order to trace the gradual curve of their evolution, but to isolate the different scenes where they engaged in different roles."[21] Genealogy does not, therefore, trace the ultimate origins of morality, asceticism, justice, punishment, and knowledge; it examines a multitude of accidental, intersecting beginnings. It refuses to regard the past as a period of lost perfections, divine creations followed by falls, or hidden truths buried under the errors of the present. On the contrary, genealogy perceives only humble beginnings and a series of errors behind the "truths" of the present. Genealogy does not, in fact, treat the question of origins at all; it studies the dispersions of descent. Unlike origin, descent reveals differences, discontinuities, and divisions. Moreover, descent locates change in the body, not the soul. It requires the genealogist to develop the diagnostic skills of a physician and to avoid the illusions of the metaphysician. Knowledge and morality are not based on reason or spirit. They emerge from the desires and struggles of the body: values reflect the domination of the strong; science arises from the jealous conflicts of scientists; and philosophy is the product of old and spiteful men too weak for action.

After transforming genealogy from a study of origins to an analysis of descent, Foucault proceeded to examine genealogical concepts of change and determined that values did not develop in an evolutionary process but emerged suddenly in a series of violent conflicts. Genealogy, he claimed, locates the points of emergence of new ideas and values in a "non-place" between conflicting forces, in the "pure distance which indicates that the adversaries do not share a common space."[22] Furthermore, genealogy examines the system of domination established after each restructuring of forces. It does not regard laws and rituals as peaceful and rational modalities of accommodation, but as the merciless institutionalization of violence—the systematic imposition of the rights of the powerful and the obligations of the weak. "Humanity does not gradually progress from combat to combat until it arrives at universal reciprocity, where the rule of law finally replaces warfare; humanity installs each of its violences in a system of rules and thus proceeds from domination to domination."[23] Each new system of domination is thus the result of the seizure of previous rules, the forced turning of rules against the rulers, and the reinterpretation of rules to suit the interests of new masters. The history of humanity is not, therefore, a purposeful development or a gradual unfolding of natural processes; it is a discontinuous sequence of interpretations that genealogy attempts to record.

In recording these justifications of power, genealogy becomes a type of history, an "effective history" (*wirkliche Historie*) that severs itself from metaphysics. It recognizes no absolutes—no eternal truths, no immortal souls, no continuing consciousness. Even feelings, instincts, and the human body itself are not constants; they too have their histories. "Nothing in man—not even his body—is sufficiently stable to serve as the basis for self-recognition or for understanding other men. The traditional devices for constructing a comprehensive view of history and for retracing the past as a patient and continuous development must be systematically dismantled."[24] In place of these traditional devices, Foucault claimed, Nietzsche hoped to constitute an effective history, one that would recognize discontinuity and allow events to be viewed as "the reversal of a relationship of forces."[25] In contrast to metaphysical histories, such an effective history would not look at the lofty peaks of the past from a distance. It would entertain a multiplicity of perspectives, examine periods of decadence, and question the purity of "the noblest periods, the highest forms, the most abstract ideas."[26] Effective history would make no claim to truth; it would not hide behind a mask of objectivity. On the contrary, it would recognize that all knowledge is relative and go on to assert its own perspective. Such a history would also scorn comprehensive histories which include everything without discrimination and which thereby reduce everything to the lowest common denominator.[27] These crude and tasteless histories, Nietzsche believed, are products of ascetic historians who suppress their individual wills in the hope of achieving greater power through "objective" knowledge.

Comprehensive histories, Foucault claimed, are based on a metaphysical affirmation of reality, identity, and truth, the "three Platonic modalities of history."[28] Nietzsche, he says, identified three types of history which correspond to these modalities: monumental history, which glorifies the realities of past accomplishments; antiquarian history, which seeks an identity of past and present through the continuity of tradition; and critical history, which, claiming to possess the truth, attempts to expose injustice and error. According to Foucault, however, Nietzsche did not accept these types of history and actually transformed each of them into an opposing form. These altered forms "imply a use of history that severs its connection to memory, its metaphysical and anthropological model, and constructs a counter-memory—a transformation of history into a totally different form of time."[29] The conversion of memory into countermemory and of the past into a "totally different form of time" involved a series of transformations. The first transformation entailed the conversion of monumental history into parody. According to Foucault, Nietzsche believed that the historian offered the "confused and anonymous European, who no longer knows himself . . . the possibility of alternative identities" from the past. The genealogist, however, knew that these revived identities were only masks.[30] Nevertheless, he would play the game; indeed, he would "push the masquerade to its limit and prepare the great carnival of time where masks are constantly reappearing."[31]

The second transformation dissolved antiquarian history by the "systematic dissociation of identity."[32] Whereas the antiquarian tries to conserve the past by tracing the continuities of his native land, language, and laws, the genealogist reveals "a complex system of distinct and multiple elements, unable to be mastered by the powers of synthesis."[33] The final transformation was the metamorphosis of critical history into sacrifice. Nietzsche began by discussing the critical use of history in terms of "its just treatment of the past, its decisive cutting of the roots, its rejection of traditional attitudes of reverence, its liberation of man by presenting him with other origins than those in which he prefers to see himself."[34] Although Nietzsche seemed, in the *Untimely Meditations*, to favor the critical use of history despite the dangers it presented,[35] Foucault believes that Nietzsche later concluded that the passion for truth was the most awesome of all threats to life. According to Foucault, Nietzsche came to view the will to truth and knowledge as a malicious force that shattered the happiness of ignorance and threatened the existence of man. In the absence of absolute truth, the will to truth questions everything, devours everything, enslaves rather than frees man. It emerges from "instinct, passion, the inquisitor's devotion, cruel subtlety, and malice"[36] and turns these monstrous passions back on man. It calls for him to experiment on himself, to sacrifice himself in an endless quest for knowledge. "The desire for knowledge has been transformed among us into a passion which fears no sacrifice, which fears nothing but its own extinction. It may be that mankind will eventually perish from this passion for knowledge. If not through passion, then through weakness. We must be prepared to state our choice: do we wish humanity to end in fire and light or to end on the sands."[37]

Foucault's apocalyptic version of Nietzsche's genealogy is in many respects similar to his own archaeology. Both genealogy and archaeology are based on enormous erudition (worn, however, far more lightly by Nietzsche). Each seeks to reveal the differences in the roles that values have played in a series of discontinuous scenes from the past. They are both concerned with conceptions of normal, good, and healthy, and both locate analyses at the level of the body (particularly the diseased, deranged, criminal, and sexual body). Furthermore, both genealogy and archaeology regard stability as well as change as fields of conflicting forces in various states of balance and disruption. Both, too, are ambivalent toward history: hostile to metaphysical histories, yet hopeful that "another" history, an "effective" history, will emerge. Finally, both genealogy and archaeology have a radically relativistic view of knowledge as perspective and are fearful of the enormous destructive power of knowledge.

Yet Foucault's archaeology, although "meticulous and patiently documentary" like Nietzsche's genealogy, is not gray. It is black; no light seems to emerge from its density. Foucault's irony, subtlety, and passion have a certain luminosity, but there is none of Nietzsche's "sunniness, sweep and assurance."[38] Nietzsche the yea-sayer, the affirmer of life, has disappeared. With Foucault criticism has no power to create and only destroys. The effort to turn the will to truth against itself is no longer intended to serve life. Its function is to separate the will to truth from the will to knowledge. Foucault's attempt to remove knowledge from the quest for truth (and from the illusion of justice) does not challenge the power of knowledge itself. It merely exposes knowledge as power and cuts knowledge off from any possibility of justifying itself.

Since Foucault's studies have been increasingly concerned with power, he refers to his most recent works on penality and sexuality as "genealogies" or "histories" rather than "archaeologies." As he explained in 1971, his current research is directed toward the formation of a "morphology of the will to knowledge."[39] He also indicated that he planned to discriminate between the will to knowledge and the will to truth.[40] Since his previous studies had isolated "the distinctive level of discursive practices," he felt prepared to develop a theoretical model for his empirical works.[41] Because he found contemporary psychological, historical and philosophical concepts inadequate, he turned at first to older philosophical theories as "initial coordinates" for the construction of a new model. He chose two opposing epistemological models: the Aristotelian, which conceived the desire for knowledge to be universal and natural, and the Nietzschean, which considered the will to knowledge to be perverse and variable in its forms. With the aid of these models, Foucault investigated the judicial system of pre-Socratic Greece and concluded that this system represented "a form of justice linked to a form of knowledge which presupposes that truth is visible, ascertainable and measurable, that it responds to laws similar to those which register the order of the world, and that to discover it is also to possess its value for purification. This type of affirmation of truth becomes fundamental in the history of Western knowledge."[42] During the next two years, Foucault directed his research and teaching toward a similar study of the relation between knowledge and power by analyzing the penal system of France in the nineteenth century and exposing its network of values and practices. In the course of this research he discovered an extraordinary document dealing with the case of Pierre Rivière, a peasant who murdered his mother, brother, and sister and who became the focus of both the power structure (judicial system) and the knowledge structure (medical opinion regarding his sanity). Rivière's own written confession, remarkable for its literary force and lucidity, challenged the established definitions of rationality and normalcy and opened the intriguing question of the relationship between words and deeds.[43]

This form of research is not, obviously, directed against knowledge. It merely indicates the points of interaction between specific types of knowledge and power. Knowledge in general, which in French is referred to as *savoir* (knowledge in the sense of understanding), is intrinsic to all social systems: it reflects the prevailing order of things. Knowledge in its particular manifestations, referred to as *connaissance* (knowledge in the sense of cognition), is a variable aspect of specific systems.[44] Foucault's archaeology seeks to locate certain forms of *connaissance* (medicine and psychiatry, for example) within the field of *savoir* and to expose these forms of knowledge as aspects of the will to knowledge while depriving them of the possibility of asserting their own will to truth. This effort may serve to check destructive forms of knowledge-power (the physical and social sciences, for example). It is, however, equally possible that if "nothing is true, everything is permitted,"[45] and Foucault may well have removed the very foundations on which he himself is standing.

Archaeology and Politics

Foucault's archaeologies have exposed the close network of interactions between knowledge and power in various social systems. He is aware, moreover, that his own discourse is itself located within the power structure of modern capitalism. But he regards his discourse as both a product of modern society and as a "box of tools" that might be used to destroy the very society which allowed its creation.[46] Foucault is also aware that his very production of discourse is a consequence of his own will to knowledge and that he cannot justify his works by claiming that they are true since he has rejected the concept of truth. Ultimately the only justification for his own will to knowledge and power is his opposition to existing forms of knowledge-power. He has no positive basis for political action and his political theory approaches not only anarchism but nihilism, since he recognizes that power will never be destroyed. This is a peculiarly self-destructive position for an ascetic "archivist" whose real interest, it seems, is not politics but science. It may, however, be a necessary consequence of the belief that science is a form of power and that it can no longer conceal its lust for knowledge under the guise of an innocent quest for truth.

The implications of this position have gradually emerged in a series of statements Foucault has made since 1968. At that time he was anxious to demonstrate that archaeology left room for political action, despite its stress on anonymous determinations of thought and practice. Since then he has discussed the type of political action he considers appropriate for intellectuals and the nature of the political choices he has himself made. Foucault is extremely resistant, indeed actually hostile, to any attempt to discuss his personal motives. He not only regards his private life as irrelevant to his public role, but he is opposed on principle to efforts to impose psychological norms on his discourse. This position is consistent with Foucault's conception of the anonymity of the "discoursing subject" and his hatred for contemporary classifications of normalcy. But Foucault's tone makes one wonder if his defense of anonymity does not indicate something other than the "absence of a problem."[47]

Among Foucault's rare acknowledgements of his own motives are two significant statements that reflect his passion for knowledge and power. In a 1967 interview he responded to a question regarding his interest in archives by mentioning a recurrent nightmare. "A nightmare has pursued me since my childhood: I have before my eyes a text which I cannot read, or of which only a small part is decipherable; I pretend to read it, I know that I am inventing it; then the text suddenly blurs entirely, I can no longer read anything or even invent, my throat tightens and I wake up."[48] Foucault regarded this nightmare as an example of the contemporary obsession with language. It seems, however, far more closely related to his own obsession with knowledge. The refusal to admit ignorance and powerlessness, even to the point of inventing meanings, is this not the boundless egotism of the ascetic? Several years later, Foucault himself drew the connection between his desire for knowledge and his passion for power. In response to a question regarding his negativism, Foucault replied by asserting that he was indeed negative, and for good reason.

> The bourgeoisie is intelligent, lucid, calculating. No other form of domination has ever been as prolific and consequently as dangerous, as profoundly rooted, as this form. . . . Fundamentally, I do not like to write; it is a very difficult activity to overcome. Writing only interests me to the extent that it unites itself to the reality of a combat, functioning as an instrument, a tactic, an illumination. I would like my books to be sorts of scalpels, Molotov cocktails, or minefields and have them carbonize after use in the manner of fireworks. . . . I am a tool merchant, a tactician, an indicator of targets, a cartographer, a draftsman, an armourer.[49]

Despite this extravagant rhetoric, Foucault recognizes that there is a considerable difference between willing power and exercising power, and he has started to outline his views on the nature of power and the possibilities for political action.

In 1968 the editors of *Esprit* presented Foucault with a number of questions. He answered in considerable length the following question, which he felt went to "the very core" of his work: "Doesn't a thought which introduces constraint of the system and discontinuity in the history of the mind remove all basis for a progressive political intervention? Does it not lead to the following dilemma: either the acceptance of the system or the appeal to an uncontrolled event, to the irruption of exterior violence which alone is capable of upsetting the system?"[50] Foucault's response was an attempt to demonstrate that "progressive political intervention" is possible, despite the determinism inherent in social systems and the discontinuous nature of change. He first corrected the editors' definition of archaeology by making the important point that archaeology is not concerned with a single totalizing system but with multiplicity. Therefore it analyzes systems and discontinuities. Moreover, archaeology does not deal with "the history of the mind" but with the histories of discourses. Archaeology thus views social systems as systems of possibilities and not as manifestations of a single closed system of necessity. Therefore political action is possible, and the real question is what kind of political practice is compatible with archaeological analysis.

Foucault approached this question by asking whether the critical operations of archaeological analysis exclude factors essential for progressive politics and whether the discourses he had chosen to analyze have any relation to progressive politics. He isolated four critical operations of archaeological analysis and concluded that they not only allow a progressive politics but are actually necessary for such a politics. The first of these critical operations entails the establishment of limits. In place of infinite hidden meanings, archaeology fixes specific visible boundaries. In place of sovereign creating subjects, archaeology defines the specific roles of discoursing subjects. Finally, in the place of an "indefinitely receding origin," archaeology analyzes the specific location and points of transformation of discursive systems.[51] By thus removing discourse from metaphysical concepts of meaning, constituent subjects, and origin, Foucault hoped "to liberate the discursive field from the historical-transcendental structure which the philosophy of the nineteenth century had imposed on it."[52] This supposedly would make possible a realistic politics rather than a politics tied to idealistic concepts of purpose, freedom, and continuity.

The second critical operation of archaeology involves the elimination of "ill-considered oppositions." In place of artificial dualities (such as tradition and invention, dead and living, static and dynamic), archaeology provides an analysis of difference. This operation, then, frees history from "the triple metaphor which has encumbered it for more than a century"—the evolutionary, biological, and dynamic metaphor.[53] Consequently, it is now possible to examine specific relations between specific discourses. The third critical operation, the lifting of restrictions on discourse, Foucault considered the most important of the four operations. Restrictions on discourse reduce discourse to "a simple place of expression for thoughts, imagination, knowledge, [and] unconscious themes" that originate outside of discourse itself.[54] Once these restrictions are lifted, it becomes possible to recognize the systematic nature of discourse. The last and most encompassing of Foucault's critical operations entails the removal of the uncertain status that has characterized the various forms of history. Instead of the conventional disciplines with their ambiguous borders, confused objects, and inadequate concepts of causality, archaeology purports to offer "a history of discursive practices in the specific relationships which link them to other practices."[55] According to Foucault, knowledge of such systematic relationships is a necessary ingredient of any progressive politics.

Archaeology, then, permits an accurate appraisal of what Foucault believes to be the real determinants of thought and action in our society. It also assumes a sufficient range of indeterminism to justify the intervention of political action. It does not, however, appear to have any necessary relation to what is usually understood as progressive politics. And despite Foucault's disclaimers, it is indeed possible that the concepts of freedom, meaning, and continuity are still essential for a progressive politics (unless that undefined term refers merely to an effective politics). There is a firmer basis for believing that archaeology implies a progressive politics if one assesses archaeology in terms of the particular discourses Foucault has chosen to analyze. Foucault studies discourses that he views as repressive in order to undermine their basic assumptions. Medicine, psychiatry, and the judiciary may not be as obvious in their repressive functions as corporations and political parties, but they are pervasive forms of power and knowledge which Foucault regards as extremely threatening. They have contributed to the establishment of complex systems of confinement (hospitals, asylums, and prisons) that install actual physical oppression under the pretense of curing, treating, and rehabilitating. Moreover, medicine, psychiatry, and law are closely tied to specific political practices which Foucault believes can be exposed through archaeological analyses. Foucault claims that by "outlining this theory of the scientific discourse, by making it appear

as an ensemble of regulated practices, being articulated in an ana-
lyzable fashion upon other practices, I am not just enjoying myself
by making the game more complicated for certain spirited souls. I
am trying to define in what way, to what extent, to what level the
discourse, and particularly the scientific discourses, can be objects of
a political practice, and in what system of dependency they can be in
relation to it."[56]

Intellectuals, Power, and Practice

Foucault's subsequent reflections on archaeology and politics have clarified the relationship between theory and practice. But
he no longer discusses "progressive" politics. He has turned instead
to an analysis of power. This concern with power, and with the role
of intellectuals in revolutionary struggles, were subjects of intense
debate after the events of May 1968. Since most French intellectuals
were surprised by this revolutionary movement, and responded to
rather than directed the uprising, they felt compelled to reexamine
the social function of intellectuals.

The increasingly marginal role of Western intellectuals had previously led sociologists and historians to trace the transformation of
this group from "ideological bulwarks of society" to "utopian critics"
standing above ordinary class conflicts.[57] In France this movement
from the social center to the periphery was complicated by the fact
that the pre-1940 *république des professeurs* combined an "institu-
tionally powerful mandarinate and an intellectual *fronde*."[58] Since
then, French intellectuals wishing to distinguish themselves from the
mandarins have felt compelled to identify with extremist political
groups (such as Maoists and anarchists) or with rejected social groups
(such as criminals and lunatics). The sociologist Annie Guédez has
even suggested that recent French intellectuals are trying to protect
their threatened group identity by making their language so esoteric
as to be inaccessible to outsiders, and that Foucault's own passage
from philosophy to archaeology and then to political action is indica-
tive of the ambivalent position of modern intellectuals.[59]

Foucault himself appears to regard this passage as part of a more
fundamental redefinition of the role of contemporary intellectuals.
In a discussion with Gilles Deleuze, published in 1972 under the
title "Intellectuals and Power,"[60] Foucault criticized the notion that

intellectuals have a privileged relation to truth and that they can maintain a position above social conflict. Both men agreed that the nature of power as well as the role of intellectuals needs to be reconsidered, and their shared views have led these two philosophers to be classified together as leaders of a new "poststructuralist" tendency in French thought.[61]

Deleuze's theory of power, like Foucault's, is an attempt to go beyond Freudian and Marxist concepts. As Foucault expressed it:

> Marx and Freud cannot satisfy our desire for understanding this enigmatic thing which we call power, which is at once visible and invisible, present and hidden, ubiquitous. . . . Who exercises power? And in what sphere? We now know with reasonable certainty who exploits others, who receives the profits, which people are involved, and we know how these funds are reinvested. But as for power . . . we know that it is not in the hands of those who govern.[62]

According to Foucault, power is not concentrated in a few centers; it is dispersed throughout society in a series of discontinuous networks. Deleuze shares this view of the dispersal of power and believes, as Foucault does, that a "wide range of professionals (teachers, psychiatrists, educators of all kinds, etc.) will be called upon to exercise functions that have traditionally belonged to the police."[63] Moreover, Deleuze does not assume that leftist political parties or unions will counter this tendency, because he believes that they respond to interests at a deeper (and more conservative) level than class interests. There are, he claims, "investments of desire that mold and distribute power" and that "function in a more profound and diffuse manner than our interests dictate . . . the masses were not deceived; at a particular time they actually wanted a fascist regime."[64] In spite of the unreliability of the masses, Foucault and Deleuze continue to regard the proletarian struggle against exploitation as essential. However, they are interested in the struggle against power and advocate the tactics of guerrilla warfare, which favor localized strikes against different constellations of power. Thus Foucault approves of the fact that

> women, prisoners, conscripted soldiers, hospital patients, and homosexuals have now begun a specific struggle against the particularized power, the constraints and controls, that are exerted

over them. Such struggles are actually involved in the revolutionary movement to the degree that they are radical, uncompromising and nonreformist and refuse any attempt at arriving at a new disposition of the same power with, at best, a change of masters. And these movements are linked to the revolutionary movement of the proletariat to the extent that they fight against the controls and constraints which serve the same system of power.[65]

This view of the need for direct action by oppressed groups against various forms of dispersed power does not leave a privileged place for intellectuals in revolutionary struggles. Intellectuals have traditionally provided overarching theories that have little relevance for localized revolutionary action. Under these conditions, and considering the isolation of intellectuals in modern society, Foucault and Deleuze attempted to define a new role for radical intellectuals. They examined, first, what Deleuze referred to as the "partial and fragmentary" relationships between theory and practice.[66] Both Deleuze and Foucault have rejected the conception of practice as an application of or an inspiration for theory. These relationships assume a "process of totalization" at variance with their own views that practice and theory are specific and limited. According to them, practice "is a set of relays from one theoretical point to another, and theory is a relay from one practice to another. . . . A theorising intellectual, for us, is no longer a subject, a representing or representative consciousness. . . . Representation no longer exists; there is only action —theoretical action and practical action which serve as relays and form networks."[67] Both Foucault and Deleuze believe that intellectuals cannot stand outside the network of relays and cannot claim a position of leadership by virtue of a special access to "truth." They themselves are part of the existing system of power and, as the events of May 1968 indicated, may even know less than the masses about the revolutionary potential of their society. Intellectuals can no longer place themselves "somewhat ahead and to the side" in order to "awaken consciousness"; they must recognize that theory is practice and join in the struggle to take power.[68] Moreover, they must reject the "stupid and hypocritical" notion of reform and realize that the present social system is totally repressive on a global as well as on a local scale. Further, intellectuals must avoid setting up "representative forms of centralism and a hierarchical structure" which would only duplicate the existing totalizing system. Instead, they must "initiate localized counter-responses" and establish "lateral affiliations and an entire system of networks and popular bases."[69] This decentralized, supposedly leaderless form of revolutionary action follows the pattern of the 1968 uprising as interpreted by Daniel and Gabriel Cohn-Bendit. They too believe that the real militant must avoid all forms of bureaucratic organization (such as political parties and unions), rid himself of the illusion that his purpose is to teach or to lead the masses, and dedicate himself to the task of helping the workers "struggle on their own behalf."[70]

Foucault's own political action is consistent with this reduced conception of the role of the intellectual. His substantial theoretical work on the nature of confinement has been paralleled in recent years by practical actions to assist those who are or have been confined. In 1971 Foucault, together with Jean-Marie Domenach and Pierre Vidal-Naquet, formed the Information Group on Prisons (GIP) in the wake of a hunger strike by leftist prisoners. During that strike the solidarity of political prisoners and "common" criminals raised hopes that the entire prison system could be challenged. The GIP distributed questionnaires to approximately a thousand prisoners and published the results. Subsequently the GIP helped to establish numerous groups investigating the conditions of prisons, not in order to effect reforms but to let the prisoners speak for themselves and to unify the struggles inside the prisons with those on the outside. A series of prison riots in 1972 suggests that these efforts have indeed been timely. The formation in 1973 of the Association for the Defense of the Rights of Detainees and the Prisoners' Action Committee (CAP), which replaced the GIP, also strengthened the prisoners' movement.[71]

Foucault has clarified the purpose of this movement in his preface to the book *From Prison to Revolt* by Serge Livrozet, himself a former convict and a founder of the CAP.[72] According to Foucault, the literature on criminals, like detective stories, usually reduces criminal acts to narratives of individual misfortune or cunning. Criminals have not been able to reflect on the meaning of crime or on the nature of the society that defines crime and that intentionally creates the conditions for crime. Reflections on crime have been the special prerogative of sociologists, psychologists, and criminologists. However, these specialists are not interested in listening to criminals; they wish to "examine" criminals, to view them as objects. Their "scientific" discourses have supported the prevailing prejudice that criminals are the products of a series of individual accidents rather than the victims of systematic social repression. Foucault hopes that prisoners' associations and a new literature by prisoners themselves will constitute a "counterdiscourse" and help to destroy the present system of crime and punishment. He praises Livrozet's book and political activities as examples of the integration of reflection and experience necessary for a new "philosophy of the people."

Although Foucault has diminished the distinction between political and nonpolitical prisoners in France, he has supported the efforts of Soviet political prisoners to maintain such a distinction. In 1976, in an interview on Russian prison camps, he contrasted the situations in France and Russia. In France, he said, the important distinction is "not between political and non-political offenders, but between the profitable illegalities perpetuated with impunity by those who use the law, and the simple illegalities that the penal system uses to create a standing army of criminals."[73] In the Soviet Union, however, the authorities deny the existence of political prisoners while simultaneously defining all crimes as political (crimes against the state). Consequently, it is necessary for Soviet dissenters to stress the difference between their political "crimes" and ordinary crimes. Furthermore, in the Soviet Union (as in France) nonpolitical prisoners are "controlled, infiltrated, and manipulated by those in power,"[74] and there are reasons for Soviet dissenters to fear them. Although Foucault has stated elsewhere that bourgeois repression is the worst form of social repression because it is pervasive and often invisible, he has no affection for the Soviet brand of visible repression. Indeed, he believes that the Soviets have

> merely adopted certain power and management techniques perfected by nineteenth-century European capitalism. . . . Moreover the prison system was only one of the techniques of power necessary to the development and control of the forces of production. The disciplined life—discipline in school, at work, in the army—is also a technical innovation of that period. And techniques are easily transplanted. Just as the Soviets adopted the principles of scientific management and other related management techniques developed in the West, they also adopted our disciplinary techniques, adding one new weapon, party discipline, to the arsenal we had perfected.[75]

Foucault's opposition to the disciplinary system of prisons is usually theoretical or organizational, but he has also participated in more direct forms of protest. After the suspicious death of an Algerian worker in the police bureau at Versailles, the Committee of Defense for immigrant workers and a number of intellectuals organized a public demonstration. The demonstration was prohibited by the police shortly before it began and thus took place illegally. Foucault, along with Claude Mauriac and Jean Genet, who were marching with him, were among those arrested.[76] Foucault's resistance to other forms of discipline and confinement also has a practical as well as a theoretical dimension. With Sartre and Maurice Clavel, he has directed the extreme leftist paper *Libération*, which carries information about abusive conditions in institutions such as factories, schools, and barracks.

In spite of the seemingly reformist nature of his political action and his own dependence on the liberal system that employs him, Foucault has been anxious to identify himself with extreme revolutionary positions at least since 1968. He has discussed the possibility for radical change in a number of interviews and debates, two of which focused on the educational system. The first, an interview with John Simon, took place in Buffalo, New York, where Foucault was teaching at the time. The second, published toward the end of 1971, was a discussion between Foucault and the editors and readers of the radical journal *Actuel*.

In the Simon interview, Foucault explained that his purpose in analyzing the "repression-suppression" systems of the past is to show that we are still trapped within these systems. He hoped to present "a critique of our own time, based on retrospective analyses," and to make visible our present "cultural unconscious."[77] He regarded his scholarly efforts as similar to the actions of students whose clothing, hair styles, and manner challenge current standards and force an awareness of the "implicit systems which determine our most familiar behavior."[78] He also claimed that, since capitalist societies need to train a large number of technicians and scientists, the universities have had to accept proletarian and lower-middle-class students. This means that "the enemy is within the gates"[79] and the universities may no longer be successful in isolating young and rebellious elements while simultaneously instilling values that serve to integrate these groups into a capitalist society.

Foucault believes that the educational system is one of the few confining structures which might be successfully challenged by the inmates themselves. By contrast, those confined in hospitals or asylums are unlikely to "make their own revolution," and prisoners, too, require help from outside. In the schools, however, the professors may be less of a help than a hindrance because they themselves are part of the established system. The position of radical professors is therefore almost untenable, and Foucault's defense of his own professorial role was not very convincing. "When I lecture somewhat dogmatically, I tell myself: I am paid to bring to the students a certain form and content of knowledge; I must fashion my lecture or my course a little as one might make a shoe, no more and no less. . . . I bring this object to the desk, I show it and then I leave it up to the audience to do with it what they want. I consider myself more like an artisan doing a certain piece of work and offering it for consumption than a master making his slaves work."[80] The role of the neutral artisan, like that of the neutral scientist, may indeed be the most comfortable position for a scholar. But Foucault himself later rejected this possibility and even presented his works as tool boxes and Molotov cocktails to be used in revolutionary battles.

The problem of the role of professors in revolutionary struggles reappeared in the discussion published by *Actuel*. Student revolts in Europe and the United States led the editors of *Actuel* to interview a number of radical intellectuals who represented contemporary forms of social analyses different from "official Marxism." Foucault as well as Marcuse, Lefebvre, Deleuze, and Guattari was among those interviewed. In a short summary of the French situation, one of the editors presented a wide-ranging social critique that included the following: the obsolescence of the Sorbonne and its failure to deal with any significant social thought later than Kant; the rigidity of the established Marxist-Leninist-Stalinist line; the barrenness of French social thought during the 1920s and 1930s compared to the creativity of thinkers such as Marcuse, Adorno, and Lukács; the "double impasse" of French Marxist scholars who have turned either toward the young Marx (Garaudy) or the mature Marx (Althusser); the new theories of society developed by the structuralists; and the new social practices represented by the counterculture of the 1960s.[81]

Foucault, who had been teaching during the late 1960s at the University of Vincennes (one of the more radical branches of the French university system), admitted that it has always been a problem for someone like me, someone who has been teaching for a long time, to decide if I should act outside or inside the university. Should we decide that the question was settled in May, that the university has broken down, and that we can now move on to other concerns? . . . Or is this merely a way of evading a fact that continues to embarrass me: namely, that the university structure remains intact and that we must continue to fight in this arena?[82]

Foucault's frank assessment of his own position as a teacher led into a discussion of the possibility that the French university system, far from being broken in 1968, was merely modernized. In the words of one of the students, the educational system after 1968 was "far more functional. It preserved the best schools, those whose primary function was the selection of technocrats." Consequently, the university now serves the "needs of neocapitalism" more effectively and is even more repressive than before.[83] Notwithstanding the possibility of an even more centralized system of repression, Foucault objected to revolutionary responses based on theoretical models and analyses of the whole of society. He claimed that "to imagine another system is to extend our participation in the present system" and that the idea of the "whole of society" is the very concept which should be destroyed.[84] He doubted that the brevity of the 1968 revolutionary movement, or even the *embourgeoisement* of the Russian Revolution, was due to a lack of theoretical models. Moreover, he rejected the argument that decentralized revolutionary movements have failed "until now" and are therefore incapable of realization. He suggested, in fact, that a future society is more likely to emerge from experiences taking place at the moment than from abstract theories of revolution. "It is possible that the rough outline of a future society is supplied by the recent experiences with drugs, sex, communes, other forms of consciousness and other forms of individuality. If scientific socialism emerged from the *Utopias* of the nineteenth century, it is possible that a real socialization will emerge, in the twentieth century, from *experiences.*"[85]

Foucault's attraction to the counterculture, like his interpretation of genealogy as a countermemory, the new literature of prisoners as a counterdiscourse, and revolutionary struggles as a series of counterresponses, is consistent with his negative political position. He is opposed both to established power and to all values that inhibit the efforts of those who do not have power to seize it. He thus defines humanism as "everything in Western civilization that restricts *the desire for power*."[86] Both humanism and reform are opposed to revolution, since "humanism is based on the desire to change the ideological system without altering institutions; and reformers wish to change the institutions without touching the ideological system. Revolutionary action, on the contrary, is defined as the simultaneous agitation of consciousness and institutions; this implies that we attack the relationships of power through the notions and institutions that function as their instruments, armature, and armor."[87] Because present revolutionary forces are not powerful enough for simultaneous attacks on all fronts, Foucault advocates a multitude of local strikes and the acceptance of a long, repetitive, and seemingly incoherent struggle on many fronts.[88]

Power and Justice

Foucault's hostility toward centralization and his conception of direct participation on a local level suggests a form of anarchism that appears to resemble Noam Chomsky's anarcho-syndicalism. This is not the case, however, for Chomsky's anarchism is based on traditional humanist values of freedom, truth, and justice whereas Foucault's anarchism is concerned solely with power. In a debate between Chomsky and Foucault, which was televised in 1971 and later published under the appropriate title "Human Nature: Justice versus Power," the differences between the political theories of these radical intellectuals became apparent.[89] The first part of the debate, which dealt primarily with theoretical issues, aroused little controversy. This was somewhat surprising, because Chomsky's views on rationalism, human nature, and the creative subject are contrary to Foucault's. The remainder of the debate, which dealt with politics, power, and justice, revealed intense differences of opinion. What was at issue throughout was the problem of defining human nature and the possibility of forming a model for a better society.

According to Chomsky, the universal, innate capacity for language is a "fundamental constituent of human nature," and he suggested that there may be "innate organizing principles" in other "domains of human cognition and behavior."[90] Foucault responded by pointing out that previous so-called universal notions claiming scientific status have been no more than "epistemological indicators" of certain ways of classifying information. For example, the nineteenth-century concept of life was not an absolute category but merely a concept tied to a specific culture. He regarded the concept of human nature in the same light and suspected that the notions of "innate" knowledge or "deep structures" are actually unfounded extrapolations from culturally determined knowledge and surface structures.

A similar exchange of differing but related views characterized their discussion of seventeenth- and eighteenth-century rationalism. Although Chomsky's *Cartesian Linguistics* and Foucault's *Order of Things* both dealt with Classical rationalism, they did so from different perspectives. For Chomsky, eighteenth-century linguistics prefigured his own belief that there are only a limited number of innate cognitive structures that nevertheless enable an enormous variety of free linguistic creations. Foucault, who studied Classical structures of perception, stressed instead the large number of potential perceptual structures and the limited number of determined responses within a specific set of structures. For Chomsky freedom and order are complementary concepts since cognitive structures indicate their compatibility. For Foucault order limits and threatens to exclude freedom since social structures indicate the repressive function of selection. Nonetheless, both men recognize that they are dealing with possibilities in linguistic and social patterns and not with completely rulebound or completely arbitrary phenomena. However, for Chomsky the individual "speaking" subject is vitally important, whereas for Foucault there are only anonymous "discoursing" subjects. This difference, as Foucault pointed out, is largely a consequence of the

state of knowledge, of knowing, in which we are working. The linguistics with which you have been familiar, and which you have succeeded in transforming, excluded the importance of the creative speaking subject; while the history of science such as it existed when people of my generation were starting to work, on the contrary, exalted individual creativity. . . . Therefore I have, in appearance at least, a completely different attitude to Mr. Chomsky apropos creativity, because for me it is a matter of effacing the dilemma of the knowing subject, while for him it is a matter of allowing the dilemma of the speaking subject to reappear.[91]

When the conversation turned to a discussion of the nature of scientific theory, Chomsky's remarks again assumed a priori cognitive structures whereas Foucault's referred to external social determinants. Chomsky maintained that if "we really want to develop a theory of scientific creation, or for that matter of artistic creation, I think we have to focus attention precisely on that set of conditions that, on the one hand, delimits and restricts the scope of our possible knowledge, while at the same time permitting the inductive leap to complicated systems of knowledge on the basis of a small amount of data."[92] The set of conditions Chomsky wishes to discover are those that create "the formal organization of [scientific] knowledge." But Foucault was discussing science as "the content of the various knowledges which is dispersed into a particular society." Therefore he wanted to know "whether one cannot discover the system of regularity, of constraint, which makes science possible, somewhere else, even outside the human mind, in social forms, in the relations of production, in the class struggle, etc."[93] Despite these differences, both men agreed that scientific knowledge is not progressive, that it alters by a series of transformations that form a "jagged pattern" of change. But Chomsky suggested that this very pattern may itself be rational.

> When we try out those intellectual constructions in a changing world of fact, we will not find cumulative growth. What we will find are strange leaps: here is a domain of phenomena, a certain science applies very nicely; now slightly broaden the range of phenomena, then another science, which is very different, happens to apply very beautifully, perhaps leaving out some of these other phenomena. . . . But I think the reason for this is precisely this set of principles, which unfortunately we don't know, . . . which defines for us what is a possible intellectual structure, a possible deep-science, if you like.[94]

Deep structures of thought and behavior, presumably constant and universal, are the assumptions central to Chomsky's view of human nature. His application of these views to social theory has involved a commitment to political structures that maximize individual creative freedom and minimize all forms of repression. Chomsky's anarcho-syndicalism (or libertarian socialism) proposes "a federated, decentralized system of free associations, incorporating economic as well as other social institutions."[95] Moreover, Chomsky favors civil disobedience against governmental orders that are immoral. Yet this does not mean that he views all laws as instruments of oppression. On the contrary, he believes that "to a very large extent existing law represents certain human values; and existing law, correctly interpreted, permits much of what the state commands you not to do."[96] Chomsky is also prepared to accept violence, but only as a last resort and only as an effort to establish a more just society. While he does not believe in ideal justice or in an ideal society, he does believe that it is possible to "imagine and move towards the creation of a better society and also a better system of justice."[97] And, finally, Chomsky believes that contemporary intellectuals are confronted by two tasks. They must first "understand very clearly the nature of power and oppression and terror and destruction in our own society." But they must also "try to create the vision of a future just society . . . [and] a humanistic social theory that is based, if possible, on some firm and humane concept of . . . human nature."[98]

Foucault's very different positions generated real controversy. Foucault refused to propose "an ideal social model for the functioning of our scientific or technological society" and recognized only the responsibility to reveal "the relationships of political power which actually control the social body and oppress or repress it."[99] He claimed that the very effort to define human nature risks making such a definition "in terms borrowed from our society, from our civilization, from our culture."[100] This, he pointed out, was what the Russian revolutionaries did in 1917, thereby entrenching nineteenth-century bourgeois values in a supposedly communist society. And, despite his own belief that theories are partial and limited, Foucault was not responsive to Chomsky's appeal "to be bold enough to speculate and create social theories on the basis of partial knowledge, while remaining open to the strong possibility, and in fact overwhelming probability, that at least in some respects we're very far off the mark."[101] Moreover, Foucault refused to recognize "justice" and "truth" as valid categories since, like "human nature," he regarded them as concepts bound to the dominant culture and thus tied today to bourgeois interests. Indeed, he flatly declared that one "makes war to win, not because it is just" and that even

the proletariat doesn't wage war against the ruling class because it considers such a war to be just. The proletariat makes war with the ruling class because, for the first time in history, it wants to take power. And because it will overthrow the power of the ruling class it considers such a war to be just. . . . When the proletariat takes power, it may be quite possible that the proletariat will exert towards the classes over which it has just triumphed a violent, dictatorial and even bloody power. I can't see what objection one could make to this.[102]

This chilling acceptance of pure power is not an isolated rhetorical comment. Foucault expanded on the theme of justice and power in a 1972 debate with militant French Maoists, which was published in *Les Temps Modernes* under the title "On Popular Justice."[103] The Maoists, who advocated setting up tribunals to judge the police, wanted to discuss revolutionary justice. Foucault's main contribution to this discussion was an effort to demonstrate that tribunals were a bourgeois conception and that revolutionary justice should be decided directly by "the people" without mediation. The issue of justice, however, quickly disappeared, given the obvious absence of any moral position among the debaters. The real question was power: how to seize it and how to consolidate it. Consequently Foucault, whose academic work is marked by great conceptual precision and who claims to resist all efforts to institutionalize power, accepted the most outrageous theoretical simplifications as well as the practical necessity for terror against both the "enemies" of the "people" and even against the "masses" themselves, who, after all, had to be "normalized."

Foucault began by contrasting the spontaneous executions (the "September Massacres") during the French Revolution, which he admired as an example of revolutionary justice, with the intervention by the newly formed Paris Commune of 1792. The commune established tribunals, which Foucault regarded as the first deformation of popular justice. By introducing a third force between the people and their enemies, the commune had reestablished the authority of the state.[104] Also, these tribunals, in both their history and structure, revealed the identification of this form of justice with bourgeois values. In a rapid survey of the development of tribunals since the Middle Ages, Foucault noted the connections between justice, money, and force. Moreover, he claimed that the very arrangement of the courtroom indicates the basic assumptions of bourgeois justice. The position of the judge between two opposing parties presupposes that the judge is "neutral" and capable of perceiving the "truth." Further, the judge's power to have his decision enforced is repugnant to Foucault. He prefers popular justice to this legal justice because "in the case of popular justice, you do not have three elements, you have the masses and their enemies. Then, when the masses recognize someone as an enemy, when they decide to punish this enemy—or to reeducate him —they do not refer to an abstract universal idea of justice, they refer only to their own experience . . . they do not rely on a state apparatus which has the capacity to validate decisions, they execute them purely and simply."[105]

The Maoists, who were represented almost exclusively by one speaker, disagreed with this conception. Since the masses were not homogeneous and might be manipulated by their enemies, the Maoists felt it necessary to develop instruments of discipline, centralization, and unification, in short, a state apparatus. Furthermore, they considered this apparatus necessary to make decisions the masses were not capable of making. For example, it might be unwise to kill all the shopkeepers; in France that would involve too many people whom the state might need. Foucault, whose works are an indictment of discipline and centralization, nonetheless capitulated to this argument. He attempted, however, to distinguish between judicial intervention by the state apparatus (which he disliked) and political intervention (which he granted might be necessary). This latter intervention could play a "positive," "educational" role by teaching the masses in such a way "that it is the masses themselves who come to say: 'Indeed, we cannot kill this man,' or 'Indeed, we ought to kill him.' "[106]

If a future revolution did install a judicial bureaucracy, Foucault warned that a system like the present bourgeois system, which divides workers from prisoners and thus fragments the proletariat, would only increase the contradictions within the masses. According to Foucault, the prison system is only one of three methods used by the bourgeoisie to divide the proletariat and make it resistant to revolution. The other two methods are the military (which creates fascists) and colonialism (which creates racists). This argument did not persuade the Maoists, who felt that Foucault was attempting to establish the distinction between the proletarianized and the nonproletarianized masses as fundamental, whereas they regarded the real division as that between individualism and collectivism.

The concept of justice reemerged toward the end of the debate in a twisted form. The Maoists distinguished between three stages of revolutionary action—revolt, subversion, and revolution—and assumed that "excesses" were necessary in the early stages. Consequently, even within the context of direct popular justice, the Maoists considered it "just" to execute the head of a factory without the agreement of the workers. In addition to this perversion of justice, Foucault suggested the possibility of a useful parody of justice. Revolutionary trials (of the police, for example) using the established tribunal form would be a way to ridicule bourgeois justice by means of a symbolic counterjustice.

In this conception of justice Foucault does not, as Nietzsche did, expose the raw power underlying moral values for the purpose of effecting a transvaluation of values. Foucault's analyses are closer to Sade's than to Nietzsche's in that they represent a simple inversion rather than a transvaluation of values. Moreover, Foucault's reduction of justice to power (like Sade's acceptance of the principles of force and destruction) has led him to that nihilism which, in the words of Camus, encompasses "universal crime, an aristocracy of cynicism and the desire for an apocalypse."[107] Yet there is a significant difference between Sade and Foucault. Sade's nihilism was consistent with a life spent largely in prisons and lunatic asylums. Foucault's nihilism is more difficult to understand. It is not theoretically coherent, but it appears to be more than just the expression of his particular personality. The precarious social position of the intellectual may indeed be a factor in the extremism of Foucault's politics and the difficulty of his language. It is unlikely, however, that sociological analyses alone can account for Foucault's theoretical or political positions since such analyses tend to explain away radical postures as mere deviations from established norms. Whatever the rhetorical dimension of his political posture may be, there can be little doubt that Foucault is intensely interested in power and is not merely engaging in verbal games. His theoretical works aim to expose knowledge as power, and his political position is geared toward the destruction of established powers. Moreover, his archaeological studies are an effort to go beyond exposing and criticizing various forms of authority. They are attempts to increase the power of knowledge by making social thought systematic. In this effort Foucault has not, like Marx, turned to the evolutionary model provided by "soft" sciences like biology. He has used instead the revolutionary model provided by "hard" sciences like physics.

 *Three*

A NEW PARADIGM

FOR SCIENTIFIC AND

SOCIAL THOUGHT

Field Concepts in Modern Physics

At the close of the nineteenth century, the classical mechanical view of the physical world was firmly established and most physicists assumed that only the details remained to be added. Twenty years later the entire system lay in ruins and a new interpretation of the physical world had replaced it. In this new version familiar Newtonian concepts such as absolute time and space, localizable objects, predictable events, and forces acting at a distance had been altered beyond recognition. Space and time were now combined into space-time and no longer served as fixed backdrops for physical events but became constitutive factors. Objects ceased to retain a constant identity and could be neither localized nor defined. Cosmological and atomic events lost both predictability and continuity to become discontinuous occurrences with variable incidences of probability. Above all, the traditional notion of forces was displaced by the very different concept of fields, which became a new organizing construct for the physical sciences.

The mechanical world view and its gradual extension to other forms of scientific and social thought are topics too well known to require elaboration here. However, two features of classical mechanics deserve mention since they mark the theoretical and practical limits of this interpretation and indicate the points of its collapse. There is, first, the mathematical system upon which the theoretical structure of mechanics was based. Second, the application of mechanics to "energetics" (heat, light, electricity, and magnetism) in the nineteenth century revealed the inadequacy of mechanical models and forced the acceptance of new concepts that were to become the bases for new interpretive systems.

The mathematical system underlying classical mechanics was Euclidean geometry, the geometry of straight lines and empty spaces. The representational power of Euclidean geometry appeared so obvious and so extensive that it became plausible to speak of the "geometric spirit" in social as well as scientific discourse. But Euclidean geometry was based upon a number of assumptions that no longer appear self-evident. It assumed, for example, that space has no intrinsic features, that it is an absence of qualities, a void. The absence of characteristics, however, is itself significant. The assumption that space is a void meant that it could not interact with matter, that it must be homogeneous (the same everywhere), isotropic (having no preferred direction), infinite, and centerless. Newton made these assumptions, although with occasional reservations,[1] and the seventeenth- and eighteenth-century philosophers who questioned such assumptions had no alternative mathematical system to offer.[2]

Non-Euclidean geometries were formulated during the nineteenth century, but they played no significant role in physics as long as the classical system seemed to work. Early nineteenth-century efforts to apply mechanics to "weightless substances" such as heat did, in fact, look promising. The kinetic theory of gases suggested that heat could be understood in terms of the motion of particles, and the newly derived laws of thermodynamics further confirmed Newton's laws of motion. Yet the second law of thermodynamics (entropy) presented special problems to physicists and carried disturbing implications for nonscientists as well. This law was disturbing because it meant that all closed systems tended toward increasing disorder and that the universe would eventually "run down." It was also problematical in a more limited sense because it imposed a constraint on energy transformations. Heat transfers require a differential; that is, the difference in temperature between substances rather than the actual amount of heat present determines heat exchange. The concept of difference (rather than substance) is central to contemporary French structuralist thought. Not surprisingly, when Foucault uses the term *entropy*, he uses it in its technical rather than its cosmic sense.[3]

The application of the principles of mechanics to the phenomena of light, electricity, and magnetism was not as successful as their application to heat. Early in the nineteenth century the Newtonian (and Cartesian) concept of light as a series of particles was replaced by the wave theory of light.[4] For some historians of science, the wave theory of light is the "first chapter" in the history of field theory, followed by Faraday's and Maxwell's work on electromagnetism and by Einstein's theory of relativity.[5] Such a view, however, obscures the fact that field theory became the foundation for a new system of thought only with Einstein. Still, the wave theory of light was an early indication of the superiority of an interpretive model in which fixed objects are replaced by interacting systems. In the wave theory, complex interactions not comprehensible in the earlier corpuscular view could now be explained. Both the nature of wave interactions and the very language in which they are expressed suggest the type of discursive relations Foucault has established in his archaeologies. Waves are *systems of dispersion* that usually occur through a series of *displacements* in a medium. Waves contained within a limited area exhibit specific features. They may, for example, interact in such a way as to form a repeating pattern (standing wave), although only a specific number of wavelengths may form such a pattern in any given area. A limited number of repetitive patterns within specified boundaries are also characteristic of Foucault's discursive formations. Further, wave behavior at boundaries reveals complex forms of change. Particles that encounter borders either bounce back or pass through, whereas waves may pass through in altered form (changed wavelength), be split, or be reflected back in inverted form. Refraction, diffraction, and reflection are also characteristic of Foucault's discursive transformations, although they do not exhaust the possibilities for discursive change.

The wave theory of light did not create a crisis in classical mechanics at first. Although mechanical constructs require "particles with forces acting along lines connecting them and depending only on distance,"[6] it was assumed not only that light waves traveled through a substance ("ether") but also that they were longitudinal waves, that is, waves undergoing displacements in the direction of motion. When the first assumption could not be verified and the second was disproved (light waves are transverse waves), then a crisis ensued. This crisis was directly related to developments in the study of electricity and magnetism. As long as physicists limited themselves to traditional concepts of substances (particles) and forces (in this case, charges, not gravity), they were unable to explain the relation between electricity and magnetism. But by shifting attention from the charged particles to the field between the charges, it became possible to relate electrical fields to magnetic fields because they have the same structure. This suggested that the field, not the charges or the particles, determines electrical action and that a change in an electrical field would create a magnetic field and vice versa. The laws describing what could now be perceived as electromagnetic phenomena were formulated by Clerk Maxwell, whose field equations are structure laws. These laws are of particular relevance to this discussion because, as Einstein explained:

> Maxwell's equations allow us to follow the history of the field, just as the mechanical equations enabled us to follow the history of the material particle. . . . In Maxwell's theory there are no material actors. The mathematical equations of the theory express the laws governing the electromagnetic field. They do not, as in Newton's laws, connect two widely separated events; they do not connect the happenings *here* with the conditions *there*. The field *here* and *now* depends on the field in the *immediate neighborhood* at a time *just past*. The equations allow us to predict what will happen a little further in space and a little later in time, if we know what happens here and now. They allow us to increase our knowledge of the field by small steps. We can deduce what happens here from that which happened far away by the summation of these very small steps. In Newton's theory, on the contrary, only big steps connecting distant events are permissible.[7]

These ideas are strikingly similar to concepts Foucault uses in his archaeologies. Indeed, Foucault's works might be seen as a series of "field histories" in which there are no material actors and which deal with the web of relationships in an immediate neighborhood. He, too, avoids causal theories connecting distant events by big steps and explores instead a multitude of small events that he views in spatial terms.

In the history of physics, field concepts made it possible not only to relate electricity and magnetism but also to combine the studies of electricity, magnetism, and light. Since electromagnetic waves travel at the speed of light and since both electrical and magnetic fields store energy, it became apparent that light itself is a type of electromagnetic "wave." Waves that are not really waves but sequences of fields propagating through space without a transmitting medium was not a concept compatible with classical notions of substance. By the close of the nineteenth century, then, "something of great importance had happened in physics. A new reality was created, a concept for which there was no place in the mechanical description."[8] A few philosophers and philosophically minded physicists also realized that conventional scientific concepts could no longer adequately represent the physical world but could only indicate systems of relationships. Men like Ernst Mach and Heinrich Hertz, for example, developed a phenomenological view of physics as a form of perception.[9] In fact, recent historians of science have maintained that Mach "moved physics as close to its revolution into relativity as philosophy alone could carry it."[10]

The revolution itself came with Einstein's two theories of relativity in 1905 and 1915. These theories are both field theories and it was Einstein's hope that eventually a unified field theory would define all physical phenomena, including matter, in terms of fields. In his first theory, the special theory of relativity, Einstein applied field equations to inertial systems, that is, to bodies moving uniformly relative to each other. In the general theory he extended field concepts to all systems, including those in nonuniform motion relative to each other. Although both theories replaced classical notions of substance and change with complex concepts of matter-energy and space-time, the special theory more radically redefined time while the general theory formulated a new concept of curved space to explain gravitation. Neither the special nor the general theory have a direct correlation to Foucault's work. Yet there are specific conceptual similarities and larger structural parallels between archaeology and relativity theory. Foucault has admitted that he does not have a "general" theory to explain relations between different epistemological systems, but his archaeologies do define relations between discourses in "uniform motion" relative to each other.

In both classical mechanics and relativity theory, as well as in archaeology, relations between inertial systems are expressed by transformation laws. Classical transformation laws assumed measurements of distance and time to be invariant and velocity to be infinitely variable. The observation that the velocity of light is constant—that it is not affected by the motion of its source or its receiver, or by its motion through "ether"—invalidated the classical transformation laws. This event had profound consequences. If velocity remained constant, then distance (space) and time must vary and a new type of transformation law was required to transpose information from one spatiotemporal system to another. Einstein used the Lorentz transformations for this purpose, because these equations could account for both field concepts and four-dimensional space-time.

According to the special theory of relativity, measurements of time and distance vary because matter in motion is not identical to matter at rest. As velocity increases, measuring rods shrink and clocks slow down relative to an observer in a slower system. Since space and time are different for observers in different inertial systems, events that appear to occur simultaneously to observers within one system will not appear simultaneous to observers in different systems. Relativity theory makes it impossible to speak of happenings in any absolute sense because, as Bertrand Russell explained, "the world which the theory of relativity presents to our imagination is not so much a world of 'things' in 'motion' as a world of *events*. . . . Causation, in the old sense, no longer has a place in theoretical physics."[11] Einstein expressed this break with the classical concept of causality in somewhat different terminology. Relativity theory, he asserted, replaced the traditional "*dynamic* picture in which positions *change* with time" with a "*static* picture" in which "motion is represented as something which *is*," as something which merely exists in a space-time continuum.[12] These concepts, which are central to relativity theory, also inform Foucault's conception of the variable role of the observer-subject, the immateriality of things, change as a series of events that exist rather than become, and the superiority of a static structural analysis over a dynamic dialectical interpretation.

The special theory of relativity, although concerned primarily with measurements of motion in space-time, also revealed the artificiality of the classical distinctions between matter and energy. Whereas classical mechanics had postulated separate conservation laws for matter and energy, Einstein demonstrated that at high velocities energy behaves like mass and matter can be transformed into energy. According to relativity theory, "matter is where the concentration of energy is great, field where the concentration of energy is small . . . the difference is a quantitative rather than a qualitative one. . . . We cannot imagine a definite surface separating distinctly field and matter."[13] As with time and space, matter and energy also could no longer be considered absolute and independent categories. All four categories were replaced by field concepts, although it was only with quantum theory that matter itself could be understood in terms of field relations. However, even before the development of quantum theory, it was clear that Einstein's special theory of relativity, by establishing field concepts as the central theoretical construct of modern physics, had revolutionized twentieth-century science. Einstein himself recognized that "the influence of the theory of relativity goes far beyond the problem from which it arose. It removes the difficulties and contradictions of the field theory; it formulates more general mechanical laws; it replaces two conservation laws by one; it changes our classical concept of time; it forms a general framework embracing all phenomena of nature."[14] Once again, a similar displacement can be perceived in Foucault's thought. For him, too, there is no distinct surface separating things and processes; traditional classificatory categories are replaced by field concepts; and a new framework for cultural phenomena is established.

The scientific framework that Einstein established with the special theory was expanded by his general theory of relativity. The general theory further revolutionized Newtonian physics by eliminating the concept of an inertial system and by defining gravitation in terms of fields instead of in terms of forces between masses at specific distances. Since inertial mass in Newtonian physics was equal to gravitational mass, Einstein came to regard the acceleration of inertial systems and gravitational attraction as identical. Thus he was able to devise laws valid for accelerating systems as well as for systems in uniform motion by viewing gravitation as a field phenomenon. Einstein's gravitational field equations are structure laws which, again, express a series of proximate rather than distant relationships. Gravitational fields, however, are determined by the density and shape of the masses involved. This meant that Einstein had to abandon a geometry based on straight lines and the absolute measurement of distance and adopt a non-Euclidean geometry in order to deal with curved space and four-dimensional space-time. In Einstein's interpretation of gravitation, the Newtonian concept of a force acting at a distance disappeared. What remained was a complicated configuration of space that determines the paths along which objects travel.

Einstein's adoption of non-Euclidean geometry and his rejection of the Newtonian concept of force have several important consequences. First of all, space can no longer be regarded as autonomous, homogeneous, and infinite. In Einstein's theory, space is related not merely to time but to matter, since it is the presence of matter that "curves" the surrounding space. And because space is unevenly curved depending on the distribution of matter, it cannot be regarded as homogeneous but must be viewed as a "heterogeneous plurality."[15] This means that "geometry reflects the condition of matter in a certain region. Geometry is 'local,' and if a universal geometry exists that underlies all the local geometries it must reflect the condition of matter *on the scale of the universe*."[16] The Riemannian geometry that Einstein used in the general theory can express a multiplicity of local curvatures of space-time, but it also implies what Einstein has called a "finite" yet "unbounded" universe.[17] Once more, these are concepts that appear, although not with exactly the same meanings, in Foucault's work. Space, as already indicated, is a prevalent metaphor in Foucault's analyses, and his imaginative spaces frequently "curve" into complex configurations. Furthermore, Foucault repeatedly discusses the problem of finite spaces and imaginative limits. And, for Foucault too, there is no "universal geometry"; his archaeologies are all expressions of the "metric" properties of many local space-times, that is, discourses at specific temporal and regional points.

The second consequence of Einstein's general theory, the rejection of the Newtonian belief that "simple forces act between unalterable particles,"[18] carries with it a number of other changes. In addition to redefining causality and substance (as mentioned above), the replacement of forces by fields meant, as Bertrand Russell expressed it, "the substitution of sight for touch as the source of physical ideas."[19] The older perception of tangible forces of attraction and repulsion is replaced, in field theory, by a visual perception of spatial configurations. This shift in the sensory mode of perception suggests a theme which not only runs through almost all of Foucault's works but which appears in the writings of many contemporary literary figures as well: the systematic exclusion of all senses except sight. In *The Birth of the Clinic* Foucault studied the examining, classifying "gaze" of the physician-scientist. In *Discipline and Punish* (the French title is *Surveiller et punir*) he analyzed the controlling and punishing eye of the political body. And in *Madness and Civilization* he traced the efforts of a measuring and watchful "rational" society to incarcerate and thus conceal the dissolving and distorting vision of the mad. Other theorists who question the rationality of the visual consciousness of technological societies include Claude Lévi-Strauss, Foucault's colleague at the Collège de France, and Marshall McLuhan, who shares Foucault's interest in varying forms of sensory perception.

The spatial basis of knowledge in the modern conception of gravitation has had a more direct impact upon the study of cosmology. Theoretical and observational developments in cosmology, particularly since 1950, have made this discipline extremely exciting. Theoretically, one of the most controversial innovations was the steady state theory, which held that the concentration of matter and energy in the universe remains fairly constant despite the expansion of the universe because new matter is continually being created *out of nothing* due to the action of a "creation field."[20] This was a shocking concept, not merely because it accepted extreme discontinuity in the universe, but because it denied the conservation of matter-energy. The steady state theory had interesting philosophical implications since, like Eastern religions, it postulated "a universe that stretches infinitely far into the past and future with many cycles of birth, death and rebirth but no permanent change."[21] Unfortunately, astronomical observations in the 1960s undermined the steady state theory and supported the theory that our universe originated in the explosion of a cosmic egg ten to twenty billion years ago. Opinion is still divided over the question of whether this "big bang" implies an ever-expanding universe or an oscillating universe that expands and contracts rhythmically. A single big bang "assumes a definite beginning resembling in a loose sense the act of creation that marks the beginning of the world in the Judeo-Christian tradition."[22] An oscillating universe, by contrast, suggests that the myth of "eternal return" is not so mythical after all.[23]

Other theoretical innovations and observational developments in cosmology have produced ideas so incredible as to appear fictional. The discovery in the early 1960s of quasars (seemingly distant objects emitting extraordinary amounts of energy) stimulated the study of collapsing stars. This involved combining relativity theory (especially gravitational field theory) and quantum theory (electromagnetic and nuclear field theories) in order to determine the effects of extreme concentrations of matter. It was already known that stars could collapse into white dwarfs, in which matter is highly condensed but atomic structure remains intact. The discovery of pulsars confirmed astronomers in the belief that stars could collapse to an even greater degree, forcing electrons to combine with protons and form neutron stars of enormous density. Further collapse, however, would mean that the "gravitational force, which normally is the weakest force in nature, now overpowers everything. Because, according to general relativity, gravity is the curving of space-time, space around the star is severely warped. As stellar collapse continues to its inevitable end, this warping becomes so great that space-time folds in over itself and the star disappears from our universe! What is left is called a *black hole*."[24]

Black holes are "black" because past a certain point (known as the "event horizon") nothing, not even light, can escape the gravitational field and no communication with our universe is possible. They are "holes" because matter has ceased to exist (although mass, charge, and momentum are preserved) and at the point of infinite density there is only an enigmatic and ominous "singularity." Black holes were predicted by Einstein's relativity theory and Einstein himself considered the implications of this concept. The Einstein-Rosen solution to the mathematical equations revealed that black holes connect to another universe by bridges called "wormholes." This idea was not taken too seriously when it was first formulated. Recent refinements of black-hole theory, however, suggest that wormholes connect to "white holes" in another universe and that perhaps quasars are "gushing up into our universe out of a white hole."[25] The newer theories of black holes also leave open the possibility that our universe may be connected to many other universes, that it may be possible to travel between universes without encountering a singularity, and that it may even be possible to return to our universe at any point in past or future space-time. But if our entire universe collapses into its own gigantic black hole, then not even mass, charge, and momentum would be preserved. The implication here is that "the universe that existed prior to the most recent big bang could have been fundamentally different from our universe today. Similarly, in the universe that will be created after the next big bang, the relative masses of nuclear particles, the electric charges they carry, and so on, could be quite different from those in our own universe."[26]

Foucault does not discuss the adventures of space travel and his earlier works predated the most recent studies of white holes and different universes. But the concept of black holes provides a dramatic image that is used today in ordinary conversation, and Foucault uses similar images. In his discussion of language, for example, he speaks of thought folding back and collapsing on itself, leaving behind mere "literature" incapable of communicating to an outside world and endlessly reflecting back on itself. He also speaks of the dangerous quest for "origins" and the emergence of "singularities" at points of extreme density. Examples such as these, of course, do not indicate exact parallels with cosmological concepts; they do, however, suggest that a common imaginative structure obtains between Foucault's archaeological studies and modern science.

The combination of relativity theory and quantum mechanics upon which current research in black holes is based really began with Paul Dirac's work in the late 1920s. Quantum mechanics itself, like relativity theory, dates from the beginning of this century with Max Planck's study in 1900 of "black body" radiation and Einstein's 1905 paper on the photoelectric effect. Relativity theory related matter, energy, time, and space to motion, but had little to say about the structure of matter or about the nature of matter-energy interactions. It was quantum theory that provided a model for atomic structure which encompassed electromagnetic and nuclear fields as well as the interaction of matter and energy. But this model introduced a number of concepts so contrary to conventional thought that even Einstein found them difficult to accept. Indeed, men such as Niels Bohr, Werner Heisenberg, and Erwin Schrödinger, who developed quantum theory, all felt compelled to discuss the inability of language to represent mathematical and scientific concepts.[27] They also frankly admitted that many quantum notions were downright bizarre. Wolfgang Pauli, who developed a theory of electron orbitals, once declared that it was "sheer madness" to believe in orbiting electrons.[28] And Bohr, after a lecture by Pauli years later, summed up the reaction of the audience by declaring: "We are all agreed that your theory is crazy. The question which divides us is whether it is crazy enough."[29]

Among the "crazy" ideas of quantum theory are a number of concepts that deserve mention here because they are similar to concepts employed by Foucault. The central feature of quantum mechanics is the assertion that change is discontinuous, that matter and energy are made up of units, or quanta, which can "vary only by jumps."[30] Other concepts associated with quantum theory include Heisenberg's uncertainty principle and the replacement of prediction by probability, Bohr's principle of complementarity, Pauli's exclusion principle and the role of conservation laws, and Dirac's theory of antimatter and related concepts of symmetry.

The discovery that matter and energy are made up of quanta and that these quanta change in a series of shifts and interact with each other and themselves in complex ways further reduced the possibility of distinguishing between matter and energy. Planck's and Einstein's studies of radiant energy disclosed that light is not uniquely a wave phenomenon. Light is emitted in quanta that Einstein called "photons" and thus light has particle as well as wave characteristics. Subsequent research in atomic structure revealed that atoms are comprised of particles which have wave properties. By the mid-1920s the equations for electron waves were formulated and the paradoxical Bohr atom—with electrons "orbiting" in a wave-state and "jumping" orbits as "particles" while simultaneously emitting or absorbing energy (in the form of photons)—became the established model for atomic physics. This model is self-contradictory within the conceptual limits of waves (forms) or particles (substances) and can only be expressed in terms of fields (relationships). Ever since Einstein adopted the concept of the field as an entity in itself and not as a vibration of a medium, fields became the closest possible approximation to "things," and "events" were thereafter interpreted as changes in fields. As Kenneth Ford explained in his discussion of elementary particles, "things and events, what is and what happens—this is the sum total of the physical world and the subject matter of science. . . . Perhaps we are approaching a merger of the description of events and the description of things . . . [perhaps] there is being *because* there is happening. A more radical departure from the classical view of the material basis for the world is hard to imagine."[31]

The interdependence of being and change on the elementary particle level presents peculiar problems. The wave nature of particles means that particles cannot be precisely located at a given time. This fundamental indeterminacy was expressed by the Heisenberg uncertainty principle, which made it apparent that orbiting electrons could not be located in an area smaller than the area of the electron wave. If electrons are forced to change energy states and thus reveal particle qualities, the very act of changing energy states alters the velocity of the electron and thereby renders velocity indeterminate. Not only is it impossible simultaneously to determine both the position and velocity of electrons, but the very existence of electrons between "jumps" is uncertain. "Electrons are indistinguishable from one another and therefore have no individuality, and one can envisage the process, not as a transition of one existing entity, but as annihilation of one electron in the first energy state and creation of another in the second state. . . . This is neither a continuous action nor an action at a distance—it is not an action at all."[32] It is not an action in the sense of uniform action through space and time; it is, rather, a discontinuous "event" of space-time. Other events permitted by Heisenberg's uncertainty principle are even more peculiar. The conservation of matter-energy can be violated within the period of temporal indeterminacy and new particles ("virtual" particles) can be created during this time. Quantum mechanics can calculate with extreme accuracy the probability that any event may occur; it just cannot predict which particle will undergo the change. Einstein explained this point as follows:

> The laws of quantum physics are of a statistical character. This means: they concern not one single system but an aggregation of identical systems; they cannot be verified by measurement of one individual, but only by a series of repeated measurements. . . . We have had to forsake the description of individual cases as objective happenings in space and time. . . . The equations of quantum physics determine the probability wave just as Maxwell's equations determine the electromagnetic field and the gravitational equations determine the gravitational field. The laws of quantum physics are again structure laws. But the meaning of physical concepts determined by these equations of quantum physics is much more abstract than in the case of electromagnetic and gravitational fields.[33]

Here again one detects basic concepts that are markedly similar to those applied by Foucault to cultural phenomena: discontinuous "jumps," aggregations of systems, a rejection of individual cases, a concern with repeated measurement, and an interest in structural laws.

The concepts of causality and determinism basic to classical mechanics which had been challenged by relativity theory were further eroded by quantum concepts of discontinuous and unpredictable change. The same disintegration applied to the classical distinction between subject and object. While relativity theory made the perception of events dependent on the spatiotemporal position of the observer, quantum theory held that fundamental characteristics of matter (such as position) exist only when measured. This interpretation of quantum theory (the "Copenhagen interpretation") is usually identified with Bohr's principle of complementarity, in which contradictory concepts (such as waves and particles) are rendered complementary by referring one of the contradictions to the act of measurement. Not surprisingly, such an interpretation has generated considerable controversy because it threatens the objectivity of scientific knowledge.[34] Although Einstein was willing to call science "a creation of the human mind" and regarded the notion of objects as "one of the most primitive concepts,"[35] he nevertheless refused to accept the postulate that reality varied not merely with the position of the observer but with the act of observation itself. Heisenberg recognized the epistemological problem involved in this issue and summed it up in his characteristically lucid manner as follows: "Natural science does not simply describe and explain nature; it is part of the interplay between nature and ourselves; it describes nature as exposed to our method of questioning. This was a possibility of which Descartes could not have thought, but it makes the sharp separation between the world and the I impossible."[36] The reconciliation of contradiction by complementary relations (in which differences remain intact) rather than through dialectical syntheses (in which differences are obliterated) is also characteristic of Foucault's methodology. More significantly, his rejection of the subject-object dualism, his hostility to Cartesian metaphysics, and his assertion that the human sciences cannot simply be described and explained but are tied to our modality of knowledge (in this case, language) are all fundamental concepts in Foucault's archaeology.

In addition to these concepts of discontinuous change, uncertainty, probability, and complementarity, quantum theory introduced new principles of exclusion and symmetry. The model of the atom that Bohr presented in 1913 did not explain why electrons stayed in orbit instead of falling into the nucleus or congregating at the lowest energy level in accordance with the contemporary theory of electrodynamics. These questions were resolved in the 1920s. Schrödinger's formulation of electron-wave functions revealed that electron waves are too large to occupy an area smaller than the circumference of the lowest orbital and thus cannot fall into the nucleus. Pauli's exclusion principle demonstrated that although some quanta (such as photon waves) can be superimposed, other quanta (such as electron waves) cannot occupy the same space at the same time. Only two electrons with opposite spins can exist in the lowest energy state of an atom, and other levels are similarly restricted. The practical implications of Pauli's exclusion principle were immediately apparent. "This restriction on the wave functions of many-electron systems, combined with the basic level structure intrinsic in the quantum theory, is responsible for the structure of the periodic table, the nature of chemical bonding, and most of the properties of matter."[37] The theoretical implications of principles based on exclusion were less apparent. But as the study of elementary particles developed, it became clear that the absence of events was more important than actual events. Nonoccurrence in elementary particle transformations pointed to the existence of conservation laws. Quantum physics is based on a number of conservation laws that are very different from laws in classical mechanics. "The classical laws of physics are expressed primarily as laws of change, rather than as laws of constancy. . . . The older view of a fundamental law of nature was that it must be a law of *permission*. It defined what *can* (and must) happen in natural phenomena. According to the new view, the more fundamental law is a law of *prohibition*. It defines what *cannot* happen. A conservation law is, in effect, a law of prohibition."[38] Since elementary particles appear to undergo all transformations that are not forbidden, the world of elementary particles is a world of continual change checked only by a limited number of constraints. This, too, presents a situation very different from the classical picture. The quantum view "is a view of chaos *beneath* order—or, what is the same thing, of order imposed on a deeper and more fundamental chaos. This is in startling contrast to the view developed and solidified in the three centuries from Kepler to Einstein, a view of order beneath chaos."[39] Once again quantum physics suggests parallels to Foucault's methodology and intellectual vision. He, too, regards absence as meaningful and searches for principles of exclusion in cultural phenomena. He also replaces a traditional picture of order beneath the chaos of events with a picture of order imposed on a more fundamental chaos. *The Order of Things*, Foucault has asserted, is the "entirely serious title of a problem; it is the ironic title of a work that modifies its own form, displaces its own data, and reveals, at the end of the day, a quite different task."[40]

The laws of quantum physics were complicated by introducing corrections into the mathematical equations to account for the relativistic effect of the rapid motion of elementary particles. When

Dirac formulated a relativistic wave equation for electrons in 1928, the solutions included both positive and negative energy states. This meant that positively charged electrons were at least theoretically possible, and four years later the predicted positrons were discovered. The existence of antimatter, which has since been demonstrated for many other particles besides electrons, introduced a remarkable symmetry into particle physics. Not only do most particles have doubles, but these doubles are created together and annihilate each other if they meet. The existence of particle pairs (although only one-half of the pair is stable in our world) has led to the suggestion that particles and antiparticles may be "different *states* of the same basic energy concentrations or mathematical singularities of some field deeper than that of the electromagnetic or the conventional meson fields."[41] Matter and antimatter may be considered different states of the same energy concentrations by regarding antiparticles as particles moving backward in time.

The search for a field deeper than the electromagnetic field or the nuclear (meson) field is the major issue in contemporary particle physics. Until recently four distinct fields were recognized, each of which was associated with specific particles whose creation and annihilation coincided with changes in the field. The electromagnetic field and the phenomenon of photon exchange dominated research for many years, primarily because the electromagnetic field is responsible for the transmission of light and the behavior of atomic electrons. The gravitational field and the exchange of "gravitons" has been the object of theoretical work, but gravitons have never been observed. Nuclear fields and the exchange of mesons for the "strong" field interactions and of neutrinos for the "weak" field interactions have been the subject of intense research since Yukawa predicted the existence of mesons in 1935. If it can be shown that these four fields are interrelated, then Einstein's dream of a unified field theory will be realized. There is evidence that the weak force is "the electric force in disguise"[42] and that the strong force may be the by-product of an even stronger force (called the color force) that binds subnuclear particles (quarks). If this is so, then the strong, weak, and electromagnetic fields might be united.[43] That would leave only the gravitational field, and recently a theory of "supergravity" has been formulated that "describes gravitation in terms of a quantum field theory . . . [and] might unify all forces in nature."[44]

In summation, the replacement of the classical mechanical view of the physical world by the field theories of relativity and quantum physics signified a shift of conceptual constructs that has a number of parallels to the conceptual structure of Foucault's archaeologies. Both field theory and archaeology replaced traditional scientific and historical concepts of continuous change and forces acting at a distance with notions of discontinuous change and proximate relationships. They have both challenged the dualisms inherent in Cartesian-Newtonian epistemology by rejecting the division of subject-object, form-substance, space-time, and matter-energy. In place of classical laws based on causality and determinism, field theory and archaeology are founded on laws that assume probability and indeterminism. Moreover, for both discourses transformation laws are based on structural principles and conservation laws are defined as prohibitory rather than permissive. In each case there has been a frank and radical admission that neither the physical sciences nor the human sciences can represent reality, that the very notion of reality cannot be divorced from the process of observation or reflection, and that ideas which are crazy enough may indeed be rational. Furthermore, in both field theory and archaeology, concepts of complementarity maintain fundamental differences without contradiction, descriptions of fields and events replace interpretations of being and becoming, and sight becomes the predominant form of perception. Finally, a number of concepts with specific meanings in modern physics create powerful images that allow their extension into other disciplines. Black holes, eternal return, symmetrical doubles, and curved spaces provide a rich source of metaphors that can be found in archaeology as well as in other disciplines. These parallels all suggest that a new concept of order and a new system of ordering phenomena are common to both field theory and archaeology. Such a reorientation of thought may, indeed, characterize other disciplines as well, giving rise to a wider cultural paradigm. In the remaining two sections of this chapter, reinterpretations in the philosophy of science, in linguistics, and in literature pointing to such a paradigm will be examined.

Reinterpretations in the
Philosophy and History of Science:
Bachelard, Canguilhem, Kuhn

The abruptness and enormity of the shift from classical mechanics to relativity and quantum theory led some philosophers and historians to speak of epistemological ruptures (Bachelard) or scientific revolutions (Kuhn) and to suggest that the new interpretation of the physical world might serve as a paradigm not just for scientific knowledge but for knowledge in general. Philosophers, who have long recognized the close relationship between science and philosophy, were quick to explore this possibility. Historians, by contrast, have been so closely tied to nineteenth-century scientific models (especially to concepts of biological evolution) that their response came later. Among the philosophers and historians who have incorporated modern scientific concepts into their disciplines, Gaston Bachelard and Georges Canguilhem have a special significance. They are major figures in French intellectual life who have greatly influenced Foucault and, except for Bachelard's literary and psychoanalytic essays, their works are little known in this country. Thomas Kuhn, who is well known in the United States and even in France, deserves to be included here because his theory of scientific change is very similar to Foucault's, although his work did not directly influence Foucault. Foucault has also been affected by other philosophers who recognized the epistemological significance of modern physics. Ernst Cassirer was one of the first European philosophers to examine the implications of relativity and quantum theories.[45] Like Bachelard, Cassirer realized that language could no longer claim to represent reality and he developed a theory of symbolic representation for both scientific and cultural forms of expression. Bachelard, too, moved from epistemology to poetics and became increasingly interested in symbolic forms.[46] Although Foucault occasionally refers to his debt to Cassirer, he has clearly been far more profoundly influenced by Bachelard.[47]

Bachelard's conception of multiple forms of rationality shifting in discontinuous jumps (as opposed to an immutable *cogito*), his conviction that only a "dispersed" philosophy is "capable of analyzing the prodigious complexity of modern scientific thought,"[48] and his insistence that such a dispersed philosophy reject fixed concepts of being in order to remain open to experience and to systems of relations, much as modern physics is open to both experimental and theoretical knowledge, are all themes that appear, in somewhat different forms, in Foucault's archaeological studies.[49] For Bachelard the abrupt break between the Newtonian and Einsteinian systems meant that the "mind has a variable structure"[50] and that philosophy must become historical. Like Foucault's archaeology, Bachelard's historical epistemology attempted to confront "the problem of the *constitution* of scientific knowledge (*savoir*), of its organization, of its *principles*"; to define regulated systems of concepts; and to examine the formation of such systems in terms of the norms of a scientific community and the imposition of extrascientific values (ideology).[51] Moreover, Bachelard was (as Foucault is) opposed to attempts by traditional philosophers and historians to reduce the novelty of new forms of thought by explaining new ideas with old concepts or by displacing attention from the new series of relationships to obsolete oppositions. Consequently, Bachelard criticized philosophical dualisms such as subject-object, concrete-abstract, and ideal-real. Not only did he claim that the concept of the object had been "revolutionized by the displacement demanded of micro-physics"[52] but, referring specifically to the modern description of electrons, he also noted that the "substance of the infinitely small is contemporaneous with its relations."[53] Bachelard even tried to replace the terms *subject* and *object* with the term *project* to indicate concrete processes rather than abstract essences. His effort "to *concretize* the abstract,"[54] as he explained in *The Rationalist Activity of Modern Physics*, was inspired by developments in quantum physics: "The meson, at the junction of the most abstract theory and the most painstaking technical research, is now a particle endowed with that double ontological status required of all the entities of modern Physics."[55]

The integration of theory and practice in modern science led Bachelard to reject the philosophical dualism of idealism and realism and to adopt what he termed an "applied rationalism" in which experience and conceptualization are dialectically related. Bachelard maintained that various schools of thought form a philosophical spectrum and that a "topographical" analysis would show that the extreme positions (realism and idealism) are inversely symmetrical, that they determine all other positions, and that they create a "*closed* field."[56] It is precisely this closure of thought which Bachelard (and Foucault) attempted to escape by abandoning empty philosophical abstractions for the concrete practices and specific theoretical formulations of modern scientific knowledge.

Foucault differs from Bachelard, however, on the question of dialectics. Although Bachelard's dialectical philosophy is not considered Hegelian,[57] Foucault has rejected all forms of synthesis in favor of a philosophy of differences. Bachelard himself did not believe that dialectical relations necessarily involved a reduction of differences. As a recent commentator has pointed out, for both Bachelard and Foucault the reality of scientific practices "resides in their *distinctness*—each having its own object, its own theory, and its special experimental protocols—and in their *uneven development*— each having its particular history."[58] Moreover, Foucault would agree with the position Bachelard took in *Applied Rationalism* that philosophical doubt must be replaced by scientific "problematics," that the "problematics of the different sciences are not wholly independent of one another, but only relatively autonomous, and that zones of partial overlap may appear."[59] The zones of overlap were particularly striking, Bachelard believed, between atomic physics and chemistry, disciplines that he examined in *The Coherent Pluralism of Modern Chemistry* and *Atomistic Intuitions*.

Bachelard's scientific and philosophical studies are usually considered one dimension of his thought and his literary and psychoanalytic writings regarded as a second, different dimension. Bachelard himself stressed the "total separation between rational life and oneiric life"[60] and his studies of earth, air, fire, and water treated these elements as symbols, even archetypes, and not as physical realities. Yet, as the titles of works such as *The Poetics of Space* and *The Experience of Space in Contemporary Physics* indicate, there are common images in Bachelard's poetic and scientific works. Dominique Lecourt, who has examined Bachelard's use of metaphors, believes that similar images are employed in Bachelard's epistemology and in his poetics and that both are based on concepts taken from modern physics. In his early epistemological studies Bachelard concentrated on absorbing the impact of the new concepts of matter, time, space, and causality introduced by twentieth-century physics. But he quickly discovered that ordinary language could not express these novel relations and, in *The New Scientific Mind*, he asked, "What poet will teach us the metaphors of this new [scientific] language?"[61] A few years later Bachelard attempted to psychoanalyze "objective" thought in order to expose the "fetishism" and the "infantile disorders" that tied language to objects, things, or substances.[62] He realized, however, that the nonobjective thought demanded by the new physics placed the imagination "under torture." Conventional words seemed incapable of expressing the juxtaposition of contradictory concepts such as waves and particles, or of explaining electron orbits and rotations that were not orbits or rotations in any usual sense. For this task a new philosophy as well as a new poetics was required. Bachelard called this new philosophy the "philosophy of no" to indicate its opposition to previous forms of thought and its intent to establish positive oppositions, as Einstein had established a positive concept on the basis of *non*-Euclidean space. Bachelard's poetics, like his epistemology, was deeply imbued with spatial metaphors taken from physics. In 1938 he wrote: "Little by little one feels the need to work *beneath* space, so to speak, at the level of the essential relations which sustain space and phenomena. Scientific thought is then led towards constructions more metaphorical than real, towards 'configurational spaces' of which sensory space is after all no more than one poor example."[63] Both Bachelard and Foucault have located their analyses at "the level of the essential relations." And for both men the region "beneath" or "between" phenomena is the field that, by its very configuration, defines space and phenomena.

Bachelard's historical epistemology has been paralleled in the last three decades by Georges Canguilhem's epistemological history. Canguilhem, who was a student of Bachelard[64] and one of Foucault's teachers, has attempted "to bring out, in Bachelardian style but on the specific terrain of biology, the philosophical categories which are at work in an actual scientific practice."[65] Canguilhem's studies of nonmechanistic models in the formation of biological concepts during the seventeenth and eighteenth centuries broke with traditional interpretations based on Cartesian models and have greatly influenced Foucault's own analyses of natural history in the classical period. Canguilhem's first book, *The Normal and the Pathological*,[66] has also influenced Foucault's conception of scientific norms in the life sciences and his understanding of the relation between scientific discourses and social values. Canguilhem, for his part, is also an admirer of Foucault's works. After the critical reaction to *The Order of Things*, he defended Foucault's theses in an enthusiastic article in which he compared Foucault first to Bachelard and then to Hume and Kant. According to Canguilhem:

In *The New Scientific Mind*, Gaston Bachelard tried to extract from the new theories of physics norms for a non-Cartesian epistemology . . . [and] in *The Philosophy of No* he outlined, à propos of new theories in chemistry, the task of a non-Kantian analytic. . . . M. Foucault extends the demands of non-Cartesianism and non-Kantianism to philosophical reflection itself. . . . *The Order of Things* may play, for a yet unknown Kant, the role of awakening which Kant accorded to Hume. . . . This work is for the human sciences what the *Critique of Pure Reason* was for the natural sciences.[67]

Their common opposition to metaphysics (especially Cartesian metaphysics) and their shared "descent" from Bachelard have led Canguilhem and Foucault in similar directions. Both thinkers are concerned with the production of scientific concepts and the relation between scientific and nonscientific theories and practices. Canguilhem's study of the eighteenth-century concept of the reflex, for example, shows how ideological values led French scientists to suppress the fact that this concept originated in the work of two foreign scientists using a vitalist model of light reflection and to attribute it to Descartes despite the fact that, in Canguilhem's view, Cartesian physiology was incapable of arriving at such a concept.[68] Canguilhem has been careful to distinguish concepts from theories, because he believes that concepts are recurring problems whereas theories are variable interpretations of these problems. He has also avoided the notions of chance discoveries and evolutionary processes in the history of science in order to explore specific transformations and distortions of concepts and abrupt ruptures in interpretive systems. Consequently, like Foucault, Canguilhem has rejected the notion of linear time and the belief that there are precursors for all scientific discoveries. Also, like both Bachelard and Foucault, Canguilhem's studies have involved a new system of classification that "reveals unexpected lines of descent, establishes new periodizations, disinters forgotten names, throws into disorder the traditional and official chronology . . . [and] draws up a 'parallel history'" in opposition to traditional histories.[69] Traditional histories of biology, for example, regard Buffon as a precursor to Darwin and view Cuvier as anomalous. Foucault and Canguilhem, on the other hand, believe that Cuvier's works provided the essential conditions for Darwin's theories and that a break in thought took place between Buffon and Cuvier.[70]

Since concepts in the biological sciences are usually expressed in words rather than mathematical equations, Canguilhem is sensitive to the role of language in the formation and transmission of concepts. Just as the physiological concept of the reflex was tied to the theory of reflection in optics, various concepts central to definitions of life have been related through metaphors to theories outside biology. Canguilhem has asserted, for example, that the "history of the concept of the cell is inseparable from the history of the concept of the individual. This has already been my justification for claiming that social and affective values preside over the development of cellular theory."[71] He has also discussed nineteenth- and twentieth-century biological concepts and noted the prevalence of models drawn from physics. In an article entitled "The Role of Analogies and Models in Biological Discovery" (1961),[72] he examined, with a certain degree of skepticism, the applicability of mathematical models to biology. Analogies, particularly those assimilating anatomy to mechanical functions, have long predominated over structural models in which the comparisons are made between the relation of part to whole in different systems. Functional analyses, however, have not been able to satisfactorily explain life processes and Canguilhem believes that they "cannot be credited with decisive discoveries in biology" even in the classical period.[73] During the nineteenth century electrical rather than mechanical models had a significant impact on neurology, as the identification of the concept of the nerve with that of an electrical current indicated. According to Canguilhem, electrical models stand midway between mechanical models and contemporary mathematical models derived from field theory in physics. "The construction of electrical (physio-chemical) models in neurophysiology constitutes an intermediary, at once historical and logical, between the mechanical model . . . and the model of a mathematical or logical type. The spirit of mathematical physics, itself progressively educated by a new mathematical knowledge, that of structures, has found an accessible path into biology, thanks to Maxwell's work in the field of electro-magnetism."[74] As Canguilhem went on to point out, Maxwell himself realized that his model of electromagnetic fields could only illustrate and not represent reality and must therefore be considered merely an analogy.[75] Canguilhem likewise admonished biologists not to confuse representation and illustration and counseled them to heed "the lesson of the mathematical physicist: what must be required of a model is the provision of a syntax to construct a transposable but original discourse."[76]

Canguilhem's own vitalist position has made him reluctant to adopt mathematical models for living systems because organisms display unique processes such as self-regulation. He noted, however, that Ludwig von Bertalanffy's general systems theory claims to resolve such problems. Systems theory has a particular relevance for this discussion because it appears to play a role in American thought analogous to that of structuralist theories in French thought.[77] It is also more explicitly related to modern physics than are theories developed in the social sciences. In his 1968 contribution to a symposium on "new perspectives in the life sciences," Bertalanffy discussed the "change in *basic categories* of knowledge" in modern science and the specific features of systems theory.[78] Bertalanffy believes that a shift in paradigms such as Kuhn described for the twentieth-century revolution in physics is now taking place in biology and that other disciplines are experiencing parallel shifts; he mentioned, in fact, that Piaget has "expressly related his conception to the general systems theory."[79]

Paraphrasing the distinctions made by Warren Weaver, one of the founders of information theory, Bertalanffy summarized three paradigms for scientific laws:

> Up to recent times, Weaver said, science was concerned with *linear causality.* . . . This was the prototype of thinking in classical physics. Somewhat later, the problem of *unorganized complexity* appeared which is essentially answered by statistical laws. . . . The paradigm of laws of unorganized complexity is the second principle of thermodynamics [entropy]. . . . Now, however, we are confronted with *problems of organized complexity* at all levels of the hierarchic structure of the universe.[80]

According to Bertalanffy, the problems of organized complexity are expressed by probability laws that are systems laws. These laws are particularly important for biology since phenomena such as organization, hierarchy, differentiation, and regulation are different in animate and inanimate systems. A major difficulty in formulating a mathematical model for biology has been the incompatibility of the principle of entropy with the fact that biological systems exhibit negentropic tendencies (increasing order). The second law of thermodynamics, however, only applies to closed systems; since open systems do not necessarily tend to diminished states of order, systems theories deal with open systems. Bertalanffy briefly discussed several types of systems theories (for example, set theory, cybernetics, information theory, and game theory) before proceeding to a critique of neo-Darwinism. Proponents of neo-Darwinism have claimed that evolution can be explained by the genetic theory of mutations combined with the theory of natural selection. Bertalanffy noted numerous instances in which natural selection failed to explain complex biological phenomena. The fact "that a theory so vague, so insufficiently verifiable and so far from the criteria otherwise applied in 'hard' science . . . has become a dogma . . . can only be explained on sociological grounds. Society and science have been so steeped in the ideas of mechanism, utilitarianism and the economic concept of free competition, that instead of God, Selection was enthroned as ultimate reality."[81] Bertalanffy was no less critical of the notion of accidental mutations. In place of chance mutations he held that there are *"parallelisms* at the genetic, developmental and organizational levels," that only "certain pathways appear to be open at the level of possible gene mutations," and that *"regularities in evolution . . .* deserve further investigation."[82] In addition, Bertalanffy pointed out that although we know "the *vocabulary* of the genetic code . . . we do not know its *grammar*" or how new genes originate.[83]

These concerns, indeed the very language in which they are expressed, indicate the close relationship between Bertalanffy and Foucault. Foucault's archaeology is also an attempt to explain organized complexity without recourse to theories of chance or evolution. He, too, has rejected concepts like linear causality and has examined parallelisms and regularities in order to discover the "grammar" of scientific discourses. Although he may not, like Bertalanffy, trace the source of these concepts to the revolution in physics, he would most likely agree that research in the life sciences "will require not less but probably much more scientific ingenuity and sophistication than theoretical physics. In its philosophic aspects, this amounts . . . to the replacement, or rather the generalization of the Newtonian universe of blind forces and isolable causal trains, and of Darwinian living nature as a product of chance, by an organismic universe of many levels, the laws of which are a challenge to future research."[84]

Foucault is not, like Bertalanffy, attempting to find the laws that govern natural phenomena, but he is trying to isolate the laws that make our knowledge of nature possible. A similar interest in the structure of scientific knowledge has led Thomas Kuhn to conclude that scientific thought does not proceed in an evolutionary pattern but alters by a series of discontinuous jumps analogous to switches of perceptual sets in Gestalt psychology. Kuhn's *Structure of Scientific Revolutions* (1962) has become extremely popular both here and abroad, and in France Kuhn has frequently been compared to Bachelard. The similarity between Kuhn's concept of paradigms and Foucault's concept of episteme, as well as numerous other parallels in their works, caused some critics to accuse Foucault of borrowing from Kuhn without citing him. Foucault responded by explaining: "It is true that I hold Kuhn's work to be admirable and definitive. But . . . when I read Kuhn's book during the winter of 1963–1964 . . . I had just finished writing *The Order of Things*. I thus did not cite Kuhn, but quoted instead from the historian of science who shaped and inspired his thoughts: G. Canguilhem."[85] For the American reader, Kuhn is much more accessible than Bachelard, Canguilhem, or Foucault, and a discussion of Kuhn's major concepts may illuminate some of the issues Foucault treats in a more philosophically rigorous fashion.

Like Bachelard, Kuhn was originally trained as a physicist and the revolutionary character of modern physics has clearly influenced his conception of scientific knowledge. He believes that we may come to view Einstein's theory of relativity "as a prototype for revolutionary reorientations in the sciences. Just because it did not involve the introduction of additional objects or concepts, the transition from Newtonian to Einsteinian mechanics illustrates with particular clarity the scientific revolution as a displacement of the conceptual network through which scientists view the world."[86] The conceptual network that determines the scientist's world view is what Kuhn has called a paradigm. He later refined his definition of paradigm to something less than a world view but more than a theory. This intermediate structure Kuhn compares to a language. Paradigms, like languages, are collective and largely unconscious forms of perception which, while systematic, are not completely rule bound. The paradigm of any specific scientific community is what Kuhn, borrowing a term from Michael Polanyi, calls "tacit knowledge," the sort of knowledge scientists acquire by the act of practicing science. The problem-solutions typical of a discipline, those found in textbooks and laboratories, provide a set of shared examples for its practitioners and these shared examples, like a language, shape perception and order phenomena.

As long as practitioners within a scientific community share the same paradigm, "normal" science is possible. Normal science is occupied with articulating accepted theories and methods and is oriented toward problem solving. To the extent that normal science succeeds in solving the "puzzles" of its own paradigm, scientific knowledge can be considered cumulative or progressive. This does not mean, according to Kuhn, that science progresses toward truth, reality, or nature. It merely means that a specialized body of information has been developed in response to questions the scientific community regards as significant. In a controversial departure from conventional assumptions about science, Kuhn claims that just as art and language no longer pretend to represent reality, so science too must be considered nonrepresentational. The belief that science can represent nature is based on a failure to discriminate between perception and interpretation. In a postscript to *The Structure of Scientific Revolutions*, Kuhn explained that what he had "been opposing in this book is therefore the attempt, traditional since Descartes but not before, to analyze perception as an interpretive process, as an unconscious version of what we do after we have perceived."[87] For Kuhn, interpretation is a rational process that begins only where perception ends. Perception is a different process, not merely because it is less conscious but also because it is not constant. The same stimulus produces different perceptions in people having different previous experiences. Consequently, there is no way of knowing what the stimulus really is, and Kuhn concluded that scientific interpretations interpret varying perceptions, not "reality."[88]

These are all concepts that have parallels in Foucault's works. Foucault too regards language as the model for knowledge; he too considers knowledge in the (human) sciences to be systematic but not wholly formalized, to be embedded in the theories and practices of specific groups, and to be incapable of representing "reality." Foucault, however, is both more ambitious and more cautious than Kuhn. He is more ambitious because he wishes to analyze the perceptual limits of discursive paradigms and the formalized as well as intuitive structures that underlie scientific thought. He is more cautious because he does not claim to be able to explain the large shifts between paradigms, although (like Kuhn) he regards these shifts as revolutionary ruptures and displacements. Consequently, Foucault's first archaeology (*The Birth of the Clinic*) describes rather than explains shifts in knowledge, and his major archaeology (*The Order of Things*) examines what Kuhn calls "normal" science in different historical periods. In this latter work Foucault's concept of episteme corresponds not to Kuhn's paradigm but to what Kuhn now calls the "disciplinary matrix."

When Kuhn decided to refine the definition of paradigm by equating paradigms with the shared examples ("exemplars") that function as models for scientific theory and practice, he introduced the term *disciplinary matrix* to indicate other aspects of scientific thought and practice previously confused with the term *paradigm*. By "disciplinary" Kuhn means the social structure of the various scientific communities. Paradigms, he claims, govern "not a subject matter but rather a group of practitioners. Any study of paradigm-directed or paradigm-shattering research must begin by locating the responsible group or groups."[89] In *The Structure of Scientific Revolutions* Kuhn did not discuss the formation of scientific communities and the social values that influence the education, initiation, and professional practices of scientists, but he has dealt with these questions elsewhere.[90] Nor did he discuss in this work the nonparadigmatic components of the "matrix" of scientific thought—the symbolic generalizations (symbols, laws, definitions), the metaphysical paradigms (analogies, metaphors), and the scientific values (simplicity, consistency, predictability)—that, like paradigms, determine scientific knowledge. However, by focusing on the concept of paradigm and by using the model of language, Kuhn has isolated a feature of scientific knowledge (and perhaps of knowledge in general) that may explain complex forms of nonevolutionary change.

In Kuhn's view, paradigms are constantly shifting so that even normal science "progresses" through a series of displacements. If these displacements affect a number of disciplines, or radically alter even a single specialty, they are recognized as "revolutionary." Paradigm shifts are an inevitable and necessary consequence of scientific activity. Not all the problems recognized as significant by a scientific community are solvable within the accepted paradigm. Usually anomalies are not considered "counterinstances" but are seen as particularly difficult puzzles that scientists hope to resolve in their traditional manner. If a number of puzzles prove unresolvable and if other paradigms are developed that offer alternative explanations, then normal science is replaced by "extraordinary" science. During this period of crisis, several paradigms compete for community approval and a general breakdown of communication between advocates of different paradigm "languages" is common. Scientists try to isolate anomalies and to push existing rules to their limits in order to magnify the problem. They may also turn to philosophy (Kuhn mentions the "thought experiments" of Galileo, Einstein, and Bohr) to make explicit the assumptions of the traditional paradigm and thereby to locate the source of weakness.[91] Ultimately the conflict is resolved when the scientific community chooses the paradigm that seems "better" than the others. The choice is not made because the chosen paradigm can be verified or measured against an external standard. It is made by comparing it to other available paradigms and the choice reflects scientific and social values that determine what the community's priorities are.

This theory of scientific change has a number of implications. It suggests, first, that factual or theoretical anomalies are not simply found or invented, but that they require a change in perception. Discoveries, therefore, are neither accidents nor sudden occurrences but "extended episodes with a regularly recurrent structure" which presuppose that "all the relevant conceptual categories are prepared in advance."[92] Second, paradigm changes indicate that nonlogical factors are at least as significant as logical ones in the choice of paradigms as well as in their formation. Paradigms are formed by modeling practice and theory on previous examples, and paradigms are chosen by comparing one to another: in both cases the criteria are internal and no assumption of "truth" is involved. The role of nonlogical factors points to a third important feature of paradigm-based knowledge: it is not rule bound. Kuhn adopted the concept of paradigms because he discovered, in examining scientific communities, that he could not "retrieve enough shared rules to account for the group's unproblematic conduct of research. . . . Shared examples can serve cognitive functions commonly attributed to shared rules. When they do, knowledge develops differently from the way it does when governed by rules."[93] This does not mean that paradigmatic knowledge is arbitrary. It may indeed be lawful and is certainly based on the same physiochemical processes that govern other forms of cognition. But paradigms do not need to be rationalized into rules in order to guide research; in fact, attempts to rationalize paradigms are rarely undertaken except during periods of crisis.

Since Foucault's analyses of the human sciences are attempts to disengage the rules of discourse from their "disciplinary matrices," it is not surprising that he views the present period as a time of cultural crisis. According to Foucault, the modern episteme, which took shape between 1790 and 1810, ended around 1950.[94] Kuhn, too, believes that research in the history of science as well as in "philosophy, psychology, linguistics and even art history, all converge to suggest that the traditional paradigm is somehow askew."[95] However, Kuhn does not think that paradigms can be understood by reducing them to sets of rules. Foucault's "thought experiment" might reveal the inadequacy of the traditional paradigm, but, according to Kuhn, the philosopher who wishes to "substitute rules for examples . . . will alter the nature of the knowledge possessed by the community from which his examples were drawn. What he will be doing, in effect, is to substitute one means of data processing for another. Unless he is extraordinarily careful, he will weaken the community's cognition by doing so."[96] Since Foucault's intention is to alter the nature of knowledge in the human sciences, he is prepared to push rules to their limits in order to hasten the destruction of the old paradigm, even without a formed alternative. An alternative paradigm, as both Foucault and Kuhn realize, must be based on a new way of experiencing the world. Unlike Foucault, Kuhn would await the emergence of a new paradigm and insist that it be based on a flexible perceptual structure with "empty spaces" between the categories to accommodate new events. According to Kuhn, formalized, rule-bound systems are closed systems; all the spaces are filled and the first exception to the established arrangement of categories destroys the system. Although Foucault's epistemes frequently resemble these closed systems, which Kuhn attributes to rule-bound cognitive structures, Foucault himself regards each episteme as a perceptual structure consisting of divergent, even contradictory, elements generated by unconscious categories of classification.

In sum, the reinterpretation of scientific knowledge and the possible emergence of a new paradigm modeled on modern physics underlies the work of Bachelard, Canguilhem, Kuhn, and (though less explicitly) Foucault. Such a reinterpretation shifts attention from homogeneous processes to discontinuous systems and challenges the distinction between thought (theory) and experience (practice). More significantly, by asserting that science, like language, is a system of classification rather than a representation of reality, these philosophers and historians have collapsed traditional distinctions between scientific and nonscientific knowledge and have indicated the points of intersection between scientific and social values. In a structural as well as symbolic sense, the new paradigm drawn from physics appears to shape thought in the natural and social sciences. In the next section, a brief discussion of the effect of this paradigm shift in the human sciences will be followed by a summary of Foucault's major literary essays. These essays suggest that for Foucault, as for Bachelard, spatial metaphors form a link between the scientific and poetic imagination.

Reinterpretations in the Human Sciences: Saussurian Linguistics and Foucault's Literary Essays

Innovations in the human sciences and the fine arts not only indicate that the traditional paradigm is askew, as Kuhn puts it, but that parallel developments are occurring in many disciplines and that a new paradigm is emerging.[97] While the Saussurian "revolution" in linguistics is perhaps the best example, innovations in psychology and anthropology reflect a similar shift away from developmental processes toward systematic relations. Serial music and nonrepresentational art likewise illustrate the replacement of expression and representation by internally structured patterns. This is not to say that all of these disciplines have been directly affected by twentieth-century physics, nor that they are all equally important to Foucault. Although he is primarily concerned with the significance of language and the life sciences, Foucault is also interested in modern art and music. Before proceeding, then, to Saussurian linguistics and Foucault's literary essays, brief consideration will be given to innovations that Foucault considers particularly relevant or that are tied to modern field theory.

Foucault once commented that serial music had been as important to his philosophical development as the writings of Nietzsche. The twelve-tone music of his friends Boulez and Barraqué provided the "first great cultural shock" that tore him from his youthful "dialectical universe."[98] Boulez himself recognized an affinity between atonal music and contemporary physics. He maintained, in fact, that the turning point in his own career as a composer came in 1945 when, listening to a piece by Schönberg, he realized that "this was music of our time . . . music moved out of the world of Newton into the world of Einstein."[99] Although Foucault continues to hold Boulez and Barraqué in high regard, his interests seem to have shifted away from music toward art. He was originally fascinated by Klee and Kandinsky because, by divorcing "signs" from meaning, they typified modern nonrepresentational art.[100] By contrast, Foucault thinks that the Classical system of representation is best symbolized by Velasquez, and he analyzed Velasquez's painting "The Maids of Honor" at length in the opening chapter of *The Order of Things*. In 1973 Foucault returned to the theme that modern art is incapable of representing "reality" in a short study of four drawings by René Magritte.[101] Unfortunately, Foucault has not discussed the works of the Dutch artist M. C. Escher (1898–1972), although Escher's drawings have been compared to structuralist thought and even to Foucault's own work.[102] Escher's designs are fascinating combinations of bizarre images, modern scientific concepts, and highly structured patterns. Some of his best-known engravings and lithographs, such as *Other World* (1947) and *Relativity* (1953), which depict multiple perspectives and radical distortions of space, now regularly appear in physics and cosmology texts. Escher is also known for figure-ground forms inspired by his interest in Gestalt psychology and for his repetitive, shifting, and duplicating structures drawn from the study of crystallography. Other Escher drawings show complex spatial configurations explicitly related to non-Euclidean geometry and perceptual distortions usually associated with madness.

Spatial and temporal relationships derived from modern physics have also directly influenced psychology, particularly in the areas of perception, social psychology, personality dynamics, and cognitive psychology. Gestalt psychology, which began in 1912 with Max Wertheimer's study of the perception of motion, developed field relationships and transformation laws similar to those formulated at the same time in physics. By the 1920s Wolfgang Köhler drew attention to this similarity and thereafter Gestalt psychologists quickly absorbed new insights from relativity theory and quantum mechanics.[103] Kurt Lewin, who had studied mathematics and physics before he joined the Berlin Gestalt group in the 1920s, later extended field concepts into the areas of personality dynamics and social psychology.[104] Jean Piaget, whose studies of cognitive psychology are now well known, was a friend of both Lewin and Einstein. Piaget has discussed the close relation between modern physics and child psychology in his article "The Child and Modern Physics." As opposed to Bachelard, who claimed that the classical concept of objects is an infantile fixation, Piaget has made it clear that such a fixation is not at all typical of infants. On the contrary, he has demonstrated that a young child's conception of objects, space, causality, and velocity is definitely not Newtonian.

Piaget's experiments reveal that "a very young baby acts with regard to objects rather like a [modern] physicist. The baby believes in an object as long as he can localize it and ceases to believe in it when he can no longer do so." Furthermore, a child's "formation of the concept of an object as a permanent thing is linked to his construction of space." Even the child's concept of causality (change in the motion of an object) is not originally associated with relations of distances or points of contact. Piaget's experiments on children's conceptions of velocity (which were, in fact, a direct consequence of a conversation he had with Einstein in 1928) prove that young children do not "think of velocity in terms of the distance-time relation" established by classical physics. Piaget even notes that "these findings, derived from researches to which the founder of the theory of relativity inspired us, return by an unforeseen route to theoretical physics," an allusion to the attempt by the physicist Jean Abelé to use concepts from child psychology to explain the invariant velocity of light.[105]

Children, physicists, and artists are not the only ones whose perceptions challenge the Newtonian world view. Dreamers, madmen, and "savages" also display thought processes very different from the supposedly normal structures of conventional rationality. Although Foucault is hostile to empirical forms of psychology and many psychologists (including Piaget)[106] are critical of him, he has long been fascinated by dreams and madness. In 1954 he wrote a lengthy introduction to the French translation of Ludwig Binswanger's essay "Dream and Existence" and in the same year he published a critical study of the concept of mental illness.[107] Four years later he helped translate Viktor von Weizsaecker's *Der Gestaltkreis*,[108] and in 1961 his own *Madness and Civilization* appeared. Foucault has also acknowledged his considerable debt to Claude Lévi-Strauss, whose study of the "savage mind" asserted that primitive thought is as logical, systematic, and complex as Western "rational" thought. But, unlike Lévi-Strauss, Foucault is not willing to consider himself a structuralist,[109] although he does recognize the importance of structural linguistics for the study of both "primitive" and "rational" thought. Since linguistic concepts such as "synchronic," "diachronic," "sign," "signifier," and "signified" not only pervade contemporary French criticism but appear in Foucault's work, it is necessary to define them within the context of Saussure's theory of language.

Saussure's lectures on linguistics, published posthumously from notes by his students,[110] were an attempt to impose order on a morass of linguistic phenomena and thus to provide conceptual and classificatory tools for analyzing language "scientifically." This involved both limiting the range of phenomena studied and making a radical distinction between arbitrary evolutionary changes in language elements and the systematic functioning of any language at a given time. Since Saussure's main contribution to linguistics was the development of the idea of language as a system, only brief attention will be given to the nature of the limits of linguistic analyses and the role of evolutionary processes.

Saussure viewed language as a psychological and social phenomenon and thus excluded from linguistics physiological questions such as the articulation of sounds. He also limited language to the spoken form and excluded writing, which he considered a separate system. Writing, he felt, was inadequate even as a representation of language because it actually obscured the real language system.[111] He also excluded individual acts of speaking, which he referred to as *parole* (speaking, not speech), and even whole groups of variations in a language (dialects) from consideration in the study of language as a system. He further distinguished linguistics from other disciplines dealing with social phenomena (such as anthropology and sociology). However, he believed that one day these disciplines would also be studied scientifically (as systems of signs) and that a general science of social signs, which he called "semiology," would emerge, with linguistics providing the master pattern.[112]

Although Saussure did not exclude the study of the evolution of languages and language families from linguistics, he made a clear distinction between this study, which he called "diachronic linguistics," and the study of language as a system, which he called "synchronic linguistics." The distinction between diachronic and synchronic lin-

guistics is comparable to the distinction he made between internal
and external elements of language. To illustrate this difference he
gave as an example the game of chess: "The fact that the game passed
from Persia to Europe is external . . . everything that has to do with
its systems and rules is internal. If I use ivory chessmen instead of
wooden ones, the change has no effect on the system, but if I de-
crease or increase the number of chessmen, this has a profound effect
on the 'grammar' of the game."[113] In this context, however, the term
grammar serves only as an illustration of a logical system of relations.
Synchronic linguistics does not deal with the abstract "proper" forms
of grammar, but with the actual system of a spoken language.

Despite Saussure's occasional reference to an absolute opposition
between diachronic and synchronic linguistics and despite his tendency to equate language exclusively with the synchronic form, the
two types of linguistics are not completely unrelated. Diachronic
changes are incorporated into synchronic relations, but this process
is not a function of the gradual accumulation of diachronic change
but of a shift in synchronic relations. To understand this, one must
first look more closely at what Saussure viewed as the basic units of a
language system and the laws governing their relations.

Synchronic linguistics, as defined by Saussure, is the science "concerned with the logical and psychological relations that bind together coexisting terms and form a system in the collective mind of
speakers."[114] The basic units of this system, which he called "signs,"
are themselves relations rather than concrete objects and thus cannot be defined in isolation. Although signs are often confused with
words, Saussure was careful to distinguish between them. Whereas
words are generally thought to be homogeneous entities that refer to
things in the world, signs are complex psychological relations shared
by a community of speakers and do not refer to things at all. Indeed,
Saussure did not even discuss the problem of what the real world is
and how one can know it or talk about it. For him a word like *tree* is
not a single unit referring to an identifiable external object. It is a
compound sign made up of a sound-image that acts as a referent
(what he called a "signifier"), referring not to a thing but to a
concept. And this concept, this idea of tree, is what is "signified."

The sign, then, is the relation between an arbitrary signifier (sound-
image) and a signified (concept). But the sign and its elements (signifier and signified) only have a linguistic meaning, what Saussure
called "value," insofar as they can be distinguished from other sig-

nifiers, signifieds, and sign groups. The value of the sound-image of the signifier tree, for example, is not the sound of tree itself but the difference between the sound tree and other similar sounds in the language. It is this difference that allows recognition, and as long as this distinction is maintained, a wide range of individual pronunciations of the word tree will be allowed. It is also the differences between the signifieds, not the signifieds themselves, which determine their value. For example, the French word *mouton* does not have the same conceptual value as the English word *sheep* because English makes a distinction between sheep and mutton.[115]

What this means is that "language is a form and not a substance"[116] and that its elements assume their meaning not from any intrinsic significance but from their relative position in a "field" of linguistic relations.[117] This field is determined not only by the pattern of differences among signifiers and signifieds, but also by the relations between signs as a whole. These relations are of two types which together order the sign field. The first set of relations is linear, that is, it is a product of the temporal nature of language—the fact that spoken language is a succession of sounds. These are what Saussure called "syntagmatic relations," by which he meant that signs acquire value by their opposition to what precedes and follows them. For example, syntagms may be comprised of units as small as *re-lire* or may involve larger groups such as *la vie humaine* or even whole sentences.[118] The second type of relation is not linear and might be considered curved. These relations Saussure called "associative relations," and by this he meant the constellation of terms surrounding any given sign. For example, the word *enseignement* may call to mind a number of words relating to education (*apprentissage*, for example) or a series of words beginning with "en-" or ending with "-ment."[119] These relations are based on similarities between concepts (signifieds) or similarities between sounds (signifiers).

The basic mechanisms of a language system, then, are relations of similarity and difference. There is one further mechanism that imposes order on language, and this Saussure called "relative motivation." Whereas many signs are absolutely arbitrary, there are also those that are only relatively arbitrary, that is, there is some degree of motivation. Thus, although *dix* and *neuf* are absolutely arbitrary, *dix-neuf* is relatively motivated.[120] All languages have some degree of motivation, and this degree changes with time. Not only does the degree of motivation change with time, but (as mentioned earlier) diachronic changes can indirectly affect synchronic relations. Although diachronic changes are arbitrary changes which in themselves affect only specific language elements and not the system, the changes introduced through time can become models for significant differences that do change the language system. For example, with the words *foot* and *feet*, speakers "took advantage of an existing difference and made it signal the distinction between singular and plural."[121] All such synchronic changes involve a shift in the relations between signifiers and signifieds. Saussure compared these shifts to the different states created when a chessman is moved (although here the change is intentional and not arbitrary): they involve jumps, not gradual changes, between synchronic states.

The relations that Saussure identified as formative of language systems raised the question of whether there were laws that would be applicable to all languages. Saussure recognized the existence of "general principles existing independently of concrete facts,"[122] which suggested that such a "panchronic" view would be possible. But he was not willing to separate language from its "material" base and felt that it would be a mistake "to think that there is an incorporeal syntax outside material units distributed in space."[123] The possibility that there may indeed be such an incorporeal syntax, however, has stimulated more recent innovations in linguistic theory. Both Noam Chomsky and Roman Jakobson believe "that there are certain phonological, syntactic, and semantic units that are *universal*, not in the sense that they are necessarily present in all languages, but . . . that they can be defined independently of their occurrence in any particular language."[124]

Saussure's concept of languages as systems of signs and his view of linguistics as the science of these sign systems have numerous implications. For present purposes, only two need be mentioned: the relation between synchronic linguistics and relativity theory, and the significance of sign systems for structuralist studies of cultural phenomena. There is probably no direct link between Saussure's and Einstein's theories, although they were formed about the same time. There seems, however, to be a similarity in the paradigms employed in each case and a similarity in the nature of the revolution each man accomplished in his discipline. Relativity and structural (synchronic) linguistics may both be regarded as "field" theories that moved analysis from a study of fixed objects to an examination of complex relations. Both theories involved a reinterpretation of the concept of time, and both viewed change in terms of shifts and jumps and not in terms of cumulative processes. Both theories, moreover, included a nonlinear concept of spatial relationships (curved space in physics and associative relations in linguistics) and both radically simplified the organization of their discipline while simultaneously rendering it more abstract. Finally, both theories had an enormous impact outside their own spheres. Relativity theory rejected traditional forms of thought in order to better apprehend reality. Structural linguistics is perhaps closer to quantum physics since it does not permit separating the process of thought from the object of thought. Consequently, language becomes both the means and the end of analysis. All thought, then, not just thought about language, is based on similar patterns of relationships (sign systems).

The pattern (or structure) of thought and the possibility of a universal structure are questions of interest to philosophers, psychologists, anthropologists, indeed, to theorists in all disciplines. These are the questions which tie together a large number of otherwise very different thinkers. Piaget's studies of cognitive development in children, Lévi-Strauss's work on the "primitive" mentality, Lacan's analysis of the structures of the unconscious, Barthes's interest in the structure of literary works, and Foucault's analyses of the structures of epistemological fields (epistemes) are all examples of this basic concern. These figures all recognize the influence of Saussure (though not necessarily that of Einstein), and some of them, especially Barthes, have seriously sought to construct a general science of signs. Saussure's key concepts, particularly his view that patterns of differences and similarities create meaning, have been adopted in other disciplines. And some of the limits he has drawn (indeed, the very concept of such limits) have been a subject of debate, especially among literary figures who, not surprisingly, are the most distressed about the inadequacy of writing as a representation of language. An even greater problem, however, has been the divorce of the sign from any referent to an external reality and its unequivocal placement in the realm of psychological processes. As Frederic Jameson noted, this makes language a "prison-house" from which there is no escape.[125]

Foucault, like other French literary critics, has pursued the implications of a concept of language that elevates the systematic aspects of language over the speaking (or writing) subject and over historical processes while simultaneously separating thought from external reality. These critics are usually associated with French "new criticism" or "new, new criticism"[126] and tend to congregate around the journals *Tel Quel* and *Critique*.[127] Foucault occasionally publishes articles in *Tel Quel*[128] and is one of the editors of *Critique*, where he has worked with such figures as Georges Bataille, Maurice Blanchot, and Roland Barthes. The latter is particularly interesting because, in addition to his study of semiology,[129] Barthes has commented on the relation between modern physics and contemporary literature. In an article on "objective literature," for example, he claimed that "Robbe-Grillet's destruction of the classical concept of space is neither oneiric nor irrational; it is based on an entirely new notion of the structure of matter and movement. The proper analogy is neither the Freudian universe nor the Newtonian—we must face instead an intellectual complex derived from contemporary art and science— from the new physics and the new cinema."[130] Although Barthes did not analyze this new "intellectual complex" at great length here, he did sketch its major features in Robbe-Grillet's writings. Barthes noted, for instance, Robbe-Grillet's exclusive concern with sight as a mode of perception and the absence in his writings of any indication that objects have a substantial reality. Objects become little more than surface configurations subject to endless description but not to depth analysis. Also, for Robbe-Grillet objects no longer exist in a fixed space or time; it is doubtful that they "exist" at all. Objects appear as indications of specific spatiotemporal relations and then they "mystify or they disappear."[131] Paradoxically, Robbe-Grillet's very "multiplication of details, his obsession with topography, his entire demonstrative apparatus actually tends to destroy the object's unity by giving it an exaggeratedly precise location in space, by drowning it in a deluge of outlines, coordinates, and orientations, by the eventual abuse of perspective . . . [and] by exploding the traditional notion of space and substituting for it a new space, provided . . . with a new depth and dimension in time."[132]

These observations could be transposed to Foucault's works with very little distortion, since his literary analyses (as well as his archaeological studies) reflect a similar concern with spatial and temporal relationships and a similar redefinition of the nature of objects and the role of subjects. Between 1962 and 1967 Foucault published a number of essays devoted to various literary figures and major themes in contemporary literature. In his article "Distance, Aspect, Origin" (1963), for example, Foucault outlined the "isomorphisms" between the works of Robbe-Grillet and recent publications by *Tel Quel* writers such as Philippe Sollers, Jean Thibaudeau, and Jean-Louis Baudry.[133] These isomorphisms, he claimed, do not define a synthetic "view of the world" but do indicate a shared "discursive articulation." Specifically, he commented on the tendency to regard objects as forms without volume or as forms with volumes that vary with the "distance" from which they are perceived. Other isomorphisms include the prevalence of mirror images (simulations), which again denote mere surface shapes without substance; spatial shifts which juxtapose two spaces simultaneously; temporal superimpositions in which the remote past is closer than the recent past; and temporal mergings in which it becomes impossible to determine what happened and what did not happen, and in which the divisions between "actual and potential, perception and dream, past and fantasy" become "moments of passage" rather than boundaries.[134] Other similarities between Robbe-Grillet and *Tel Quel* writers refer to the substitution of ordering systems based on resemblance or succession by a system based on networks (fields); a refusal to regard fiction as representative of either the real or the unreal and, despite close ties to surrealism, a refusal to look for a hidden reality; a tendency to define the fictive in terms of trajectories or points of intersection; and a determination to abolish the language of dialectics, which divides subject and object, interior and exterior, reality and imagination.[135] Still other isomorphisms reflect similar notions of "origin" and "aspect" between Robbe-Grillet and many *Tel Quel* writers. These writers describe multiple, fragmentary precedents instead of seeking an "original" enunciation. They also have adopted the grammatical category of "aspect," in which order is given by a spatiotemporal relation based on an indeterminate time and a spatial field. Finally, both Robbe-Grillet and the *Tel Quel* group recognize that with the dispersion of language comes the inability to name things and the necessity to locate language in the space outside of things.

Foucault again stressed the significance of spatial images for contemporary literature the following year in his article "The Language of Space."[136] In this essay he maintained that space has become an obsessive literary metaphor and that spatial relations such as distance, dispersion, and difference are not just themes in modern literature but fundamental characteristics of language itself. The relationship between language and literature, which Foucault analyzed in *The*

Order of Things (1966), was also the subject of several articles he published at about the same time. In an important essay on Blanchot,[137] Foucault discussed the incompatibility of language and consciousness and the need for a new form of thought that does not function in the interior of knowledge but at its limits. Since this type of thinking requires a language continually moving "outside" itself, literature then becomes the system of networks that defines the outward passage of language (much in the way that light is defined as a sequence of electromagnetic fields).

Thought at its limits was also the theme of "A Preface to Transgression" (1963), an essay Foucault wrote on Georges Bataille.[138] For Bataille sexuality marks the transgression of limits, but, as Foucault expressed it, "we have not in the least liberated sexuality, though we have, to be exact, carried it to its limits: the limits of consciousness because it ultimately dictates the only possible reading of our unconscious; the limits of law, since it seems the sole substance of universal taboos; the limits of language, since it traces that line of foam showing just how far speech may advance upon the sands of silence."[139] Limits, however, are no longer fixed borders. In Bataille's thought the absence of external (divine) limits means that limits are established and transformed in a continuing process by the excesses that create and transgress them. Transgression ceases to have an ethical meaning; it merely delineates the fragile line separating "same" from "other" while simultaneously forcing an inclusion of what had previously been excluded. Foucault believes that philosophy cannot express the transformations of transgression because philosophy is so deeply enmeshed in dialectics. But he hopes that a different philosophy, a "philosophy of eroticism," will follow Sade and Bataille's literature of eroticism and replace the contradictions of dialectics with the experience of difference that encompasses both finitude (limit) and being (transgression).

The effort to extend language "outside" itself and to thereby escape the endless cycle of self-reflection was examined in Foucault's essay "Language to Infinity" (1963).[140] Like Saussure, Foucault believes that language does not represent the world but is instead a system of self-representation. Literature is a more abstract form of self-reflection than language because writing represents speech, which itself represents language, and language only represents itself. Literature, trapped within its own system of signs, engages either in endless doublings, mirror images, and repetitions or (as with Sade) in a desperate attempt to push language to extremes and to go outside language. Language imprisoned within itself suggests the image of the library, and for Foucault "the space of language today is not defined by Rhetoric, but by the Library: by the ranging to infinity of fragmentary languages . . . [which] postpones death indefinitely by ceaselessly opening a space which is always the analogue of itself."[141] This theme of self-reflection embodied in the image of the library reappeared in Foucault's later essay on Flaubert's *Temptation of Saint Anthony*.[142] The bizarre figures that populate the *Temptation* were not the product of a delirious imagination but instead attest to Flaubert's meticulous scholarship. Since Flaubert copied these monstrous images from other books, the *Temptation* is, in a very real sense, located within the space of the library. The *Temptation* is also itself a seemingly infinite series of books within books and thus contains an extremely complex internal structure. Moreover, this work has created new spaces in literature and has thereby reordered the Library.

The rational bases of the fabulous and the paradoxical relation between rational and imaginative thought were also mentioned in an article Foucault published in 1966 on Jules Verne.[143] This relationship had been explored in depth, however, in Foucault's study *Raymond Roussel* (1963).[144] While Roussel's bizarre literary fantasies passed largely unnoticed during his lifetime, his works were revived during the 1950s and Roussel himself was acclaimed as a precursor of the "new novel."[145] Shortly before his suicide in 1933, Roussel explained how he constructed his extraordinary tales.[146] His method consisted of repeated decompositions and recompositions of language: he took phrases at random, reduced the words to their phonetic elements, and went on to construct entirely different words from these elements. Although his stories were endlessly descriptive, they only described images; thus Roussel's fiction, like much of modern literature, revealed language doubling back on itself. It also revealed an effort, made by both Roussel and Verne (Roussel adored Verne's works), to "abolish time by the circularity of space."[147] For Foucault, time and space in Roussel's works are embodied in the inversely symmetrical concepts of metamorphosis and labyrinth. He claims that Roussel's language "advances to infinity in the labyrinth of things, but its essential and marvelous poverty brings it back to itself by giving it its power of metamorphosis: to say something else with the same words, to give to the same words another meaning."[148]

The self-referential nature of language (*langue*), speaking (*parole*), and writing (*écriture*) and the redefinition of spatial and temporal relationships are not the only characteristics of modern literature. Another major feature is the effacement, even the destruction, of the subject. In "What is an Author?"[149] Foucault discussed the "kinship between writing and death" and the transformation of writing from a means of insuring immortality to an act of sacrifice. Whereas Greek epics and Arabian tales once functioned to postpone oblivion and death, Foucault believes that writing today "attains the right to kill, to become the murderer of its author. Flaubert, Proust and Kafka are obvious examples of this reversal. . . . If we wish to know the writer in our day, it will be through the singularity of his absence and in the link to death which has transformed him into a victim of his own writing."[150] According to Foucault, the contemporary writer is anonymous, his identity is fragmented and dispersed, and it is no longer meaningful to ask who is speaking. The relevant question has become: what is the function of the author?

Foucault previously referred to specific "author-functions" in articles on Rousseau, Bataille, Hölderlin, and Klossowski. His introduction to a new edition of Rousseau's *Dialogues* entitled *Rousseau, Judge of Jean Jacques*[151] analyzed the plurality of Rousseau's speaking and writing voices as well as the different spaces in which they functioned. The *Confessions* contain the speaking voice of the "real" Rousseau, a voice that moved horizontally in an unbroken line through open space. This voice, however, was suffocated by the silence of "others" (the *philosophes*) and Rousseau was forced to assume the new voice that appeared in the *Dialogues*, a voice that no longer moved along a single horizontal plane but ran vertically through numerous planes in a closed space. The voice of the *Dialogues* is not a speaking but a writing voice, and the transparent, ever-present subject of the *Confessions* disappeared. In its place several dissociated, opaque, and often absent subjects emerged—the various "Jean-Jacques" of the *Dialogues* whom the "real" Rousseau attempted to judge. But Foucault maintained that by the end of the *Dialogues* Rousseau had fled the harsh prospect of judgment and had turned instead to a mythical world that increasingly closed in on him.

Rousseau had, perhaps, gone mad but Foucault insisted that Rousseau's work was not mad. Literature and delirium may share analogous structures, but literature cannot take place in delirium. Literature can, however, lead to madness as well as death, and Foucault believes that this is the risk Hölderlin took in his effort to transgress the limits of language. The relation between Hölderlin's life and his works was the subject of a study by Jean Laplanche, and Foucault's review of that work[152] examined the similarity between the repressive role of Hölderlin's punitive father and the linguistic prohibitions which Hölderlin attempted to challenge in his poetry. Hölderlin's desire to recover all that was forbidden (and thus absent) in his life and language marks the trajectory that leads him "to the absence of the father, that directs his language to the fundamental gap in the signifier, that transforms his lyricism into delirium, [and] his work into the absence of a work."[153]

In conclusion, Foucault's literary essays, structural linguistics, relativity theory, quantum mechanics, and various "field" theories in the human sciences all point to "isomorphisms" in diverse disciplines which suggest the formation of a new paradigm. This paradigm replaces Newtonian-Cartesian conceptions of causality, time, space, subject, and object with systematic relations in which the subject is merely a variable function, objects have no fixed substance, space and time interact, and change is discontinuous. Old oppositions that divided rational from imaginative thought, form from content, and history from structure are collapsed in this new paradigm and replaced by the coexistence of differences. Old certainties, however, have been sacrificed. There is no longer the assumption of a fixed external reality subject to the progressive revelation of modern science. Nor is there a basis for belief in a fixed ego capable of knowing the essence of nature or man. In this new interpretation, thought and reality are not perceived as stable, homogeneous entities but have become fragmented, variable forms defined by a multiplicity of discursive languages.

FROM A CRITIQUE OF

MENTAL ILLNESS TO AN

ARCHAEOLOGY OF MEDICAL

PERCEPTION

Psychological Conceptions of Mental Illness

Shortly after completing his formal education in philosophy and psychopathology, Foucault published a small book under the title *Mental Illness and Psychology* (1954).[1] This work marks his passage from phenomenology to history and suggests his later transition to "archaeology." It also reveals a tightly structured and eloquent style that is devoid of the repetitions and qualifications which characterize Foucault's more complex later works. Furthermore, this early study prefigures many of the themes Foucault subsequently developed at length in *Madness and Civilization* (1961). Unfortunately, *Mental Illness and Psychology* was largely ignored when it first appeared[2] and has since been eclipsed by Foucault's other publications. It is nevertheless worth discussing, both as a prelude to Foucault's historical and archaeological studies and in its own right as an incisive critique of modern conceptions of mental illness.

In the rigorously systematic manner that typifies much of his writing, Foucault began by reducing conventional interpretations of mental illness to their underlying assumptions, then went on to indicate the limitations of each type of analysis, and finally stated his own position. In rapid (perhaps too rapid) fashion, he dispatched the view that relegated mental illness to the status of organic pathology. The classification of mental illness established early in this century, which included categories such as hysteria, psychasthenia, obsession, mania and depression, paranoia, chronic hallucinatory psychosis, hebephrenia, and catatonia—the last three categories later grouped together as "dementia praecox" and then as "schizophrenia"—was based, in Foucault's view, on two untenable assumptions. Behind the symptoms that defined each category was the assumption of a disease entity, a "thing" that invades the body. Behind the apparent changes in each form of illness was the assumption that mental illness is an evolving disease that, like a biological species, develops into various subspecies. Neither assumption could be verified and the attempt to establish a "psychosomatic totality" by integrating mental and organic pathology into a "metapathology" failed. Foucault implied that this failure was inevitable, that the same concepts cannot be used for physical and mental phenomena, and that madness will never be reducible to an organic disorder. But since Foucault was not primarily concerned with either the organic bases of madness or with the treatment of mental illness, he admitted frankly that "I have purposely not referred to the physiological and the anatomicopathological problems concerning mental illness or to those concerning techniques of cure. It is not that psychopathological analysis is independent, de facto or de jure, of them. . . . But neither physiology nor therapeutics can become those absolute viewpoints from which the psychology of mental illness can be reduced or suppressed."[3]

In addition to the attempt to define mental illness as a disease, modern psychology tried to define this "illness" as a functional disorder. By viewing mental illness as a partial or total disturbance of a structured personality, all mental disorders were reclassified as either neurotic or psychotic. Again, pathological personalities were compared to pathological organisms, but here too Foucault considered this comparison artificial. In organic (unlike mental) pathology, cause and effect relationships can be isolated, clear distinctions can be made between normal and pathological processes, and the sick organism can be studied by isolating it from its environment. Since Foucault held that mental illness cannot be understood simply as a form of organic pathology, he concluded that it was necessary to "analyze the specificity of mental illness, seek the concrete forms that psychology has managed to attribute to it, then determine the conditions that have made possible this strange status of madness, a mental illness that cannot be reduced to any illness."[4]

Foucault's desire to isolate concrete forms of scientific discourses, like his critique of fixed objects (such as disease entities) and traditional systems of classification (such as those that define mental illness), is characteristic of his later archaeological studies. Moreover, Foucault already signaled his intention to replace stable concepts with systems of relationships by attempting "to show that the root of mental pathology must be sought not in some kind of 'meta-pathology,' but in a certain relation, historically situated, of man to the madman and to the true man."[5] The concept "true man" disappears in Foucault's later works, although he continues to believe that the relationship between rationality and madness determines the different forms of mental illness and the conditions under which they appear. Foucault's analysis of the modern forms of mental illness, which constituted the first half of *Mental Illness and Psychology*, drew heavily on phenomenological concepts of consciousness and being, concepts that gradually dropped out of his more developed thought. An analysis of the historical conditions that determined the appearance of specific types of madness comprised the last half of his study and anticipated in both method and substance his subsequent history of madness.

Since psychology has defined mental illness as a personality disorder, Foucault examined the nature of this disorder and identified three psychological dimensions of mental illness. Psychological interpretations, he claimed, regard mental illness as an evolutionary regression to childlike or primitive behavior, as a regression in the afflicted individual's personal history to defense mechanisms formed early in life, or as an existential retreat from being-in-the-world to the security of a private world. Since these three aspects of mental illness are frequently confused and since each is a limited expression of madness, Foucault was careful to point out the differences between them and to indicate the weaknesses of each interpretation.

Evolutionary theories stem from the obvious functional disorders found in extremely sick people. In such patients complex, integrative, and conscious functions are suppressed while simpler, less voluntary functions emerge and dominate behavior. Foucault characterized this suppression of higher functions and augmentation of lower functions as a loss of "syntax" and spatiotemporal orientation. "The complex synthesis of dialogue has been replaced by fragmentary monologue; the syntax through which meaning is constituted is broken and all that survives is a collection of verbal elements out of which emerge ambiguous, polymorphic, labile meanings; the spatio-

temporal coherence that is ordered in the here and now has collapsed, and all that remains is a chaos of successive heres and isolated
moments."[6] By this description Foucault did not mean to suggest
that madness resembles modern literature (broken syntax) or modern physics (chaos of successive heres and nows), although these
parallels may well hold. He intended to indicate that, insofar as
mental illness is a regression to lower functions, it is "not an essence
contra natura, it is nature itself, but in an inverted process."[7] The
various evolutionary theories of mental illness, Foucault maintained,
all presuppose such an inverted process and merely differ on the
type of regression involved. The British neurologist John Hughlings
Jackson held that mental illness was an organic regression, what he
called a dysfunction of "the highest cerebral centers." A great deal of
Freud's work was devoted to describing stages of libidinal development and examining the types of neurosis associated with regressions
to these various stages, a project Foucault referred to as an "archaeology of the libido." Finally, the French psychiatrist Pierre Janet
regarded mental illness as a regression to a more primitive level of
social evolution.[8] While Foucault granted that theories of evolutionary regression and comparisons of the mentally ill to children or
primitives might provide useful descriptions of mental illness, he did
not believe that they could satisfactorily explain mental illness. As he
phrased it:

> On the horizon of all these analyses there are, no doubt, ex-
> planatory themes that are themselves situated on the frontiers of
> myth: the myth, to begin with, of a certain psychological substance
> (Freud's "libido," Janet's "psychic force") . . . the myth, too, of an
> identity between the mentally ill person, the primitive, and the
> child—a myth in which consciousness, shocked by the sight of
> mental illness, finds reassurance and is reenforced in the en-
> veloping prejudice of its own culture.[9]

Although there may indeed be functional regressions in mental
illness, Foucault insisted that this does not entail a regression to
"archaic personalities." The sick personality has its own unique structure that cannot be grasped unless the evolutionary dimension of
mental illness is supplemented by the individual's psychological history. Foucault did not yet question the concept of time that underlay
both the evolutionary and historical perspectives, and he still appeared to accept, with reservations, the coherence of traditional

psychological theories. However, he wished to distinguish between psychological evolution which "integrates the past in the present in a unity without conflict" and psychological history in which "it is the present that detaches itself from the past, conferring meaning upon it."[10] In Foucault's view, Freudian theory recognized that regression was not really a return to an archaic state of nature, but a recourse to a specific set of defensive mechanisms that substituted an imaginary past for a threatening present. But the complex defensive systems and the intricate pattern of substitutions and metamorphoses characteristic of pathological thought processes do not resolve psychic conflict.[11] Indeed, pathological regression actually intensifies such conflict and establishes a vicious circle that dramatizes the morbid inability to integrate past and present. Again, psychology describes but does not explain this morbid process. Foucault refused to believe that the destructive circularity of pathological conflict can be understood as an expression of Freud's mysterious "death instinct." Moreover, if psychological regression is interpreted as a defense against underlying anxiety (a theory Foucault accepted), then the nature of that preexistent anxiety must be examined. This, however, requires the addition of a third dimension to the psychological definition of mental illness.

Pathological anxiety, Foucault claimed, cannot be understood in terms of evolutionary regression or in terms of regressive defense mechanisms. It can only be apprehended from within, from within the experience a person has of his own sickness and of the world he inhabits. This kind of understanding requires a different method from that provided by conventional psychology. Consequently, "discursive logic is out of place here. . . . Intuition goes further and more quickly when it succeeds in restoring the fundamental experience that dominates all pathological processes. . . . This new reflection on mental illness is above all 'comprehension' (understanding). It is this method that phenomenological psychology has practiced."[12] With the exception of extreme dementia, Foucault insisted that the "sick consciousness" is still a consciousness that perceives its own sickness. Nothing, he said, "could be more false than the myth of madness as an illness that is unaware of itself as such. . . . The doctor is not on the side of health, possessing all the knowledge about the illness; and the patient is not on the side of the illness, ignorant of everything about it including its very existence."[13] The patient's consciousness of his illness, however, is an ambiguous consciousness that arises from the illness itself. The illness is sometimes perceived merely as an accidental, organic process and no recognition is given to its psychological aspects. Sometimes it is regarded as a destiny, the consequence of some tragic event in one's past. At other times it is viewed as a separate experience in which the consciousness of a morbid world is detached from the coexisting consciousness of the real world. Even in acute cases, when it appears that the patient is unaware of the outside world, he still has a dreamlike awareness of "a distant, veiled reality."[14]

The patient's subjective experience of his illness and the capacity of others to grasp this experience through intuition were not, however, Foucault's main concerns even in this seemingly humanistic work. He was already more interested in the way the mentally ill structure their world than he was in either comprehending their experience of morbidity or assessing the significance of their experiences for therapeutic purposes. Consequently, despite the similarity of Foucault's approach to the phenomenological psychiatry of the 1950s and the antipsychiatric movement of the 1960s,[15] his perspective was, and remains, epistemological rather than psychoanalytic. Yet his epistemological focus has shifted from this early phenomenological acceptance of concepts such as intuition, consciousness, personality, and being to an analysis of "pathological" and "normal" perceptual structures.

The structure of the pathological world is characterized by spatial and temporal distortions and by distorted perceptions of others and of oneself. The phenomenological studies by Eugène Minkowski and Ludwig Binswanger[16] offered Foucault insights into the spatio-temporal organization of the morbid world. For the seriously ill, "time is rendered instantaneous by fragmentation; and, lacking any opening on to the past and future, it spins round upon its axis, proceeding either by leaps or by repetitions. . . . The schizophrenic's temporality is thus divided between the fragmented time of anxiety and the formless, contentless eternity of delusion." And again:

> Space, as a structure of the experienced world, lends itself to the same kind of analysis. Sometimes distances disappear, as in the case of those delusional subjects who recognize here people they know to be somewhere else, or those subjects suffering from hallucinations who hear their voices, not in the objective space in which sound sources are situated, but in a mythical space, in a sort

of quasi space in which the axes of reference are fluid and mobile.
. . . In other cases, space becomes insular and rigid. Objects . . .
are affirmed in their isolation, without any real or potential link to
other objects. . . . Objects have lost their cohesion and space
has lost its coherence.[17]

These temporal and spatial distortions, which are characterized by
repetitions, discontinuous jumps, excessive fluidity, and bizarre rigidity, did not yet provide Foucault with the conceptual tools for a
critique of "pure reason." He recognized, however, that these morbid
mental structures represented an important form of knowledge that
had been systematically suppressed by Western concepts of rationality. Similarly, pathological experiences of society and morbid perceptions of the body are based on perceptions of alienation from the
rational world. Social relationships disintegrate once others are perceived as unreal, threatening strangers. For the mentally ill, the
outside world assumes "the heaviness and distance of an inhuman
universe in which things freeze when expressed, in which significations have the massive indifference of things, and in which symbols
assume the gravity of enigmas."[18] Even the patient's own body appears alien and is experienced as an exterior thing or as an absence of
substance. Such morbid perceptions, Foucault concluded, cannot be
understood simply as a withdrawal into a private world. They must
also be recognized as a retreat from a hostile "normal" world, a retreat that psychological theories cannot explain because psychology
locates madness in the personality, not in the world. In order to
understand the relation between reason and madness, Foucault decided to go beyond the limitations imposed by psychological concepts of mental illness and to seek out the historical conditions that
determined the various forms of madness.

While Foucault never precisely defined the terms *mental illness*
and *madness*, the latter is obviously the more general category. Yet
madness appears to refer both to a single entity and to a variable
experience that happens to be equated in our culture with the concept of mental illness. This issue is further complicated by the introduction of the term *insanity* as an even more general category.
Foucault claimed, for example, that the historical constitution of
mental illness can be seen as a social "experience of the Insane, which
gradually, through successive divisions, becomes *madness*, *illness*, and
mental illness."[19] Although he did not develop this concept of in-

sanity, Foucault seemed to regard madness and the experience of insanity as more or less equivalent and he took the Renaissance perception of madness as a model. He believes that during the Renaissance madness was recognized as different but was not viewed as pathological, whereas during the so-called Age of Reason (approximately 1650 to 1789) it was considered an illness. After the French Revolution, madness came to be viewed not just as an illness but as a disorder of the psyche (meaning both soul and mind); that is to say, it was classified as "mental illness" with specific moral connotations. Madness is still regarded as mental illness and has increasingly been associated with the negative concept of deviancy; sociological notions of statistical abnormality and anthropological theories of atypical social types are examples of this trend. This development gave rise to two questions that Foucault addressed in the remainder of his study: "How did our culture come to give mental illness the meaning of deviancy and to the patient a status that excludes him? And how, despite that fact, does our society express itself in those morbid forms in which it refuses to recognize itself?"[20]

Madness has been retrospectively defined as mental illness for earlier societies by interjecting the concept of "possession" into previous perceptions of madness. But according to Foucault, there was, and is, no necessary connection between possession and madness. Possession is a religious concept that was first confused with medicine when the Catholic church solicited the medical profession in its efforts to suppress heretical opinions. The concept of mental illness is a recent construct; in fact, Foucault maintained that "before the nineteenth century, the experience of madness in the Western world was very polymorphic."[21] In the medieval period only a few forms of madness were subjected to medical treatment. During the Renaissance, too, medical treatment was the exception and "madness was allowed free reign; it circulated throughout society, it formed part of the background and language of everyday life, it was for everyone an everyday experience that one sought neither to exalt nor to control."[22] Foucault viewed this open attitude as an extraordinary sign of social flexibility. After experiences of terror and death during the fourteenth and fifteenth centuries, Renaissance society might well have turned in fear upon the mad. Instead, faced with madness, "Renaissance culture put its values to the test and engaged them in a way that was more ironic than tragic."[23] The strange and different were recognized as bizarre, but the bizarre became strangely familiar (for example, in Bosch's paintings). The dialogue between reason and unreason remained open and the great Renaissance writers (Foucault cited Erasmus, Shakespeare, and Cervantes) all recognized the wisdom of madness.

With the emergence of bourgeois values in the mid-seventeenth century, this tolerant attitude abruptly ended. The mad, as well as others unable or unwilling to work, were confined in "hospitals" whose purpose was not to offer medical treatment but to exclude nonproductive social elements from society at large. Consequently, madness "entered a phase of silence from which it was not to emerge for a long time; it was deprived of its language; and although one continues to speak of it, it became impossible for it to speak of itself. Impossible at least until Freud, who was the first to open up once again the possibility for reason and unreason to communicate in the danger of a common language, ever ready to break down and disintegrate into the inaccessible."[24] In addition to reducing madness to silence, internment associated madness with crime and thus burdened the insane with undeserved guilt.

Curiously, repression increased rather than decreased with the coming of the French Revolution. The Revolution freed impoverished, disabled, and criminal groups from the hospitals but kept the mad imprisoned. Moreover, Foucault did not regard the late eighteenth- and nineteenth-century reforms that began with men like Philippe Pinel in France and William Tuke in England as either humane or rational.[25] On the contrary, he believed that these reformers liberated many of the physical constraints on the mad but further imprisoned their minds. By regarding madness as social and moral deviancy, "enlightened" reformers introduced the psychological definition of madness as "mental" illness and set up punitive systems to coerce the mad to conform to social standards. In nineteenth-century asylums the mad were "cured" by inculcating "proper" moral values. Shame and punishment were common therapeutic methods; in fact, all means were used that "might both *infantilize* the madman and *make him feel guilty.*"[26] Foucault concluded:

It is hardly surprising, then, that an entire psychopathology—beginning with Esquirol, but including our own—should be governed by the three themes that define its problematic: the relations of freedom to compulsions, the phenomena of regression and the infantile structure of behavior, [and] aggression and guilt.

What one discovers under the name of the "psychology" of madness is merely the result of the operations by which one has invested it. None of this psychology would exist without the *moralizing sadism* in which nineteenth-century "philanthropy" enclosed it, under the hypocritical appearances of "liberation."[27]

The experience of confinement during the nineteenth century, then, produced both the conditions that allowed a "science" of psychology to develop and the specific types of madness that emerged. Madness became mental illness and was thereafter characterized by infantile regression, defensive regressions to ward off anxiety and guilt, and compulsive fears of restraint—pathological forms that Foucault considers more historical than psychic in origin. Moreover, none of these pathological forms are accidental; they all reflect the values of the "rational" society from which they emerged. If regression to childhood is a dominant pathological feature, it is because "normal" society has made the integration of past and present problematical. The "whole development of contemporary education," Foucault claimed, is aimed at "preserving the child from adult conflicts" and thereby "exposes him to a major conflict, to the contradiction between his childhood and his real life."[28] If regression to defensive mechanisms which lock the mentally ill into endless cycles of self-conflict characterizes contemporary forms of mental illness, this type of regression is only possible in a society permeated by internal conflict. The competitive, conflictual relations that pervade modern business and social life are transmitted through the family to the child. According to Foucault, the Oedipus complex, "the nexus of familial ambivalences, is like the reduced version of this contradiction: the child does not himself bring this love-hate that binds him to his parents; he meets it only in the adult world."[29] Finally, if retreat to a private world characterized by alienation from self and others typifies mental illness, that too reflects a society in which "mechanistic rationality excludes the continuous spontaneity of the affective life."[30] The manifestations of madness in the modern world, then, mirror the conflicts of bourgeois society. According to Foucault, the "science" of psychology that was born in the asylums of the nineteenth century will never be able to integrate the experiences of madness and reason because psychology by definition excludes madness. The dialogue between reason and unreason, Foucault concluded, must be sought elsewhere, in the works of Hölderlin, Nietzsche, Artaud, and Roussel, for example, which offer the hope that man will one day "be able to free himself of all psychology and be ready for the great tragic confrontation with madness."[31]

Despite this appeal to Nietzsche and to various romantic and surrealistic critics of rationalism, *Mental Illness and Psychology* stands within the rationalist tradition. What Foucault rejected, however, was the elevation of reason to the status of an essence that defines human nature by excluding madness as unnatural and inhuman. In this work, as in much of Foucault's subsequent writing, the tension between his literary imagination and his epistemological concerns occasionally obscures the logic of his argument. The multiple metaphorical uses of abstract terms like *reason, unreason, madness, man, nature,* and *consciousness* often result in dramatic images with contradictory meanings. Moreover, many questions remain unanswered as Foucault makes the transition from phenomenological psychology to intellectual history. If madness is not an illness but a relationship between rational men and madmen, what determines this relationship? And if Foucault rejects scientific psychology because it is associated with a punitive moralism, why does he not question the morality of philosophical and historical analysis? Although he admits that "all knowledge is linked to the essential forms of cruelty,"[32] it is not at all clear how his analysis is less cruel than that of earlier "humanists." They, at least, were interested in the madman as well as in madness, however imperfect their motives may have been. Also, Foucault's rejection of psychology was not as absolute as it appeared. While he claimed that psychology cannot communicate with madness, he praised Freud for reopening the dialogue between madness and reason.

Finally, Foucault's identification of psychology with nineteenth-century bourgeois values is not, in this study, a well developed theory or even a particularly original idea, although it does strengthen the epistemological critique of psychology made in the first part of this work. It also suggests the direction of his later research, which has been less an attempt to integrate Marx and Freud than an effort to isolate the functions of specific "scientific" discourses in Western thought and practice since the Renaissance. The periodization Foucault established here—Renaissance, Classical, and Modern—is, with little variation, the periodization he used later. And, although *Mental Illness and Psychology* is based on philosophical and historical methodologies that Foucault later rejected, this work already points to his subsequent semistructural and archaeological methodologies. Not only does Foucault later transform this early combination of logical analysis and narrative exposition into a systematic methodology based on intersecting "fields," but ideas he mentions in passing here emerge as major themes in his later works. The association of madness and crime refers here almost exclusively to the creation of guilt and aggression in the mad. Later Foucault examined the impact of this association on the judicial system. The image of madness as a language signifying itself refers here to a defective language; in subsequent works Foucault argued that all thought is a self-referential linguistic system. But despite these anticipations of his later studies, *Mental Illness and Psychology* represents a break with the past as much as it does an opening to the future. Foucault's main concern at the time was not to create a new discourse, but to establish a critical distance from the phenomenological psychology that dominated his own early intellectual life.

Perceptions of Madness in the Age of Reason

In *Mental Illness and Psychology* Foucault claimed that madness was a relation between rational man and the madman rather than an entity in itself. Yet madness was usually treated in this work as a continuous, if changing, phenomenon. In *Madness and Civilization* (1961)[33] madness no longer has a constant identity. It has been dissolved as an object and exists only as a function, a function of the concrete relations between the "rational" and "mad" groups in society and a function of the abstract relations between the concepts of reason and madness. As Roland Barthes commented, "Foucault never defines madness; madness is not the *object* of knowledge, whose history must be rediscovered; one might say instead that *madness is nothing but this knowledge itself*: madness is not a disease, it is a variable and heterogeneous *meaning*, according to the period; Foucault never treats madness except as a functional reality."[34]

Madness, then, is a variable perception, and Foucault has attempted to unearth the Classical knowledge of madness by identifying various forms of perception during this period. In so doing, he has examined a wide range of political, economic, social, philosophical, artistic, literary, and medical data and has isolated both structures of perception (synchronic relations) and sequences of events (diachronic relations). Perceptual structures fall into two main groups: the general, often contradictory, cultural perception of madness and the specific medical perception that determines both the classifications of madness and the established therapeutic practices. Diachronic relations refer to the nondiscursive political, social, and economic developments that form a background to the perception of madness but do not themselves determine its emergence. Above these structures and events runs a metaphysical tension between Reason and Unreason which is the most encompassing of the "fields" within which madness functions. Before turning to the diachronic relations or to the general and specific structures of madness in the Age of Reason, it is necessary to examine the metaphysical assumptions that provide the framework for Foucault's study.

Foucault obviously wishes to reduce the metaphysical aspect of this work because he has subsequently deleted many of the most speculative sections from an abridged French edition (upon which the English translation is based). Yet even the abridged text indicates that Foucault had not separated himself from romanticism, Hegelianism, and phenomenology. Note, for example, his statement in the preface that "we must try to return, in history, to that zero point in the course of madness at which madness is an undifferentiated experience, a not yet divided experience of division itself. We must describe, from the start of its trajectory, that 'other form' which relegates Reason and Madness to one side or the other of its action as things henceforth external, deaf to all exchange, and as though dead to one another."[35] This attempt to return to a mythical origin, a period of undivided wholeness, reveals the profoundly romantic bias of Foucault's study.[36] For Foucault (as for Rousseau, Nietzsche, Freud, and Marcuse) civilization is associated with repression and "progress" has meant a progressive reduction in the range of human expression. Consequently, Foucault's study of the Classical period is really an investigation of the transition from an idealized pre-Classical period in which madness and reason were integrated to a dehumanized Modern period in which these two forms of knowledge have been almost completely separated. The "zero point," however, is not the Renaissance, as it was in *Mental Illness and Psychology*. It has been moved further back into the Middle Ages, although Foucault often refers to a combined Medieval-Renaissance "experience" of madness. The two ruptures in Western sensibility have been symbolically fixed at the dates 1657 (with the creation of the *Hôpital*

Général) and 1794 (with the freeing of the insane from the "hospitals" and their incarceration in asylums). Between these two dates reason and unreason moved further apart and madness was increasingly distinguished from other forms of unreason (disease, crime, and poverty).

For Foucault, the relation between madness and reason in the Classical period is similar to that between tragedy and reason in Nietzsche's view of Greek classicism, except that Descartes rather than Socrates embodies the cleavage between two forms of experience. Madness, however, does not stand in a simple relation of opposition to reason. Reason and unreason emerge together and define each other, forming an inverted and symmetrical pair. Like the contemporary physical notion of matter and antimatter, they are mutually dependent categories that differ from each other merely by a positive or negative sign. Moreover, reason and unreason constitute only one of many mirror-image pairs that can exist in different states or disappear completely but cannot metamorphose into a third form. Like many structuralists and phenomenologists, Foucault has adopted a binary model whose "deep structure" appears to be defined by the pair same-other.[37] The relation between same and other can also be expressed in complementary pairs such as inclusion-exclusion, being-nonbeing, and, of course, reason-unreason. Although Foucault does not discuss the theological pair good-evil, here too a parallel relationship may be drawn. Furthermore, Foucault is less interested in the content of these pairs than he is in the boundaries between them. For Foucault, as for Bachelard and Saussure, meaning comes from form (defined by boundaries) rather than from content.

In *Madness and Civilization* the relation between reason and unreason is particularly important during the Classical period because the border between reason and unreason gradually shifted during this time. Disease and poverty were progressively liberated from unreason and assimilated into reason. Crime was partially liberated from and partially identified with madness. By the end of the eighteenth century, the diffuse and general experience of unreason had been reduced to madness, which alone became otherness, nonbeing, and the very essence of exclusion and evil. Not only was unreason reduced to madness, but between the Medieval and Modern periods madness was systematically divorced from the world, from nature, and from society, until it was located exclusively in the personality of the madman. This internalization of madness paralleled the shift from the medieval belief in God to the Enlightenment concept of Nature and the later shift to nineteenth-century notions of History and Man.

During the Middle Ages madness was associated both with the forbidden knowledge of the Fall and with the divine madness of Christ's redemption; that is to say, it was regarded as a divinely inspired or satanic form of knowledge. During the Classical period madness came to be viewed as a violation of the orderly and rational laws of Nature. Since the concept of Nature did not, at this time, imply a violent struggle for survival, madness was associated with "unnatural" bestiality. Consequently, although madmen in the Classical period were exhibited as monsters or disciplined as wild beasts, they were not viewed as sick men. It was only at the end of the eighteenth century, when madness became associated with delirium (a mental derangement) rather than with passion (a physical and emotional phenomenon), that the mentally ill were "freed" by Enlightenment reformers. It was then, too, that madness assumed another role; henceforth it was to be regarded as alienation from society and from the self. This concept of alienation coincided with new views of history (Hegelian and Marxist concepts of alienation) and psychology (the separation of psychic from physical phenomena). As a result of these transformations, the concept of madness no longer possessed any real content; it merely indicated absence, nothingness, nonbeing. Thus, the last chapter of *Madness and Civilization*, devoted to Goya's and Sade's violent efforts to emerge from the void of nonbeing, is neither an enigmatic nor a careless afterthought, as some commentators have charged, but a natural conclusion to Foucault's "history" of unreason.[38]

The metaphysical relation between reason and unreason and the progressive identification of madness with nonbeing are aspects of Foucault's study that have generally been satirized or ignored by Anglo-American reviewers. French critics take this dimension of Foucault's thought much more seriously. Maurice Blanchot, for one, discusses Foucault's concept of madness as nonbeing in terms of his own theory of forgetfulness (*oubli*), which denotes neither presence nor absence but a state analogous to the unconscious.[39] Roland Barthes views the theme of inclusion and exclusion in Foucault's work as a basic structure (what he calls a "form of forms"), but he believes that this structure establishes a "complementarity which opposes and unites" and that therefore an "implacable dialectic is set up."[40] Michel Serres also calls attention to the Hegelian features in Foucault's thought, although he does not believe that Foucault has established a dialectic.[41] Instead, Serres interprets Foucault's categories of inclusion and exclusion in terms of spatial relationships, and he views Foucault's concept of unreason as a "geometry of negativities." The pre-Classical period, Serres suggests, can be imagined as an original chaotic space in which madness had many points of contact with the world. The Classical space, by contrast, was dualistic, with the space of unreason (hospitals and later asylums) functioning as a negative image of the space of reason (society, in particular the family). Serres further argues that the progressive reduction of unreason to madness can be visualized as a shrinking of a once large circle of unreason within a still larger circle of reason until only a miniscule sphere of madness remained at the heart of reason. Although Serres does not go so far as to suggest that this residue of unreason might have collapsed into a "black hole" whose absence nonetheless warps the surrounding space, he does recognize a similarity between Bachelard and Foucault and calls Foucault's history of madness an "archaeology of psychiatry" comparable to Bachelard's "archaeology of physics."[42]

Other critics have focused on reason rather than unreason in their assessment of *Madness and Civilization*, but these terms cannot really be separated in Foucault's study since a "rational" definition of "irrationality" defines both simultaneously. The madman is precluded from contributing to this definition because, according to Foucault, madness has been silenced since the Renaissance. Still, even reviewers who agree with Foucault's main argument have disagreed with him on just how the definition of reason and unreason was made during the Age of Reason. Jacques Derrida, for example, has criticized Foucault's interpretation of Cartesian epistemology in a lengthy article entitled "Cogito and the History of Madness."[43] And Hayden White, in one of the few significant analyses available in English, has concluded that Foucault is writing an archaeology of Western consciousness.[44] Like Barthes and numerous other critics, White believes that Foucault can be classified as a structuralist, with certain qualifications. Unlike them, however, White distinguishes between two branches of structuralism, what he terms the "positivist" wing (Saussure, Piaget, Althusser) and the "eschatological" wing (Lacan, Lévi-Strauss, Barthes, Foucault). According to White:

The positivist wing has been concerned with the scientific determination of the structures of consciousness by which men form a
conception of the world they inhabit. . . . The eschatological wing,
by contrast, concentrates on the way in which structures of consciousness actually conceal the reality of the world and, by that
concealment, effectively isolate men within different, not to say
mutually exclusive, universes of discourse, thought, and action.
The former wing is, we may say, *integrative* in its aim, insofar as it
envisages a "structure of structures". . . . The latter wing is ultimately *dispersive*, insomuch as it leads thought into the interior of
a given mode of consciousness, where all of its essential mystery,
opaqueness, and particularity are celebrated as evidence of the
irreducible variety of human nature.[45]

Foucault would probably not concede that he had written an archaeology of Western "consciousness" or that he was an "eschatological
structuralist." But White has captured the romantic and apocalyptic
tone of Foucault's writing, the "dispersive" features of his philosophy, and Foucault's conviction that scientific and poetic modes of
knowledge are not ultimately separable.

Most critics, certainly most historians, have been more receptive
to Foucault's analysis of the Classical perception and treatment of
madness or to his interpretation of the political, economic, and social
conditions of the period than they have been to his metaphysical
thesis. Although the Classical perception of madness is the major
theme of Foucault's work, historical conditions also played a role:
the consolidation of royal absolutism, the transition from mercantilism to an industrial economy, and the growth of the bourgeoisie all
contributed to the "great confinement." According to Foucault, the
establishment by royal decree of the first *Hôpital Général* in 1657
installed a "third order of repression" between the police and the
courts.[46] These hospitals, reflecting royal power, were autonomous
and absolute forms of authority under civil (rather than religious)
administration. They were never intended to offer medical treatment and functioned instead like a combination prison-workhouse.
The general hospitals in France were similar to the sixteenth- and
seventeenth-century English workhouses and to the seventeenth-
century German *Zuchthäusern* (houses of correction), which were
intended to provide relief for the poor and social control. By the
mid-seventeenth century, the wars of religion, the European eco-

nomic crisis, and the declining power of the guilds had created an enormous number of beggars and rioters. The poor and the homeless constituted the majority of those confined in the hospitals, although a variety of other social undesirables were also rounded up. The hospitals lumped together the poor, the sick (particularly those suffering from venereal diseases), the insane (about ten percent of the total), and certain types of criminals (including wastrels, blasphemers, and homosexuals).[47] Since no particular distinction was made among these groups, the mad consequently suffered from their identification with poverty (social uselessness), disease (especially diseases associated with immorality), and crime.

By the end of the eighteenth century, the mad were separated from other groups in the hospitals, but this was not the result of special compassion for the innocent insane (traditional accounts notwithstanding). It had more to do with the alarming increase in the numbers of the confined, the desire to protect the sane criminal from the madman, the wish to "liberate" the poor for use in the new factories, and the plan to free the capital tied up in the general hospitals so that it could circulate. Nor, in Foucault's account, did the French Revolution liberate the insane. On the contrary, the revolutionary decrees freed almost everyone from the general hospitals except certain criminals and the mad. During the Revolution the insane were actually legally classified as "marauding beasts" and both outside and inside the general hospitals they were subjected to strict control.[48] Even when the general hospitals were abolished in 1794, the revolutionary government failed to provide medical centers for the mad. The insane were herded into prisons, where confusion and disorder reflected a general uncertainty regarding their status. This condition prevailed until the insane were finally confined in asylums modeled on the moral order of the bourgeois family rather than on the impersonal authority of royal absolutism.

This history of the general hospitals, which is scattered throughout Foucault's study, does not play an important role in his history of madness. Although confinement itself was a critical factor, Foucault does not believe that political and economic events can really explain the establishment of the great houses of confinement, much less account for their long duration or for the transformations that occurred during one hundred and fifty years of internment.[49] These issues were related instead to a "social sensibility common to European culture" which united "a new sensibility to poverty" and "a new ethic of work . . . within the authoritarian forms of constraint."⁵⁰ What, then, was this "social sensibility" that gave birth to a new perception of unreason? And how did this understanding differ from the perception of madness before and after the Classical period?

During the Middle Ages the madman was not a focus of social fear and systematic exclusion. Most often he was portrayed as a "ridiculous and familiar silhouette in the wings," and madness ranked low in the medieval "hierarchy of vices."⁵¹ Yet the medieval world was not open to all forms of humanity. Throughout Europe great lazar houses were built in an effort to ward off both death and evil by isolating lepers. After the Crusades leprosy withdrew from Europe, but the leprosariums and the memories remained to haunt the European imagination.

> For centuries, these reaches would belong to the non-human. From the fourteenth to the seventeenth century, they would wait, soliciting with strange incantations a new incarnation of disease, another grimace of terror, renewed rites of purification and exclusion. . . . Poor vagabonds, criminals and "deranged minds" would take the part played by the leper. . . . With an altogether new meaning and in a very different culture, the forms would remain—essentially that major form of a rigorous division which is social exclusion but spiritual reintegration.⁵²

Between the closure of the leprosariums and the opening of the general hospitals, a new perception of madness was formed. During the late Middle Ages and the Renaissance, madness became a tragicomic experience capable of expressing essential truths about man and the world before being abruptly silenced during the Enlightenment by a sudden rejection of all forms of unreason.

The tragic perception of madness and its links to the late medieval fear of death merged, during the fifteenth and sixteenth centuries, with the Renaissance perception of madness as a great mockery of death—an ironic celebration of the futility of life and the frailty of reason. The symbol of this tragicomic experience of madness was the famous Ship of Fools, a vessel that existed both in the imaginative literature of the period and in the experiences of daily life. Communities rid themselves of their mad by placing them on special ships, a banishment that served not merely as a form of social exclusion but also as a ritual of spiritual purification:

> It is possible that these ships of fools, which haunted the
> imagination of the entire Renaissance, were pilgrimage boats,
> highly symbolic cargoes of madmen in search of their reason. . . .
> What matters is that the vagabond madmen, the act of driving
> them away, their departure and embarkation do not assume their
> entire significance on the plane of social utility. Other meanings
> much closer to rite are certainly present. . . . The madman's
> voyage is at once a rigorous division and an absolute Passage.[53]

Although the mad were expelled, they were neither completely
separated from the world nor silenced. They still carried a message
from another realm, a world before or beyond reason, and this message embodied both the awesome temptation of forbidden knowledge and the comic pathos of the non-sense of this world. The dark
temptation of madness and the link between madness and themes of
violation, punishment, and death were more evident in the plastic
arts (Bosch, Brueghel, and Dürer) than they were in Renaissance
literature and philosophy.[54] The ironic experience of madness as
illusion, which gradually dominated the Renaissance perception of
madness, was reflected in Erasmus's satire *In Praise of Folly* as well as
in popular literature and drama.[55]

Then, quite suddenly in the mid-seventeenth century, this Renaissance perception gave way to a new and very different perceptual
structure. Foucault offers no real explanation, he merely marks the
fissure:

> Madness has ceased to be—at the limits of the world, of man,
> and death—an eschatological figure. . . . Oblivion falls upon the
> world navigated by the free slaves of the Ship of Fools. Madness
> will no longer proceed from a point within the world to a point
> beyond, on its strange voyage; it will never again be that fugitive
> and absolute limit. Behold it moored now, made fast among things
> and men. Retained and maintained. No longer a ship but a
> hospital.[56]

The "great confinement" which initiated the Classical period signaled
the end of a distinct perception of madness. Madness was merged in
the more general perception of unreason, which mingled images of
poverty, disease, crime, and madness into a more or less unified
structure. Clearly, however, the perception of poverty dominated
the initial stages of the Classical perception of unreason. Neverthe-

less, a specific perception of madness remained, finding expression in the medical theories and practices of the period. The general structure of unreason and the transformation of this structure during the Age of Reason are themes that appeal to cultural historians and were the basis for enthusiastic reviews by such *Annales* scholars as Robert Mandrou and Fernand Braudel.[57] The medical perception of madness is a theme more attractive to historians and philosophers of science.

Foucault's analysis of the intersection of medical theory and social practice, as well as his careful delineation of the complex displacements of medical concepts, bears the stamp of Canguilhem's influence. This is not surprising, because Canguilhem not only was Foucault's teacher but he also read and corrected the original draft of *Madness and Civilization.*[58] In Foucault's analysis, however, the Classical perception of madness was never completely divorced from the structure of unreason. Indeed, Foucault insisted that it "was in relation to unreason and to it alone that madness could be understood. Unreason was its support; or let us say that unreason defined the locus of madness's possibility."[59] These two themes can nonetheless be isolated to some extent, and Foucault himself stressed one or the other in various sections of his work.

The Classical perception of unreason paralleled a shift in the European attitude toward poverty. In Christian mythology, man's expulsion from the Garden of Eden carried with it the curse of labor, which became both an economic necessity and a spiritual penance. Until the Reformation and the growth of capitalism, however, the moral imperative to labor did not displace the simple necessity to work to overcome poverty. But by the mid-seventeenth century, the association of idleness with sin blurred the distinction between poverty and crime. The incarceration of the poor was not merely a defensive measure to prevent begging and rioting or a charitable effort to aid the unfortunate poor. It was also a form of penance, clearly expressed in the requirement that the confined work regardless of the economic advantages of such labor. Since the deranged and disabled were conspicuous by their inability to work, they too were subject to the general condemnation of idleness.

The great confinement, then, like the medieval confinement of lepers, signified both exclusion and penance and the "old rites of excommunication were revived, but in the world of production and commerce."[60] According to Foucault, this was an ominous event that certified the success of the bourgeoisie in establishing for "the first time . . . an astonishing synthesis of moral obligation and civil law."[61] It was to be particularly ominous for the madman as the perception of unreason shifted during the Classical period. With the emergent industrial society, poverty was increasingly defined as an economic inevitability rather than as a moral failing. The need for a large, subsistence-level work force gave the poor a redeeming social function that freed them of much of the moral stigma associated with their original confinement.[62] This stigma, however, was increasingly transferred to the mad.

While poverty diminished as a factor in the Classical perception of unreason, disease, crime, and madness became more closely intertwined. This too had repercussions on the perception of madness. When the general hospitals were first established, madness was not completely identified with either disease or crime. Although other inmates of these hospitals were hidden to conceal the shame of their presumed guilt, the mad were exhibited for profit and regarded not as guilty humans but as monsters. This discrepancy between the treatment of the mad and the other prisoners of the general hospitals revealed several important features of the early Classical perception of unreason. First, the very desire to conceal the evil of all forms of unreason except madness suggested that evil was too awful and too contagious to be dealt with publicly. This view stood in marked contrast to Renaissance attitudes toward evil; during the pre-Classical period, punishment was still a public rather than a private affair that carried with it the possibility of absolution and reintegration into society. Second, the perception of the insane as wild beasts meant that the mad were still subject to cruel treatment, but not as punishment for social crimes. They were instead disciplined like wild animals for their refusal to conform to the orderly laws of Nature. Confinement and discipline were expected to break the will of the madman and to check his unreasonable passion for freedom. A third consequence of the perception of madmen as wild animals was that the insane were not considered sick. On the contrary, it was believed that "the animal solidity of madness, and the density it borrows from the blind world of beasts, inured the madman to hunger, heat, cold, and pain. It was common knowledge until the end of the eighteenth century that the insane could support the miseries of existence indefinitely."[63] Finally, the perception of the mad as mere animals implied that madness no longer expressed anything meaningful.

Whereas madness had once conveyed the tragic truth of the Fall or the ironic truth of human illusions, during the Enlightenment reason alone expressed truth, and the mad became dumb beasts devoid of all knowledge.

The mad continued to be perceived as monsters throughout the Classical period, but gradually madness became identified with disease and crime as well. By the middle of the eighteenth century, the madman appeared in the popular imagination as both monster and man and was associated with vague fears of physical and moral corruption. The first sign of this perceptual shift, Foucault claimed, was the belief that crackpot social theorists (caricatures of Enlightened reformers) were simultaneously mad, sick, and criminal. Diderot's satire *Rameau's Nephew* (1762) gave voice both to this changed perception of madness and to its corollary, the erosion of rational man's self-confidence. During the 1770s and 1780s the dread of unreason reached such proportions that even before the French Revolution a "great fear" swept France. The general hospitals were widely regarded as sources of contagious diseases, centers of vile debaucheries, and scenes of brutal bestiality. Thus, "the circle was closed: all those forms of unreason which had replaced leprosy in the geography of evil, and which had been banished into the remotest social distance, now became a visible leprosy and offered their running sores to the promiscuity of men."[64] An entire fantastic imagery combining long-repressed memories of a fearful disease and a Boschlike iconography of madness reemerged at the close of the eighteenth century. But these new images were not simply recapitulations of older ones. During the long confinement the perception of disease and madness had united with a new perception of criminal sexuality. According to Foucault, the Marquis de Sade symbolized this altered perception:

> Sadism is not a name finally given to a practice as old as Eros; it is a massive cultural fact which appeared precisely at the end of the eighteenth century, and which constitutes one of the greatest conversions of Western imagination: unreason transformed into delirium of the heart, madness of desire, the insane dialogue of love and death in the limitless presumption of appetite. Sadism appears at the very moment that unreason, confined for over a century and reduced to silence, reappears, no longer as an image of the world, no longer as a *figura*, but as language and desire.[65]

This transformation in the perception of unreason included a rupture in the perception of madness. On the one hand, the fantastic and forbidden features of madness (such as bestiality and freedom) were combined with images of disease and crime to the point that unreason was reduced to madness. On the other hand, the new association of madness with disease permitted certain aspects of madness to be separated from unreason and treated "scientifically" by seeking physical and historical explanations for what in the nineteenth century would be called "mental illness." This new conception of madness as mental illness was thus dissociated from the perception of unreason and thereafter "the time of unreason and the time of madness receive two opposite vectors."[66] Unreason appeared sporadically in art and literature but disappeared as a general social sensibility; madness was reduced by physiology and psychology to either a physical infirmity or a mental disorder mirroring social conflict. Earlier in the eighteenth century certain popular explanations of madness had already tied mental derangement to contemporary social conditions. What the French considered excessive freedom in England, for example, was frequently blamed as the cause of English melancholia and suicide. Likewise, an excessive religious sensibility or cultural sophistication was held to be deleterious to mental health, and idleness (excess time) seemed a natural explanation for a variety of nervous disorders. Slowly, then, "the eighteenth century constituted, around its awareness of madness and of its threatening spread, a whole new order of concepts. . . . Madness was no longer recognized in what brings man closer to an immemorial fall or an indefinitely present animality; . . . madness became possible in that milieu where man's relations with his feelings, with time, with others, are altered."[67]

The transformation from madness as bestiality to mental illness as alienation was only possible given the simultaneous transformation in the Classical conception of illness. Medical theories and practices during the Age of Reason were developed largely outside the general hospitals, since these hospitals were neither research nor treatment facilities. Medical theories during the seventeenth and eighteenth centuries all assumed the fundamental unity of body and soul and sought to explain the interaction of physical and emotional states. Not only was medicine based on the perception of psychosomatic integration, but Classical medicine was not, in Foucault's view, a scientific discipline founded on observation rather than imagination, as most histories of medicine assert. On the contrary, medicine was based on images rather than observable phenomena. "Humors," "spirits," "qualities," and "nerves" provided a series of images that formed "a perceptual structure, . . . not a conceptual system." This structure underwent a series of displacements during the Classical period and left behind a classificatory system that persisted even after the explanatory myths disappeared.[68]

The early seventeenth-century theory of humors assumed a mutual interaction between various physical substances and different mood states. Thus, bile was believed to cause anger and anger to disperse bile. By mid-century the theory of humors had been largely replaced by the theory of spirits, in which less tangible substances were held to determine physical and mental health by their regulated movement and proper distribution through the body. In the late seventeenth and early eighteenth centuries, the theory of spirits was displaced by the theory of solids and fluids. The interaction between body and soul no longer depended on substances or on motion but on qualitative states (such as "heavy" blood) that determined physical and mental conditions simultaneously. By the close of the eighteenth century, the theory of nervous sensibility superseded the theory of qualities and introduced a spatial conception of the body. It was then thought that nervous fibers too close together (thus subject to sympathetic vibrations) or too sensitive to stimuli (particularly sexual sensations, but also mental stimuli such as novels and the theater) "explained" madness.[69]

The assumption of an integrated body-soul system and the various interpretations of interactions within this system also shaped the classification of diseases in the Classical period. Mania and melancholia were grouped together, for example, not on the basis of similar observable symptoms but because both could be explained by the same "scientific" constructs. Thus mania was attributed to excessive mobility of the spirits, to dryness in the brain, or to tension in the nervous fibers, whereas melancholia was explained by postulating the opposite conditions (slow spirits, excessive humidity, or lax nerve fibers). Moreover, as these explanatory theories changed, so too did the definitions of mania and melancholia. For instance, melancholia in the early Classical period referred to a delusional state, but in the late eighteenth century it meant a nondelusional stuporous condition. Such changes cannot be credited to a progressive refinement of scientific knowledge; they merely indicated a series of shifts in the perception of madness.

While earlier categories of illness were redefined, disorders not previously considered forms of madness emerged in the new nosography of this period. Hysteria was perhaps the most important of these additions, since the interpretations of hysteria represented the transition from Classical conceptions of illness to Modern concepts of mental illness. Before the eighteenth century hysteria was regarded as a female physical disorder caused by an irregular motion of the uterus. During the eighteenth century hysteria was classified as a form of madness because it could be assimilated to the theory of nervous sensibility (nerve vibrations seemed to explain diffuse physical complaints). A similar explanation for hypochondria suggested that hysteria and hypochondria, like mania and melancholia, were merely different aspects of the same disorder. But the interpretation of hysteria as a female nervous disease carried with it the implication that weak nerves were due to moral as well as physical debility. Such an interpretation gave madness "a new content of guilt, of moral sanction, of just punishment which was not at all a part of the classical experience."[70] By the end of the eighteenth century, then, medical theory as well as the experience of confinement had identified madness with disease and social deviancy.

A similar series of shifts took place in the medical treatment of the mad. Therapeutic measures, inspired by medical theories, were chosen not because of observed efficacy but on the basis of metaphorical relationships. Iron was thus administered to "strengthen" the nerves; bleeding and cauterization were used to purify the body; water in the form of drinks, baths, and showers was expected to purify and to establish a proper fluid balance; and exercise or travel was prescribed to regulate the motion of the spirits or to tone nerve fibers. Many of these methods for treating madness were retained in the later treatment of mental illness, but as punitive rather than therapeutic measures. For example, a rotary machine that spun the patient at varying speeds was used in the Classical period to regulate the motion of spirits. In the nineteenth century it was a means to regulate behavior through punishment.

This transformation from treatment to punishment required a perception of madness as a mental disorder different from disorders of the body-soul. Classical medicine made this distinction by identifying delirium as a mental derangement and passion as a physical and emotional state. During the Classical period little attention was given to the delusional content of mad thought, although delirium was carefully distinguished from other imaginary experiences (such as fantasy and dream). In fact, according to Foucault, there was a clear recognition that "the man who imagines that he is made of glass is not mad, for any sleeper can have this image in a dream; but he is mad if, believing he is made of glass, he thereby concludes he is fragile, that he is in danger of breaking. . . . Such reasonings are those of a madman; but again we must note that they are neither absurd nor illogical."[71] What defined delirium as madness was not the form or the content of this type of thought. It was the madman's insistence that his delusion was true which elicited a punitive response from those who claimed to possess both reason and truth. The madman who assents to error was not regarded as "the victim of an illusion, of a hallucination of his senses, or of a movement of his mind. He is not *abused*; he *deceives himself*."[72]

Although the madman was recognized as someone who held false ideas, these ideas were not regarded as immoral until late in the eighteenth century. Consequently, the role of the physician during the Classical period was not to converse with his patient but to restore him to a natural relation to truth. Those physicians who attempted to treat the delusional ideas rather than the diseased body and soul of the madman therefore did not rely on analysis but on intervention. Treatment thus included efforts to awaken the patient to reason (sometimes by scare tactics), attempts to play along with his delusion in the hopes of thereby abolishing his fears, and placement of the patient in a rural environment where the orderly cycle of daily labor and seasonal change would restore his reason.[73] Again, although similar methods were used in the nineteenth century, they served a different function. Shock, pretense, and isolation were then used to force the mentally ill to conform to a moral order rather than a rational one.

The replacement of a supposedly rational order by a moral order is the theme which repeats at all four levels of Foucault's interpretation of the Classical perception of madness. The metaphysical relation between reason and unreason altered during the course of the seventeenth and eighteenth centuries until unreason was stripped of everything except its moral content and condensed into the perception of madness. The historical changes during this period resulted in the substitution of a bourgeois moral order for the arbitrary and superficial monarchical order. The popular perception of madness shifted from an image of bestiality to a perception of corruption. And the medical perception of madness had already split between the perception of a diseased body-soul and the perception of a deranged mind. Consequently, while the rupture between the Renaissance and Classical periods appears in Foucault's history as a sudden, inexplicable loss of wholeness, the rupture between the Classical and Modern periods seems to follow from an inexorable determinism at many levels. The final break, symbolized by Tuke and Pinel's lunatic asylums, occurs in Foucault's study as the concluding act in a tragic play.

Although Tuke's Retreat and Pinel's asylum were functionally equivalent, Tuke established his moral regime within a religious (Quaker) setting whereas Pinel's vision was founded upon a purely secular moral order. Both men freed the mad from the physical restraints of the old general hospitals and established instead a "family" environment. In their new role as children, watched over and punished by their physician-fathers, the insane were "treated" by being forced to recognize and accept responsibility for their guilt. The asylums were so structured around the concepts of surveillance and judgment that the mad were viewed not only as guilty children but also as strangers whose gestures were carefully observed and evaluated. In Pinel's asylum the inmates were not merely observed and judged by others but were required to examine and judge themselves. And the physician, who had played an insignificant role in the old general hospital, became a central figure in the asylum, not because he represented scientific knowledge but because he possessed power through his function as father and judge. During the course of the nineteenth century, however, this source of the doctor's authority was forgotten and his quasi-magical powers were attributed to his position as a scientist or to the imagination of his patients. Even Freud, who broke through the asylum structures of silence, observation, and judgment by listening to his patients, did not destroy these structures. He merely transferred both their disciplinary functions and the moral authority on which they rested to the physician and thereby substituted the analyst's office for the asylum. Thus Foucault again concludes that "psychoanalysis has not been able, will not be able, to hear the voices of unreason" and that, since the end of the eighteenth century, only a few poets have been capable of "resisting by their own strength that gigantic moral imprisonment which we are in the habit of calling, doubtless by antiphrasis, the liberation of the insane by Pinel and Tuke."[74]

Foucault himself does not pretend to hear the "voices of unreason"; in fact, the mad never speak in this history of madness. What Foucault does do is to systematically undermine the concept of reason. Social and scientific thought during the Age of Reason (and by implication, in our time also) do not appear in *Madness and Civilization* as rational structures but as shifting forms of perception. Unlike cognition, perception cannot be altered merely by presenting new evidence or new theories, and Foucault does not limit himself to these scholarly functions. Instead, his strategy has been to arm himself with theories already available, ransack the archives for evidence excluded from conventional histories, and launch into an intense and sustained effort to change the way madness is perceived. As a result, Foucault's history of madness is frankly polemical and relies on constant repetition and brilliant, if contradictory, images and associations. This outrages historians who regard history as an objective science as much as it delights literary critics who view Foucault as a master craftsman. Psychologists and sociologists have generally taken a middle position and are impressed by Foucault's critique but disappointed that he offers no solutions.[75]

Although Foucault does not present a blueprint for social change, he has certainly attacked important social issues. It will now be more difficult to justify the exclusion of the mentally ill and current treatments based on sedation or analysis by appealing to science. Moreover, madness is not the only disease that reflects the ideological basis of scientific knowledge. In fact, one could argue that today cancer has replaced madness as the modern equivalent of leprosy. The same vague fears of contamination and death, the same desire to exclude and conceal, now appear to be focused on the cancer victim instead of the madman. In this case, too, the scientific perception of disease is mythical rather than rational and intersects with prevailing social values. Modern medicine persists in regarding cancer as an invasive "thing," despite substantial evidence to the contrary, and treatment is based on the same "search and destroy" methods that characterized the American military fiasco in Southeast Asia. Since a crude dualism (them-us) once again underlies both scientific knowledge and power relations, it is not surprising that medical and political strategies have had similar results: the simultaneous destruction of "them" (whether enemy or cancer) and "us" (whether ally or patient).

Unfortunately, Foucault does not analyze current medical theories and practices. But two years after *Madness and Civilization* he published an "archaeology" of medical perception in the nineteenth century. In this work Foucault examined the general perception of disease (not the particular perception of mental illness) and articulated for the first time his developed archaeological method. Several features of this method had already been formulated in *Madness and Civilization*: the replacement of the "object" of analysis (madness) with systematic relations (reason-unreason), the repetition of "measurements" from different perspectives, and the (not yet systematic) suspension of conventional causal relationships in favor of complex and discontinuous forms of change. Yet Foucault had not really broken with evolutionary concepts of time and had expressed only a limited sense of spatial relationships. With *The Birth of the Clinic: An Archaeology of Medical Perception* (1963), Foucault severed his remaining ties to history and restructured his analyses around new conceptions of space and time.

An Archaeology of Medical Perception

"This book is about space, about language, and about death; it is about the act of seeing, the gaze."[76] With this opening sentence Foucault announces the major themes of his first "archaeological" study, *The Birth of the Clinic*. The spatial and temporal forms of medical perception; the language in which medical knowledge is expressed; medical conceptions of life, death, and disease; and the role of the senses in various perceptual structures together constitute the epistemological bases of Foucault's idiosyncratic history of medicine. Thematically, although not methodologically, *The Birth of the Clinic* complements *Madness and Civilization*. Whereas Foucault studied the origin of the modern science of mind (psychology) in the earlier work, he now examines the origins of the modern science of the body (physiology). And, as he previously related the nineteenth-century perception of madness to the creation of the asylum, he now associates the nineteenth-century perception of disease with the clinic, a teaching hospital where medical theory and practice united to form modern medicine. But in *The Birth of the Clinic*, unlike *Madness and Civilization*, Foucault analyzes the "mutation" in Western culture that took place at the close of the eighteenth century by focusing on a limited chronological and geographical cross-section of the past, the period roughly between 1770 and 1820 in France.

Before proceeding to a discussion of the shifting structures of medical knowledge in this period, it is important to pause and listen to the expressions Foucault uses in his descriptions. Words like *fields*, *configurations*, and *geometry* recur continuously in this work. Although these terms refer to diverse relationships, they indicate a repeating pattern: medical perception is a field within a larger social space; it is determined by the relative positions occupied by subjects (doctors) and objects (diseases or patients); its distribution of concepts and theories constitute configurations that shift in a series of discontinuous displacements.

A few examples may serve to illustrate the style (and substance) of Foucault's argument. Note first the following use of the term *field*, taken from the chapter entitled "The Free Field," which deals with the abolition of the old medical institutions during the French Revolution: "This medical field . . . is strangely similar, in its implicit geometry, to the social space dreamt of by the Revolution, at least in its original conception: a form homogeneous in each of its regions, constituting a set of equivalent items capable of maintaining constant relations with their entirety, a space of free communication in which the relationship of the parts to the whole was always transposable and reversible."[77] Although this usage of the term field may be closer to Gestalt psychology than to field-theory physics, other passages suggest mathematical models. For instance, in a reference to the "space of origin and distribution of disease," Foucault asserts that disease has not always been, and will not always be, identified with the body. He asks rhetorically: "Has anyone ever drawn up the specific geometry of a virus diffusion in the thin layer of a segment of tissue? Is the law governing the spatialization of these phenomena to be found in a Euclidean anatomy? . . . Every great thought in the field of pathology lays down a configuration of disease whose spatial requisites are not necessarily those of classical geometry."[78]

The mathematical model is even more explicit in Foucault's analysis of the transformation from the established eighteenth-century perception of diseases as natural "species" to the first stage of the new clinical perception, in which diseases were regarded as combinations of symptoms. Foucault attributes to this early clinical perception the same two epistemological models that inform his own thought—linguistics and mathematics. "The clinic is a field made philosophically 'visible' by the introduction into the pathological domain of grammatical and probabilistic structures. . . . The grammatical model . . . is a question of a *transference of the forms of intelligibility*. The mathematical model . . . is a question of the *contribution of themes of formalization*."[79] The probabilistic structure in question refers to the early clinical method of studying "cases" in terms of degrees of frequency rather than through close examination of individual patients. Although Foucault appears to discuss statistical frequencies, his choice of terms suggests probability theory. As he puts it, "medicine discovered that uncertainty may be treated analytically, as the sum of a certain number of isolatable degrees of certainty that were capable of rigorous calculation."[80] When the individual patient, rather than the statistical "case," emerged in the later anatomical form of clinical medicine, Foucault describes this crucial event in terms that suggest modern cosmological concepts of black hole formation. "On the line on which the visible is ready to be resolved into the invisible, on that crest of its disappearance, singularities come into play. A discourse on the individual is once more possible, or rather, necessary."[81]

More general than these specific statistical and geometrical concepts is the relation between time and space, which runs as a constant theme throughout *The Birth of the Clinic*. In comparing the clinical to the anatomo-clinical "gaze," for example, Foucault uses the notions of temporal series and spatial volumes. "The clinician's gaze was directed upon a succession and upon an area of pathological events; it had to be both synchronic and diachronic, but in any case it was placed under temporal obedience; it *analyzed a series*. The anatomo-clinician's gaze has to *map a volume*; it deals with the complexity of spatial data which for the first time in medicine is three-dimensional."[82] Although anatomo-clinical medicine was primarily spatial, it also had a temporal dimension. The study of corpses involved a conception of death which was not that of a sudden cessation of life but of a continuing, living process in its own right. "Death is therefore multiple and dispersed in time: it is not that absolute, privileged point at which time stops and moves back; like disease itself, it has a teeming presence that analysis may divide into time and space."[83]

Spatial concepts also determined the relationship between the subject and object of medical knowledge. In Foucault's schema the subject of knowledge is not the personality or the consciousness of the physician; it is the position of the physician in a social and professional field at a given moment.[84] The objects of medical knowledge (life, death, disease, and perhaps the patient) are also not fixed entities but functions of the varying perceptual structures that define medical knowledge. Foucault thus describes the shift from clinical to anatomo-clinical medicine in these terms: "What is modified in giving place to anatomo-clinical medicine is not, therefore, the mere surface of contact between the knowing subject and the known object; it is the more general arrangement of knowledge that determines the reciprocal positions and the connexion between the one who must know and that which is to be known."[85] This "more general arrangement of knowledge," which Foucault calls a perceptual structure, might also be regarded as a field. Such fields have complex spatio-temporal forms, alter through a series of discontinuous transformations, and exist within a larger social space. Before proceeding to a more detailed examination of Foucault's fields, however, a second pause is in order. Foucault's study of medicine is significant not just for its methodological novelty but also for the implications this methodology has for philosophical, historical, and scientific studies.

Foucault's main philosophical purpose seems clear: he is seeking the temporal and spatial a prioris of knowledge. This archaeology can thus be viewed as a modern form of Kantianism, relativized to deal with a series of specific and variable structures of rationality rather than presuming to define the structure of knowledge in general. According to Foucault, "we belong to an age of criticism" devoid of a "primary philosophy" and philosophical thought must therefore become historical. Like Bachelard, Foucault is attempting to establish a historical epistemology, which he justifies in these terms: "For Kant, the possibility and necessity of a critique were linked, through certain scientific contents, to the fact that there is such a thing as knowledge. . . . We are doomed historically to history, to the patient reconstruction of discourses about discourses, and to the task of hearing what has already been said."[86]

Yet Foucault does not believe that we are doomed to traditional histories. He wishes to avoid historical constructions based on analogy (as in the history of ideas) or on hermeneutics (as in psychological histories that deny stated meanings in search of hidden meanings). *The Birth of the Clinic*, then, represents an attempt to write a new history, a history Foucault alternately referred to as "archaeology," "structural history," or a new systematic history of ideas. Although he later rejected these last two labels, there can be no doubt that archaeology is related to structuralism in *The Birth of the Clinic*. Foucault himself has admitted that this work is a "structural study" in which "the meaning of a statement would be defined . . . by the difference that articulates it upon the other real or possible statements, which are contemporary to it or to which it is opposed in the linear series of time."[87] Since the meanings of statements in *The Birth of the Clinic* really are dependent on their relationships to proximate statements, it is almost impossible to discuss Foucault's ideas apart from these relations. Nevertheless, a few ideas need to be pulled out of the overall structure, since they suggest a radical redefinition of nineteenth-century science.

Foucault claims that the human sciences are the product of a recent mutation in Western culture that established man as the object as well as the subject of "positive" knowledge. Clinical medicine contributed to nineteenth-century positivism by making patients instead of diseases the focus of investigation. But, according to Foucault, this was only possible given the transformation in the medical perception of death, a transformation that occurred in the literary as well as the scientific imagination. Consequently, Foucault believes that nineteenth-century science and poetics were founded on the same epistemological ground and that the history of positivism needs to be rewritten. A "vertical investigation of this positivism" exposes linguistic structures, corporeal spatiality, and finitude (language, space, and death) as basic to the "genesis of positivism."[88] Moreover, Foucault's vertical investigation reveals that the "positivist" sciences in the nineteenth century were not modeled on biological concepts, as is generally believed, but on new theories that emerged with clinical medicine. Classical medicine had studied disease and valued health; clinical medicine studied sick bodies and valued normalcy. This new medical perception of a normal-pathological polarity, rather than the biological conception of life, informed nineteenth-century social thought.

> The prestige of the sciences of life in the nineteenth century, their role as a model, especially in the human sciences, is linked originally not with the comprehensive, transferable character of

biological concepts, but, rather, with the fact that these concepts were arranged in a space whose profound structure responded to the healthy / morbid opposition. When one spoke of the life of groups and societies, of the life of the race, or even of "psychological life" one did not think first of the internal structure of *the organized being* but of *the medical bi-polarity of the normal and the pathological.*[89]

The introduction of medical conceptions of normalcy and abnormality is a muted but vital theme in Foucault's history of medicine. Like other themes, it is so embedded in the tight logical structure of his argument, so nearly dissolved by systematic qualifications, and so well camouflaged by Foucault's extraordinary language that it becomes difficult (perhaps meaningless) to disengage it from the field in which Foucault has placed it. However, despite the risks of falling into either banal reductions of Foucault's complex ideas or unintelligible efforts to express their complexity, the remainder of this section will be an effort to impose a melodic line on Foucault's amazing polyphonic, even atonal, composition.

Although each of Foucault's chapters deals simultaneously with the interaction of discursive and nondiscursive relations, these internal and external networks receive differing stresses. In the first two chapters Foucault moves from an examination of the structure of eighteenth-century classificatory medicine to the social and political ideologies that intersected with this form of medicine. He then devotes three chapters to the projected and actual reforms of medical theory and practice during the French Revolution. This is followed by four extremely dense chapters charting the formation of clinical medicine and its transformation into anatomo-clinical medicine. The final chapter describing the spatial and temporal structures of "fevers" marks the consolidation of nineteenth-century clinical medicine. Throughout this "history," names appear as simple signposts to different forms of perception. Great men clearly play no role in the anonymous formation of perceptual structures, and the figures Foucault has selected as symbols of perceptual shifts are not always those generally considered important. This hardly bothers Foucault; in fact, he seldom refers to any other historical study (Canguilhem's works are important exceptions) and concentrates almost exclusively on primary sources. It is highly unlikely that Foucault is unaware of conventional interpretations. He seems instead to be intentionally ignoring them in order to write his own antihistory in conscious opposition to smug narrations of the "progress" of science.

Foucault refers to the established paradigm of eighteenth-century medical knowledge as "classificatory medicine" or the "medicine of species." The major nosologies of the period were concerned with identifying diseases in much the same way that Linnaeus identified and classified botanical species.[90] The underlying assumption was that diseases were independent entities with no necessary relation to the human body. Medical perception therefore distinguished three forms of disease "spatialization": the disease in relation to other diseases, the disease in the space of the human body, and the disease in the social body. The first type of spatialization, which Foucault calls the "primary configuration of disease," was based on four principles which assumed that diseases were natural structures visible to the medical "gaze." The presence of diseases in the body constituted the "secondary spatialization of the pathological" and required a theory of sympathetic transmission to explain the effects of diseases on the human organism. What was transmitted were not fragments of disease entities, but nonspatial disease qualities such as lightness and dryness. Since these qualities interacted with the "temperament" of the patient, the individual, regarded as a mere obstacle to the natural development of diseases at the level of primary spatialization, became an essential factor at the level of secondary spatialization. The third type of disease spatialization refers to the assumed distribution of diseases through society and the appropriate social spaces for treatment. In the medicine of species, "unnatural" environments were believed to complicate and multiply diseases; therefore peasants and laborers were presumed to suffer from a few simple diseases while the upper classes were supposedly afflicted with numerous and complex diseases. Recovery, too, was considered more likely if the patient were left in the natural space of the family than if he were exposed to other diseases in the artificial environment of the hospital. Likewise, medical practice was based largely on the effort to allow the disease to follow its natural course with a minimum of intervention.

The eighteenth-century conception of disease "species" and the associated concepts of family care and minimal medical intervention coincided with contemporary economic theory, which aimed at abolishing the hospitals and providing financial aid directly to the families of the sick. Such a policy, however, implied a centralized program of assistance that would delegate to the physician the right to judge family needs. The role of the physician had already been politicized, on a smaller scale, in the eighteenth-century medicine of epidemics. Government officials had appointed doctors throughout France to chart the range of epidemics and to examine the environmental conditions surrounding each outbreak. Epidemics, unlike diseases, were not regarded as fixed entities but as changing combinations of external circumstances such as climate, soil, and famine. Despite the different perceptions of diseases and epidemics in the eighteenth century, both forms of medical thought acknowledged the need for state regulation. Nevertheless, little was done to implement a national medical program until the French Revolution, and even then the role of medicine in society was a matter of heated debate and utopian daydreaming.

> The years preceding and immediately following the Revolution saw the birth of two great myths with opposing themes and polarities: the myth of a nationalized medical profession, organized like the clergy, and invested, at the level of man's bodily health, with powers similar to those exercised by the clergy over men's souls; and the myth of a total disappearance of disease in an untroubled, dispassionate society restored to its original state of health.[91]

Foucault further claims that these apparently divergent myths were really isomorphic forms of the same desire to regulate and perfect society. Nationalized medicine was expected both to cure the "sick slaves" of the Old Regime and to establish the moral as well as physical conditions for the elimination of disease in the new society.

During the Revolution the converging demands of doctors and statesmen resulted in the abolition of all intermediate structures (medical associations, university faculties, and hospitals) that obstructed the "free gaze" of the physician and the watchful eye of the body politic. But despite lengthy debate and a plethora of suggested reforms, the laws of 1794 which terminated the old institutions failed to create new ones. On the political level, the revolutionary government had not been able to resolve the contradictory demands of abolishing privileged organizations such as medical schools and also protecting the public from unqualified practitioners. On the medical level, the physician's demand for freedom to observe diseases in a natural environment likewise delayed the establishment of new institutions. Ironically, "scientific" medicine based on free observation was not the ally of clinical medicine, as legend has it; on the contrary, it was "scientific, political, and economic *liberalism* . . . [which] was the ideological theme that prevented the organization of clinical medicine."[92]

Under the pressure of acute need—large numbers of sick and wounded, few competent physicians, and almost no hospitals—the Revolution finally opened clinics. These clinics were not merely revivals of the protoclinics that had existed in Europe since the mid-seventeenth century; they represented new political and medical structures. Politically the clinic served to bypass the old corporate structures while simultaneously instituting state control over medicine. Significantly, this control was established in the medical realm, as in the economic, over the person of the producer (physician) rather than over the product (physician's practice). As Foucault phrased it, "the state must verify his capacity, his moral value."[93] The moral issue was a very real one. The clinics both treated and displayed their patients, and when the physician's desire to teach and his obligation to protect his patients conflicted, accommodations were made. The poor or other undesirable groups (unmarried pregnant women, for example) were used for teaching purposes, and the exchange of medical care for medical knowledge was justified in economic terms (the poor "paid" with their bodies).

As a medical institution, too, the clinic born during the Revolution had little in common with the earlier protoclinics, which had not combined medical theory and empirical practice. Although these earlier clinics were teaching hospitals, students were taught to observe diseases rather than patients and to learn to classify illnesses in accordance with the established nosography. Consequently, the protoclinics actually interfered with, rather than contributed to, the development of modern clinical medicine. Then, abruptly at the end of the eighteenth century, the protoclinic "was to undergo a sudden radical restructuring: detached from the theoretical context in which it was born, it was to be given a field of application that was no longer confined to that in which knowledge was *said*, but which was coextensive with that in which it was born, put to the test, and fulfilled itself: it was to be identified with the *whole* of medical experience."[94] Thereafter medical knowledge assumed a completely new structure. Although the medicine of species persisted, it did so no longer as the dominant paradigm but as a displaced form of knowledge. The new medical paradigm that emerged underwent a succession of internal transformations and then became the model for medical thought in the nineteenth century. In this new paradigm, "not only the names of diseases, not only the grouping of systems were not the same; but the fundamental perceptual codes that were applied to patients' bodies, the field of objects to which observation addressed itself, the surfaces and depths traversed by the doctor's gaze, the whole system of orientation of this gaze also varied."[95]

Foucault calls this first stage of clinical medicine the "medicine of symptoms," which, unlike the medicine of species, viewed diseases as processes rather than entities.[96] The "fundamental perceptual codes" of this new form of knowledge were the linguistic structure of signs and the statistical structure of cases. In the medicine of symptoms, diseases were viewed as varying combinations of symptoms, not as fixed species. Diseases became words in a complex pathological language, and the physician's gaze was not focused on all symptoms equally but on those that revealed the syntax of this language. Consequently, certain symptoms were considered signs, that is, they explained the past and present configurations of diseases and predicted their future courses. A medicine based on signs introduced a new temporal dimension into medical knowledge. While the medicine of species sought to draw up a "table" and to locate each disease in a classificatory chart with fixed borders, the medicine of symptoms set up a horizontal series of relationships limited only by the temporal poles of life and death.

Temporal relations also characterized the study of cases. Eighteenth-century clinical medicine did not regard the individual as a sick person but as a "pathological fact," one of a series of such facts that could, in principle, be predicted on the basis of a calculation of probabilities. Such a calculation obeyed four rules. To begin with, the relevant symptoms must be identified. In the medicine of species, diseases were identified by noting diffuse disorders such as pain and coughing. In the medicine of symptoms, diseases were identified by noting functional disorders such as muscular weakness. Secondly, the physician, like the mathematician and the philosopher, must be able to analyze combinations, in this case combinations of medical symptoms. Thirdly, the study of cases required scanning a large number of cases rather than observing a small number closely. Numerical scanning also meant that extreme variations were merely infrequent, not "abnormal," and that the normal-pathological polarity did not yet exist. Finally, a medicine based on calculation required an evaluation of the combination of symptoms, not each symptom separately. In Foucault's view, the introduction of these four mathematical concepts of calculation coincided with a shift in medical practice. Whereas in the medicine of species doctors had resisted "artificial" intervention, in the medicine of symptoms they were willing to intervene, but only after (very literally) calculating the risks.[97]

The medicine of symptoms did not represent a lasting structure in Foucault's archaeology. It was quickly transformed into a new form of medical knowledge that Foucault calls the "medicine of tissues" or "anatomo-clinical medicine." The series of displacements that transformed clinical medicine into anatomo-clinical medicine is described by Foucault in terms of shifting relations among the senses of sight, sound, and touch. In clinical medicine the doctor looked, questioned, and listened: his gaze was that of a "speaking eye." Through a series of complex shifts touch became a major form of perception and the medical gaze moved from the surface of the body to its invisible and silent interior. The doctor ceased to ask, as he had in the medicine of species, "What is the matter with you?" and began to ask "Where does it hurt?"[98]

The displacements that made this last question characteristic of nineteenth-century medicine took place in the linguistic and mathematical structures of the medicine of symptoms. These structures concealed four "epistemological myths," all of which assumed that sight and sound were a sufficient basis for medical knowledge. The first myth was that diseases, like words, were made up of a small number of elements comparable to the letters of the alphabet and that these elements were visible to the doctor's diagnostic eye. The second myth was that diseases, again like words, had no essence but embodied a set of relations that could be apprehended by knowing the "sound" of the pathological language. The third myth figured as a particularly critical factor in the transition from clinical to anatomo-clinical medicine; it referred to the assumption that diseases, like chemical combinations, could be decomposed by the "fire" of the physician's gaze. Such a gaze did not merely read surface symptoms, it probed to hidden depths. The physician's gaze, then, was the fourth epistemological myth of clinical medicine to dissolve at the end of the eighteenth century. It was gradually replaced by a different mode of perception, the "glance." According to Foucault, "the gaze implies an open field . . . it records and totalizes . . . it spreads out over a world that is already the world of language."[99] The glance, by contrast, "does not scan a field: it strikes at one point . . . [and] therefore goes beyond what it sees. . . . It is not burdened with all the abuses of language. The glance is silent, like a finger pointing, denouncing. . . . Hence that metaphor of 'touch' by which doctors will ceaselessly define their glance."[100] With the glance, clinical medicine was restructured around a new space, "the tangible space of the body," and the medicine of symptoms was replaced by a "medicine of organs, sites, causes . . . a clinic wholly ordered in accordance with pathological anatomy. The age of Bichat has arrived."[101]

By attributing the birth of modern clinical pathology to this perceptual shift, Foucault has inverted conventional interpretations of the history of medicine. According to conventional wisdom, it was the triumph of reason over religion that resulted in the practice of autopsy, the establishment of the clinic, and the birth of modern empirical medicine. Foucault, however, maintains that religion did not prevent the practice of autopsy during the eighteenth century and that modern anatomy was the result rather than the cause of a new form of medical knowledge.[102] Foucault claims that the dissection and study of corpses were commonplace in the eighteenth century and that there was "no need to rob graves or to perform anatomical black masses."[103] By the mid-eighteenth century a medicine of organs already existed, yet neither this medical theory nor the practice of autopsy led to clinical medicine because "anatomy and the clinic were not of the same mind."[104] It was the incompatibility between a temporally based medicine of symptoms and a spatially based medicine of organs, not a conflict between science and religion, that prevented the formation of anatomo-clinical medicine in the eighteenth century. Only after the epistemological myths of the medicine of symptoms were dissolved was it possible for Bichat and his contemporaries to rediscover the earlier medicine of organs and to incorporate anatomy into a new medicine of tissues. By so doing, Bichat combined the spatial and temporal structures that together constituted the anatomo-clinical synthesis.

Although Bichat's *General Anatomy* (1801) established a classificatory system for the interior of the body, this system was not based on a specific knowledge of organs but on the distribution of twenty-one different types of tissues throughout the body.[105] In the medicine of tissues, diseases no longer referred either to species or to combinations of symptoms; they indicated instead the presence of lesions in specific tissues. Diseases ceased to be regarded as "words" (symptoms) or "things" (species) and came to be viewed as aberrations of the body. The physician's gaze now focused on the individual patient rather than on the statistical case. Yet this gaze had to explore the body of the dead man in order to see and to know the living patient. Thus death assumed a new role in medical perception. Whereas "in eighteenth-century medical thought death was . . . the end of life and . . . the end of disease,"[106] in nineteenth-century anatomo-clinical medicine disease processes and life processes were carefully distinguished from the processes that decomposed the body at death. Death processes appeared as distinct life forms, preceding the actual death of the patient, continuing after this brief moment, and dispersed in corporeal space as well as time. Since the decomposition of the body provided the perspective for unraveling the secrets of life and disease, death became "the great analyst. . . . Analysis, the philosophy of the elements and their laws, meets in death what it had vainly sought in mathematics, chemistry and even language: an unsuperable model, prescribed by nature; it is on this great example that the medical gaze will now rest."[107]

Nineteenth-century anatomo-clinical medicine thus defined disease, like death, as a life process. Like death, disease was also viewed as a degenerative process, but one that was usually limited to those tissues sharing a similar structure. Diseases therefore were classified on the basis of structural rather than functional disorders, and signs pointed to the site of tissue damage rather than to the disease itself. Moreover, signs were no longer necessarily symptoms. In anatomo-clinical medicine, signs could be made to "appear artificially where there had been no symptom," for example, by tapping the chest to hear the sounds of lung congestion.[108] As Foucault observes, "the medical gaze embraces more than is said by the word 'gaze' alone. It contains within a single structure different sensorial fields. The sight/touch/hearing trinity defines a perceptual configuration in which the inaccessible illness is tracked down. . . . The 'glance' has become a complex organization with a view to a spatial assignation of the invisible."[109]

The effort to make the invisible visible lies at the heart of clinical anatomy. Significantly, it was life that obscured the medical gaze and death that revealed the truth: "obscure life, limpid death, the oldest imaginary values of the Western world are crossed here," intersecting in the space of the individual body.[110] Death, life, the individual, and the body: these four concepts were redefined in the new medicine that emerged at the end of the eighteenth century, just as they were in the literature of eroticism born at the same time. Thereafter the medical experience and the lyrical experience constituted parallel structures in the Modern episteme, although the romantic basis of positivist science was systematically suppressed during the nineteenth century.

By the beginning of the nineteenth century, only two steps remained for the anatomo-clinical perception to achieve its paradigmatic form. Time and space could not be integrated into a new perceptual structure until fevers were classified in spatial as well as temporal terms and until the causal relationship between disease processes and tissue lesions was established. According to Foucault, this synthesis began in 1816 when François Broussais published his *Examination of Medical Doctrines*. Broussais, an ex-army surgeon who is regarded by most medical historians as a minor, even reactionary figure, is remembered primarily for reintroducing the use of leeches.[111] Yet Foucault believes it was Broussais who faced the problem of explaining apparently nonorganic diseases (fevers in particular) within the conceptual possibilities of a medicine of tissues. Broussais regarded fevers as inflammations of tissues and considered inflammation merely an indication of the site of tissue damage. He sought the cause of this damage not in the presence of a disease but in the reaction of the body to a foreign irritant. Thus, Foucault concludes, "the medicine of diseases has come to an end; there now begins a medicine of pathological reactions, a structure of experience that dominated the nineteenth century, and, to a certain extent, the twentieth, since the medicine of pathogenic agents was to be contained within it, though not without certain methodological modifications."[112] The "medicine of pathological reactions" does not represent, in Foucault's opinion, the culmination of a series of refinements in medical knowledge. It represents a repressive, rather than a progressive, form of knowledge that is part of a larger system of cultural repression. Modern culture defines all human behavior, social as well as physical, in terms of normal or abnormal functioning. In *The Birth of the Clinic*, as in *Madness and Civilization* and *Mental Illness and Psychology*, Foucault has attempted to expose the recent and ultimately nonrational foundations of modern "scientific" thought.

Again, as in *Madness and Civilization*, Foucault has offered a critique but not an alternative to a "science" of pathological reactions. But *The Birth of the Clinic* is a far more ambitious work than *Madness and Civilization.* In his history of madness Foucault attempted to change the conventional perception of madness but not our conventional ways of thinking about the past in general. In *The Birth of the Clinic*, however, Foucault makes it impossible to view the past historically if history requires a linear, temporal consciousness. By introducing spatial concepts into the temporal perception of the past, Foucault created a complex four-dimensional history that is both strange and familiar. The familiar aspects appear almost mundane; the differences appear bizarre. Unfortunately, a single path through Foucault's labyrinthine study threatens to make the unfamiliar familiar by suggesting that Foucault has merely changed historical periodizations or conceptual classifications (such as those dividing science from literature) and not the concept of history itself. To appreciate Foucault's unhistorical history, one must confront his text directly. Generally such an experience creates more frustration than enlightenment, but a few readers seem to have "decoded" Foucault. Again, Hayden White goes to the heart of the matter by noting that

> Foucault celebrates the spirit of creative *dis*ordering, *de*structuration, *un*naming. His whole effort as a historian can be characterized as a sustained "*dis*remembrance of things past." . . . He is an anti-historical historian, as Artaud was the anti-dramatist dramatist and Robbe-Grillet is the anti-novelistic novelist. Foucault writes "history" in order to destroy it, as a discipline, as a mode of consciousness, and as a mode of (social) existence.[113]

Even without such decoding skills, it is possible to decipher Foucault well enough to catch an occasional glimpse of a different "order of things." In *The Birth of the Clinic* this strange order is limited to too narrow a field to command general interest. But Foucault's next archaeology, *The Order of Things: An Archaeology of the Human Sciences* (1966), opens a site three centuries deep and wide enough to include all the "sciences" of man.

FOUCAULT'S ARCHAEOLOGY

OF THE HUMAN SCIENCES

The Order of Things

Les mots et les choses was translated into English as *The Order of Things* rather than *Words and Things*, as the French title would suggest.[1] Both titles, however, indicate Foucault's effort to identify different systems of ordering language (words) and perceptions of reality (things) from the Renaissance to the present. Since it is Foucault's intention to describe different structures of knowledge (epistemes) rather than to narrate what "really" happened, this work cannot be regarded as a historical study in any conventional sense. In fact, Foucault does not deal with objective reality at all. He examines various perceptions, and thus his "archaeology" of the human sciences is a form of idealism that draws heavily from speculative philosophies of history and in particular from the Hegelian tradition.

Although Foucault does not, like Hegel, offer a theory of change, the transformations he perceives in the history of Western thought parallel Hegelian conceptions of the progress of Spirit through History. Foucault, however, regards this transformation as a regression rather than a progression and he refers to Being rather than Spirit. Consequently, while Foucault's periodization conforms to traditional historical divisions, it refers to different modes of being and not to social, economic, or political relationships. This means that certain historical periods are almost unrecognizable in Foucault's scheme. The Renaissance, for example, refers neither to the revival of Greek and Roman learning nor to the birth of a secular humanist culture. Instead it functions here, as in Foucault's earlier works, as a mythical past, a period in which Being was still undifferentiated and in which time and space had no significant function. The Classical period, by contrast, marks the real beginning of Western culture, the first great disruption of the unity of Being. Although Foucault does not call the Classical form of knowledge "being-in-itself," his description of the Classical episteme places thought on the level of perception rather than on the level of consciousness. The period of consciousness ("being-for-itself") appears only in the nineteenth century, when man became conscious of himself as a historical being. Therefore the human sciences, those Modern sciences which take man's life, labor, and language as their objects, emerged less than two centuries ago, as did the concept of Man, which humanists believe to be of ancient origin. The last epistemological structure in Foucault's archaeology, one barely mentioned in this work and not clearly distinguished from the Modern episteme, is the Contemporary age. This period ("being-in-and-for-itself") is the stage of self-consciousness and self-criticism. It is here that the human sciences (psychology, sociology, and literature-myth) are confronted by new counterhuman sciences (psychoanalysis, ethnology, and linguistics) which seek the unconscious structures that make the human sciences themselves possible. Foucault's own archaeology is a product of this episteme and, like the counterhuman sciences, it seeks the deep structures that make thought possible.

Despite this similarity to Hegelian thought, Foucault does not acknowledge the relationship between his archaeology and philosophical idealism. Instead he considers his work "positivistic" because it studies the formation of systematic discourses or "positivities."[2] He even claims, rather unconvincingly, that he has learned more from Cuvier, Bopp, and Ricardo than from Kant or Hegel.[3] The original inspiration for *The Order of Things*, however, came neither from philosophy nor from the history of science, but from Foucault's reading of a passage by Jorge Luis Borges on a bizarre Chinese method of classifying animals. According to this extraordinary taxonomy, categories such as "fabulous," "embalmed," "innumerable," "having just broken the water pitcher," and "drawn with a very fine camelhair brush" were criteria for classifying animals. *The Order of Things*, Foucault explains, was born from "the laughter that shattered, as I read the passage, all the familiar landmarks of my thought—*our* thought" and from the sudden awareness of "the stark impossibility of thinking *that*" within the confines of our own very different system of thought.[4] As a consequence of this insight into incompatible systems of ordering phenomena, Foucault turned to an examination of the different ordering systems in Western culture. Much as an ethnologist studies foreign cultures, Foucault has studied the unconscious forms by which the "natives" represented to themselves their systems of exchange (labor), their classifications of plants and animals (life), and their speech (language).

By writing an "ethnological" history of Western culture, Foucault has concentrated on the similarities within each episteme and considers the breaks between periods as ruptures irrevocably and inexplicably dividing diverse archaeological layers. Thus, although the human sciences of the nineteenth century shared the same epistemological ground and spoke the same "language," they cannot be traced backwards (downwards) because the preceding layer of knowledge is qualitatively different. The positivities that structured the knowledge of life, labor, and language in the earlier periods have different configurations and occupy different spaces in the archaeological field. The closest neighbors to the human sciences are the empirical sciences (biology, political economy, and philology) which were formed around 1800 when the Modern episteme emerged. These sciences, however, did not take man as their object of study; they studied organic functions, economic production, and the history of languages.

Below the empirical sciences, at the next archaeological layer, lie the sciences of the Classical period: natural history, the analysis of wealth, and general grammar. These sciences, formed in the midseventeenth century, did not take either man or history as their objects; they examined physical, economic, and linguistic structures. Despite the apparent similarities between the Classical structural episteme and the Contemporary structuralist counterhuman sciences, the Classical sciences were based on the assumption that classificatory systems (words) represented real things in the world. Contemporary structuralist thought, by contrast, deals exclusively with internal relationships in which words represent other words, not things. Finally, at the earliest and most inaccessible level lie the mythical sciences of the Renaissance period. Words and things in this episteme all symbolized the divine order: knowledge consisted of recognizing the correspondence between the microcosm of this world and the macrocosm of God's order. Words, like things, were marks or signatures; ultimately everything referred to the same thing, and thus everything was essentially identical.

Foucault's archaeology focuses primarily on the Classical and Modern epistemes and particularly on the natural and empirical sciences characteristic of these epistemological systems. Yet he does not actually discuss what the knowledge of life, labor, and language was in these periods; he examines instead the isomorphic forms of knowledge within each period. Thus he describes how identities and differences (same-other relations) were perceived and how space and time functioned as categories of thought. These two pairs of relationships run through his study like two axes upon which knowledge revolved.

In the Classical period knowledge was knowledge of the visible differences between static structures: natural history consisted of a taxonomic table of relationships; the analysis of wealth referred to an examination of objects (like coins) that could be represented in a system of exchange; and grammar was regarded as a logical system in which each element maintained a specific function. In Classical philosophy, as in the natural sciences, spatial relationships predominated and time usually functioned as a fixed background. The primary form of perception in an epistemological structure based on spatial relationships was sight. But, like Marshall McLuhan, Foucault does not believe that perceptual knowledge, or any other form of knowledge, can be regarded as constant.[5] Sight in the Classical period meant to see through, to grasp the essence of a relationship, to understand.[6] This form of vision should therefore not be confused with sight in the Contemporary period, which refers to seeing surfaces rather than perceiving essences. Nor should it be confused with sight in the nineteenth century, when vision penetrated into the dense interior of things which were neither transparent (as in the Classical period) nor reflective (as in the Contemporary period).

In the Modern episteme, which coincided with the emergence of history, time moved to the foreground of knowledge and space receded into the background. Knowledge no longer meant learning the relations among visible differences; it meant understanding how the same differentiated into the other. The new sciences of life, labor, and language, then, were fundamentally new forms of knowledge. Unlike natural history, biology was not concerned with charting the external structures of plants and animals; it was occupied with anatomical studies and with tracing the evolution from inorganic forms to organic beings. Political economy, unlike the analysis of wealth, did not seek the source of value in things or the exchange of things but in the process of production. The study of language shifted from general grammar to philology, and changes in grammatical forms rather than constant structures were the object of study. Finally, although sight still functioned as a mode of perception, touch became the characteristic modality of knowledge in the Modern period. Hence one did not "see" the truth, as Descartes did; one "felt" it, as the Romantics did.

In the Contemporary period, which is barely sketched in this work, the same-other relationship is reversed. Structuralism begins with differences and proceeds to similarities. The oppositions characteristic of the human sciences—psychological concepts of conscious and unconscious, sociological concepts of normal and abnormal, and literary concepts of form and content—dissolve as the structure supporting these oppositions is revealed and differences are assimilated into the system. More remarkably, since time and space emerge together into the foreground of knowledge, there is no background and consequently no grounding for thought. There are only fragmented moments and local configurations suspended in a void.

In addition to these same-other relations established in *The Order of Things*, similar relations exist between Foucault's works. In *Madness and Civilization* he was "investigating the way in which a culture can determine in a massive, general form the difference that limits it," whereas in *The Order of Things* he was concerned with "observing how a culture experiences the propinquity of things." *Madness and Civilization*, then, is "the history of the Other—of that which for a given culture is at once interior and foreign, therefore to be excluded," whereas *The Order of Things* is the "history of the Same—of that which, for a given culture, is both dispersed and related, therefore to be distinguished by kinds and to be collected together into identities."[7] Foucault maintains that his histories of madness (disorder), disease (orderly disorder), and epistemic fields (order) in the Classical period together expose the "deepest strata of Western culture," the strata that mark the threshold of Modern thought and the emergence of the concept of Man. Man, he believes, has dominated Western thought for a relatively short time and Foucault considers it "a source of profound relief to think that man is a recent invention . . . a new wrinkle in our knowledge, and that he will disappear as soon as that knowledge has discovered a new form."[8]

Such apocalyptic comments, of which there are many in this work, contributed to the bitter controversy surrounding *The Order of Things* and to the surprising popular success of so difficult a book.[9] Even Foucault's staunchest admirers, however, have asked how it is pos-

sible to recover previous forms of thought if the mutations in Western thought have been as radical as Foucault claims and the various
systems of knowledge are indeed incommensurable.¹⁰ To even discuss an archaeology of knowledge these critics believe that there
must be some fragment of continuity or some hidden deep structure
common to present and past systems of thought. Such a deep structure does, in fact, appear to exist in this work. Language does not
function for Foucault as merely one of the positivities that shape
human experience; it functions as the model (and perhaps the substance as well as the form) of all thought. In this respect Foucault's
archaeology can be regarded as the philosophical equivalent of Lévi-
Strauss's structural anthropology and Lacan's structural psychoanalysis, which, like other structuralist studies, assume that all sign systems
are coded in the way linguistic systems are.

The grammatical structure that serves as the deep structure of
Classical and Modern epistemology is what Foucault has termed the
"quadrilateral of language." The four sides of this quadrilateral are
formed by two sets of theoretical segments. The first pair, which
determines the structure of thought, consists of *attribution* and
articulation. The term *attribution* designates those language elements
that attribute "being" to statements, a function performed by verbs
(modeled, of course, on the verb "to be"). The term *articulation*
refers to those grammatical structures that describe, identify, and
name; this function is performed by nouns, with the assistance of
adjectives and other secondary grammatical elements. The Classical
period, in Foucault's view, was dominated by "articulation." The great
taxonomies, encyclopedias, and economic projects all reflected the
same modality of thought, the same fundamental effort to exhaust
the power of nomination. The Renaissance episteme, by contrast,
was dominated by "attribution." Knowledge in this epistemological
structure meant knowledge of the relationship of specific beings
to being in general through what has been called the "great chain
of being."

The two other sides of the quadrilateral of language, which determine the relation of thought to the world, Foucault has labeled *derivation* and *designation*. While articulation and attribution constitute a
representation of thought, derivation and designation constitute a
duplicated representation by projecting thought into the world.
Derivation refers specifically to grammatical theories that explain
change. In the Classical period language changes were explained as

random events made possible by the alphabetical (and thus arbitrary) nature of Western script, as contrasted to the more stable images of figurative writing. Foucault compared the various forms of figurative writing (curiologics, hieroglyphics, and symbolic writing) to the tropes of rhetoric (synecdoche, metonymy, and metaphor).[11] This suggests that a theory of tropes may be the basis for a concealed theory of change in Foucault's own work, as Hayden White has claimed.[12] Designation, the remaining segment of the quadrilateral, refers to theories that explain what words designate, or signify, in the outside world. In the Classical period words were presumed to have an original signification in a primeval relationship between words and primitive cries or gestures.

Theories of derivation and designation, however, did not dominate Classical thought. Rather, Foucault implies that these two categories respectively characterize Modern and Contemporary thought. The Modern episteme was based on a new temporal dimension that was paralleled by a shift from an analysis of nomenclature to philological theories of verb inflection and root changes. This concern with derivation not only typified linguistic studies (symbolized by the shift from Port-Royal general grammar to nineteenth-century philology), but other "positive" studies as well. Thus the analysis of wealth was displaced by the history of labor, symbolized (provocatively) not by Marx but by Ricardo. And the classifications of natural history were replaced by a new conceptual structure that made evolutionary theory possible. Again, this shift was marked by an unexpected figure. Foucault did not choose Darwin but Cuvier, who is usually regarded as an antievolutionary thinker.

Just as derivation seemed to characterize Modern thought, designation appears in Foucault's work as the fundamental construct in Contemporary thought. With the end of Classicism, the order of words no longer represented the order of things. During the nineteenth century, the search for a connection between words and things was expressed in numerous interpretations of the past claiming to have found hidden meanings. According to Foucault, the human sciences of this period (sociology, psychology, and literature-myth) were among these hermeneutic exercises. Yet they failed to establish a consistent relation between thought and reality and consequently revealed that there is no Being (essence) in man or the world. Contemporary thought is thus limited to the being of language, and language does not signify anything beyond itself and surely does not signify man. In fact, Foucault claims that the "Being of Man" is incompatible with the "Being of Language." It is not man who speaks (the individual and conscious subject, the Cartesian *cogito*), as Nietzsche had already suspected. It is the Word that speaks (collective and unconscious language), as Mallarmé had realized.

Foucault portrayed the quadrilateral of language and its function of ordering knowledge between the seventeenth and nineteenth centuries in two detailed diagrams (see fig. 1). These diagrams are typical of Foucault's thought—abstract yet precise and based on spatial relations. An important feature of the two figures represented is the relative location of the filled and empty spaces in each. As Foucault explains:

> Philology, biology, and political economy were established not in the places formerly occupied by *general grammar, natural history,* and the *analysis of wealth,* but in an area where those forms of knowledge did not exist, in the space they left blank, in the deep gaps that separated their broad theoretical segments and that were filled with the murmur of the ontological continuum. . . . Inversely, a new philosophical space was to emerge in the place where the objects of Classical knowledge dissolved.[13]

Although characteristic of the relationships he establishes and appropriately focused on the Classical and Modern epistemes that constitute the bulk of his study, Foucault's diagrams do not give a sense of the archaeological layers of his work. For this purpose the diagram in figure 2 may be useful; it is less elegant than Foucault's but hopefully more accessible.[14] While the four epistemes are represented here as separate strata with no connecting structures, there are transition figures. Don Quixote marks the break between the Renaissance unity of words and things and the Classical system of representation, in which the order of words represented the order of things. In a similar fashion, Sade marks the break between the Classical period and the Modern episteme, in which the order of words did not represent real things but man's representation of things. Likewise, Nietzsche prefigures the Contemporary episteme, in which words only represent other words or, in structuralist terminology, in which signs signify other signs without external referents.

The various positivities that define the perception of life, labor, and language are portrayed here, with a few exceptions, in Foucault's own terms.[15] Although Foucault frequently refers to Classical

Figure 1. *Foucault's Quadrilateral of Language*

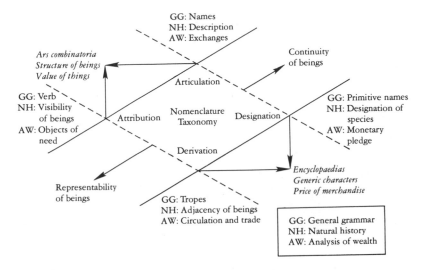

SEVENTEENTH AND EIGHTEENTH CENTURIES

GG: Names
NH: Description
AW: Exchanges

Ars combinatoria
Structure of beings
Value of things

Continuity
of beings

Articulation

GG: Verb
NH: Visibility
of beings
AW: Objects of
need

Attribution

Nomenclature
Taxonomy

Designation

GG: Primitive names
NH: Designation of
species
AW: Monetary
pledge

Derivation

Representability
of beings

Encyclopaedias
Generic characters
Price of merchandise

GG: Tropes
NH: Adjacency of beings
AW: Circulation and trade

GG: General grammar
NH: Natural history
AW: Analysis of wealth

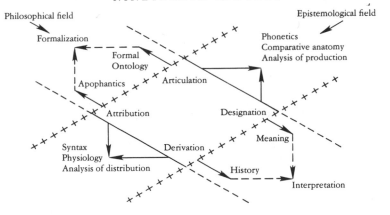

NINETEENTH CENTURY

Philosophical field

Epistemological field

Formalization

Phonetics
Comparative anatomy
Analysis of production

Formal
Ontology

Apophantics

Articulation

Attribution

Designation

Syntax
Physiology
Analysis of distribution

Derivation

Meaning

History

Interpretation

Source: *The Order of Things: An Archaeology of the Human Sciences*, by Michel Foucault, translated by Alan Sheridan-Smith, p. 201. Copyright © 1970 by Random House, Inc. Reprinted by permission of Pantheon Books, a Division of Random House, Inc.; Editions Gallimard; and Tavistock Publications Ltd.

Figure 2. *Archaeological Chart of the Human Sciences*

Episteme	Form of Knowledge	Same-Other	Time-Space	Dominant Grammatical Structure	Object of Knowledge
Contemporary	Self-Reflection	Other ↓ Same	Space-Time	Designation	Language

NIETZSCHE

| Modern (1800–1950) | Self-Representation | Same ↓ Other | Time | Derivation | Man / History |

SADE

| Classical (1660–1800) | Representation | Other | Space | Nomination | Nature |

DON QUIXOTE

| Renaissance (1500–1660) | Resemblance | Same | | Attribution | God |

Positivities	Life	Labor	Language	Philosophy
Counterhuman Sciences	Psycho-analysis	Ethnology	Linguistics	"Archaeology"
	Structuralism			

	Life	Labor	Language	Philosophy
Human Sciences / Empirical Sciences	Psychology / Biology	Sociology / Political Economy	Literature / Philology	"Anthropology"
	Hermeneutics			

	Life	Labor	Language	Philosophy
Natural Sciences	Natural History	Analysis of Wealth	General Grammar	Rationalism
	Sign Systems			

	Life	Labor	Language	Philosophy
Cosmographies	Histories of Nature	Knowledge of Value	Commentaries of Texts	Theology
	Symbolism			

representations as sign systems and in other essays has discussed nineteenth-century hermeneutics, he does not actually characterize the four forms of encoding knowledge as symbolic, semiotic, hermeneutic, and structuralist, as indicated in figure 2. However, he would probably agree that there is a superficial resemblance between the Classical and Contemporary epistemes (in both epistemes form determines content) and an analogous resemblance between the Renaissance and Modern epistemes (both are interpretive modes of thought).

Besides the positivities of life, labor and language, Foucault also examines the philosophical systems characteristic of each episteme. But he does not discuss these systems in an easily recognizable fashion, nor can they be said to constitute a secondary rather than a primary concern, as he claims. Foucault obviously wishes to avoid the vague "isms" common to the history of ideas. Renaissance humanism, seventeenth- and eighteenth-century rationalism, nineteenth-century romanticism, idealism, vitalism, and positivism, and twentieth-century structuralism are terms that rarely appear in Foucault's work. In fact, despite an almost obsessive desire to break with Cartesian rationalism, Foucault seldom mentions either Descartes or rationalism. When the term *rationalism* does occur, it is quickly dismissed, as in the following reference to the shift from the Renaissance to the Classical episteme: "This new configuration may, I suppose, be called 'rationalism'; one might say, if one's mind is filled with ready-made concepts, that the seventeenth century marks the disappearance of the old superstitious or magical beliefs and the entry of nature, at long last, into the scientific order."[16] Foucault's intention, clearly, is not to rely on ready-made concepts but to discover the unconscious structures that made these diffuse and unsystematic conceptions possible. For example, he does not consider the distinction between rational (scientific) and magical (religious) thought in the Renaissance to be significant, since he views both forms of knowledge as reflections of a more fundamental epistemological configuration. Nor does Foucault believe that the highly conscious systemizations of knowledge in the Classical period, such as Newtonian physics and Cartesian epistemology, shaped Classical thought. Indeed, he thinks that mathematical and mechanical models had only a limited influence, affecting relatively few areas of thought for only a short period of time.[17]

Foucault's study of philosophy, then, is not intended to assert the primacy of rational thought. On the contrary, he is more interested in the often unconscious conceptions of being that lie at the heart of diverse philosophical systems. For the Renaissance period philosophy is not even discussed, perhaps because Foucault's interpretation of the Renaissance rests on the belief that being was assumed and thus did not become an issue. But in the Classical period Foucault believes that a narrow concept of being was flatly asserted, thereby excluding the possibility of interpreting modes of being. The Cartesian formula "I think therefore I am" simply declares being as a fact ("I am"). It also identifies being with the individual subject ("I") and with consciousness ("I think"). Such an epistemology excludes, almost by definition, unconscious phenomena (dreams and madness), collective phenomena (language), and changing states of being (historical experiences). It is this epistemology and its triple commitment to the individual, consciousness, and atemporal existence that preoccupies Foucault. On the one hand, he claims to reject all three assumptions; on the other, his own thought remains deeply imprinted with the logical, almost axiomatic, structure of Cartesian rationalism.

Despite his critique of Enlightenment rationalism, Foucault does not claim adherence to any of the philosophical systems of the Modern period that sought to interpret man's "being-in-the-world." Foucault refers to all these man-centered philosophies as "anthropology," an explicit reference to Kant's concept of anthropology. Kant, he claims, was not the final expression of Classical rationalism but the philosophical manifestation of the first phase of the shift from the Classical to the Modern episteme. Like Lamarck in biology, Adam Smith in political economy, and William Jones in philology, Kant was a link between Classical representational thought and the historical consciousness of nineteenth-century culture. The paradigmatic form of Modern thought was established during the second phase of this cultural "mutation," and the philosophical equivalent of Cuvier, Ricardo, and Bopp was Hegel. But while Kant and Hegel contemplated the being of man, they were more concerned with being than with man. The thinkers who paralleled the formation of the human sciences were Freud, Marx, and Husserl, all of whom sought man's essence in his history. Contemporary philosophy, by contrast, does not affirm transcendental being. Man no longer has an essence and philosophy has become "archaeology," limiting itself to describing discontinuous modes of being.

Since Foucault's archaeology of the human sciences is really an ontology and an epistemology, he rarely discusses social, economic, or political events. This naturally shocks historians who expect the study of science to include a consideration of technological innovations, general cultural changes, and the contributions of individual scientists. It is particularly startling in a work that examines the history of the social sciences to find only a passing reference to industrialism and the French Revolution. But, according to Foucault, social and political upheavals can only determine the content of discourse; the "intrinsic possibility" of these forms of knowledge cannot be referred to external factors or to conscious choices but to deep epistemological "configurations."[18] Likewise, there are few heroes in Foucault's archaeology, although Nietzsche and Freud occasionally burst out of Foucault's neat categories. Archaeology does not easily accommodate individual creativity and even Marx has been calmly bypassed. In Foucault's view, "at the deepest level of Western knowledge, Marxism introduced no real discontinuity. . . . Marxism exists in nineteenth-century thought like a fish in water: that is, it is unable to breathe anywhere else."[19] Similarly, Foucault dismisses the controversy between bourgeois and revolutionary economics during the nineteenth century as having "stirred up a few waves and caused a few surface ripples; but they are no more than storms in a children's paddling pool."[20] Again, the real action takes place elsewhere, at the unconscious level of thought that made both forms of economics possible.

Apart from the polemical nature of such phrases, there are methodological reasons why Foucault has ignored the usual landmarks of Western culture. Although Foucault's methodology is not explicit in this work,[21] a number of principles are nevertheless apparent, both in the relationships he establishes and in the metaphors he employs. These suggest that linguistics is not the only model for *The Order of Things*, perhaps not even the major one. The epistemological fields Foucault examines are spatial and temporal fields, structurally similar to physical fields and described in similar terms. As already indicated, a spatiotemporal axis runs throughout this work. Not only do spatial and temporal relations shape epistemological fields, but geometric images are used as metaphors for each episteme. The Renaissance, for example, an almost prehistoric period in this study, is represented by a sphere signifying the circularity of knowledge. The Classical and Modern periods are symbolized by a quadrilateral, although the shape of this figure varies. Knowledge in these two epistemes is circumscribed by the same four planes (the quadrilateral of language), but the surrounding spaces undergo a perpendicular displacement relative to each other: previously empty spaces become filled and the filled spaces become empty. This, it may be recalled, is precisely how electromagnetic fields are described. They also share identical structures but undergo perpendicular displacements that occur as quantum jumps rather than gradual transitions. Moreover, for both epistemological and physical fields, observable phenomena (epistemic or wave functions) are determined not by the substantial content (socioeconomic events or particles) or mysterious forces (ideas or charges) but by the form of the field.

For the Contemporary period, Foucault does not refer to a quadrilateral of knowledge but to a triangle whose planes are formed by mathematics and the physical sciences, by the empirical sciences of biology, economics, and philology, and by philosophy. Again, he does not employ a two-dimensional image. He suggests that this episteme "should be represented rather as a volume of space open in three dimensions . . . it is in the interstices of these branches of knowledge, or more exactly, in the volume defined by their three dimensions, that the human sciences have their place."[22] Although in Foucault's imagery the human sciences lie closer to the empirical sciences than to the other two planes, the counterhuman sciences lie closer to mathematics. With linguistics, "the relation of the human sciences to mathematics has been opened up once more, and in a wholly new dimension; . . . the question that arises is that of knowing whether it is possible without a play on words to employ the notion of structure, or at least whether it is the same structure that is referred to in mathematics and in the human sciences."[23]

The possible correlation between epistemological and scientific structures is a fundamental question that Foucault poses openly here and that exists in this work as more than a mere "play on words." The concept of fields (or structures) seems also to have shaped Foucault's response to three basic issues, what he calls the three problems that cannot be solved by traditional methodologies and perhaps cannot yet be solved by any method: the problems of change, causality, and subject. These are the problems that modern physics has "solved" by substituting the concept of probability for predictable change, by describing regional spatiotemporal configurations rather than invoking magical causes acting at a distance, and by collapsing the distinction between the acting subject (scientist) and the observed object.

Foucault has taken a similar approach to these problems in his archaeology of the human sciences. On the question of change, for example, he commented that "it seemed to me at the outset that different kinds of change were taking place in scientific discourse. . . . I tried to describe the combination of corresponding transformations that characterized the appearance of biology, political economy, philology, a number of the human sciences, and a new type of philosophy, at the threshold of the nineteenth century."[24] By "the combination of corresponding transformations" Foucault means the field interactions which determine the probability that certain positivities will emerge. By assuming a significant degree of probability (Foucault uses the term *regularity*), he has implied that change in the social sciences is neither arbitrary nor completely determined, although the range of freedom has little to do with human action; it is inherent in the system itself. Also, by selecting only those positivities with an intermediate incidence of regularity and thereby excluding those with a high incidence (the physical sciences) or a low incidence (the arts), Foucault has made the assumption that the "sciences" of life, labor, and language represent the characteristic forms of thought in each period. Moreover, once these sciences emerge, Foucault assumes that they exclude other forms of thought and that they remain constant during the entire period in question. Now it is true that in physics and Gestalt psychology fields may preclude the simultaneous presence of other fields in the same space and may maintain a constant structure for a specific period of time. But for the historical sciences these are difficult assumptions to maintain. For example, it is hard to believe that, "in any given culture and at any given moment, there is only one *episteme* that defines the conditions of possibility of all knowledge, whether expressed in a theory or silently invested in a practice."[25]

Foucault had not, in fact, previously made such an extreme assertion. In *The Birth of the Clinic* he examined a period of change and found three forms of clinical medicine that coexisted in time and space. And despite his aggravating tendency to refer to all three—the protoclinic, the "mere" clinic, and the anatomical clinic—as simply "clinic," he treated these forms of medicine as competing structures of thought. In *The Order of Things*, however, Foucault studied established structures and eliminated almost all nonparadigmatic formulations. He also identified each episteme with a long period of time so that in spite of his claim to preserve differences he imposed a uniformity of thought on periods as long as a century and a half.

Similar difficulties are associated with the related question of causality. Even if one can predict probable changes, determining their causes may not be possible. Consequently, Foucault does not have a causal theory.

> The traditional explanations—spirit of the time, technological or social changes, influences of various kinds—struck me for the most part as being more magical than effective. In this work, then, I left the problem of causes to one side; I chose instead to confine myself to describing the transformations themselves, thinking that this would be an indispensable step if, one day, a theory of scientific change and epistemological causality was to be constructed.[26]

The absence of a theory of causality means that archaeology, despite its highly theoretical features, is a descriptive discipline similar to field-theory physics before the quark model was developed.[27] Moreover, both archaeology and physics have broken with older, magical conceptions of forces acting at a distance and both describe proximate relationships. Yet Foucault's style frequently obscures this fact because he often makes sweeping generalizations suggesting a return to the conception of "world views." He has tried to correct this impression by insisting that *The Order of Things* is not "an analysis of Classicism in general, nor a search for a *Weltanschauung*; but a strictly 'regional' study."[28] By this he means a study of specific epistemological "spaces," not a narration of events in an actual physical area at an exact moment.

Furthermore, Foucault does not really confine himself to "describing the transformations themselves." He attempts to determine the pattern of these transformations, and here again he employs concepts found in the physical sciences. He discusses, for example, the isomorphisms among the sciences of life, labor, and language and the symmetrical structures of certain discourses (such as psychoanalysis and ethnology) or certain categories of thought (such as sympathy and antipathy). He also suggests that the laws underlying knowledge in the counterhuman sciences (like those in modern physics) express systems of prohibition. Thus, psychoanalysis and ethnology seek meaning in taboos, and linguistics locates meaning in the systematic spacings (the absences, the forbidden places) between sounds or concepts. Foucault refers to these negative coding devices as Death, Desire, and Law, the three figures which shape the contemporary mode of being and which "designate the conditions of possibility of all knowledge about man."[29]

The third problem mentioned by Foucault concerns the concept of the subject. Since Foucault deals with collective and largely unconscious structures of perception, individuals play almost no role in his work. He is not concerned with the discoveries of "great men"; he is not even interested in the conscious evaluations scientists make of their own work. Ricardo, Cuvier, and Bopp, for example, are not depicted as real people; no reference is made to their lives and little consideration is given to the controversies surrounding their ideas, since these issues are regarded as merely surface phenomena. As Foucault explains, he has "tried to explore scientific discourse not from the point of view of the individuals who are speaking, nor from the point of view of the formal structures of what they are saying, but from the point of view of the rules that come into play in the very existence of such discourse."[30]

This stress on discursive systems rather than on creating subjects has involved a number of difficulties. First, it is almost impossible to locate anyone who perceives, thinks, or acts in Foucault's anonymous archaeology. Physical systems may function in isolation, but it is difficult to imagine the human sciences without specific individuals. This dehumanization has other consequences as well. There are few subjects to Foucault's sentences. Abstractions such as "Classicism" and "the nineteenth century" frequently function as subjects, but sometimes the problem is simply avoided by creating extraordinarily long sentences that provide complex series of relations with no precise referents. Also, Foucault's own status as an author-subject is brought into question. If language rather than man speaks, as he claims, and if the statement "I am writing" is a contradiction comparable to "I am lying," then who is the author of *The Order of Things*?[31] Is Foucault the "voice" of our time or is he speaking for himself? If the latter, is he then "lying"? This may not be a relevant question for him, since he believes that truth and falsehood both express possible statements within a system and that the significant categories are those of exclusion (what cannot be said) and inclusion (what can be expressed). Yet truth is still widely regarded as a relevant category and Foucault's rereading of history and his idiosyncratic use of the "archive" have aroused suspicion. A "proper" use of sources, however, implies that there are criteria of verification apart from logical coherence, whereas Foucault does not seem to recognize either an absolute standard or standards established by convention.

Again, these problems exist in the physical sciences as well as in history, philosophy, and archaeology. Kuhn, for example, has pointed out that the paradigms which shape scientific thought are collective, often unconscious, and are not accepted because they conform to an external standard of verification. And, as quantum physics makes clear, subject and object are no longer meaningful categories. The scientist (subject) is part of the process he observes and the act of observation is a factor in the results. Moreover, the objects observed are not real "things." To use a term common to both physicists and structuralists, objects are "traces" of presumed events. These events are themselves merely functions of fields, which also do not represent things but refer to methods of ordering knowledge. Fields and epistemes are thus isomorphic forms of ordering thought. As Foucault has explained in a paradox common to both archaeology and physics, order is simultaneously given and constituted.

> Order is, at one and the same time, that which is given in things as their inner law, the hidden network that determines the way they confront one another, and also that which has no existence except in the grid created by a glance, an examination, a language; and it is only in the blank spaces of this grid that order manifests itself in depth as though already there, waiting in silence for the moment of its expression.[32]

The order that Foucault examines is not the order of nature but the mental order that made the concept of Man possible. This order, he believes, did not result from the progress of reason but from a sudden reorganization of the perceptual structure of Western culture. It is this catastrophic event, as well as the structures that preceded and followed it, which concerns Foucault and which can now be examined more closely.

The Renaissance Episteme

Although traces of the Classical episteme survive in the "archive," the Renaissance episteme appears so remote as to be almost completely lost. It exists in Foucault's archaeology as an imaginary beginning situated in a distant time (comparable to those mythical origins postulated by Rousseau, Marx, and Freud) and in an unfamiliar space (comparable to those foreign and primitive societies studied by anthropologists). There is no indication here of a culture that prefigures our own. The great scientists (Copernicus, Kepler, and Galileo) and humanists (Erasmus and Montaigne) of the Renaissance do not figure in the brief chapter devoted to this period. Instead Foucault describes "the prose of the world," the unity of words and things in the network of correspondences ("resemblances") that presumably structured knowledge in this period.

For Foucault knowledge in the sixteenth century was knowledge of the connections between things. There were four major forms of resemblance that connected everything in the world and tied this world to the universe. These four forms can be imagined as four concentric circles of "similitudes," which Foucault labels *convenientia, aemulatio*, analogy, and sympathy. *Convenientia* refers to the resemblances between things connected in space, that is, to the correspondences born of proximity. Thus the body and soul interact and everywhere in "the vast syntax of the world the different beings adjust themselves to one another; the plant communicates with the animal, the earth with the sea, man with everything around him."[33] *Aemulatio* refers to resemblances based on simulation, a form of resemblance that does not require spatial proximity. Thus the sky and the human face mirror each other, both having two eyes (sun and moon), a mouth (Venus), and a nose (the pattern formed by Jupiter and Mercury).[34] Analogy is a still more general form of resemblance because it is not bound by space or by specific images. It can bind things together merely on the basis of similar relations. Thus "the relation of the stars to the sky in which they shine may also be found . . . between living beings and the globe they inhabit."[35] The most powerful form of resemblance, however, is sympathy, a sort of free association by which any quality can connect one thing to another. Thus fire is dry like earth, but in rising becomes moist like water, and then, turning to vapor, becomes air.[36] Sympathy is a force that collapses all differences; its power of attraction is so strong that if it "were not counter-balanced it would reduce the world to a point, to a homogeneous mass, to the featureless form of the Same." There- fore sympathy is opposed by antipathy, which keeps things apart and "encloses every species within its impenetrable difference and its propensity to continue being what it is."[37]

These four similitudes, then, tied everything to everything else while simultaneously maintaining the identity of things. But there was one further form of resemblance necessary to complete the Renaissance episteme. Foucault calls this form "signature" and con- siders it both a resemblance (a sign) and a sign of other resemblances. Since the connections among the different parts of the cosmos were often hidden, it was believed that God had placed a mark, or signa- ture, on things to indicate their relation to one another. For example, the usefulness of the plant aconite for the treatment of eye diseases was revealed by the signature on the seeds, whose coloration made them resemble the human eye.[38] To know the "order of things" during the sixteenth century, therefore, one needed both a herme- neutics that indicated which signs were signatures (a form of knowl- edge that appears to us magical or mad) and a science that explained the relation between things in this world (a form of knowledge we wrongly regard as an early stage of modern science or as a primitive semiotics). During the sixteenth century *divinatio* and *eruditio* were not, in Foucault's view, conflicting modes of thought. They were complementary and necessary expressions of an episteme based on resemblances.[39] Although Foucault does not claim that our own science might be magical in the way that sixteenth-century magic was scientific, his description of the Renaissance conception of sympathy and antipathy is expressed in terms analogous to current descriptions of the symmetrical relation between forces in nature such as matter and antimatter.

Within an episteme of resemblance, the discourses of life, labor, and language all reflected the infinite, but essentially identical, pat- tern of the cosmos. But the apprehension of this pattern required a form of perception different from that characteristic of our age. Studies of plants and animals included everything that was seen (ob- served) or heard (fabled) and thus there was no natural history in this period; there were only histories or stories about natural beings. Foucault even insists that, on the archaeological level, there was no difference between the legends of naturalists like Ulisse Aldrovandi and the science of naturalists like Pierre Belon, whose studies of human and bird skeletons are usually regarded as an early form of comparative anatomy.[40] Furthermore, natural magic, intended to control things by manipulating the marks that identify them, should not be regarded as a marginal form of knowledge. Consequently, magicians such as Giambattista della Porta and Paracelsus, whose works are not generally treated seriously, figure for Foucault as representative thinkers in the sixteenth-century discourse on life.

Foucault's interpretation of the late Renaissance discourse on language is similarly unconventional. Words, like things, were signs, and written words (since they are visible and durable) had more signifying power than spoken words. Again, on the archaeological level, there was no difference between Claude Duret's history of languages, which compared the known spatial arrangements of script with the order of the heavens and the shape of the cross, and Peter Ramus's scholarly grammar. Both were studies of resemblances, since even grammarians believed that "words group syllables together, and syllables letters, because there are virtues placed in individual letters that draw them towards each other or keep them apart, exactly as the marks found in nature also repel or attract one another."[41] Words were thus bound by the same forms of similitude as things. They also functioned within the same ternary system of signs that characterized all of Renaissance thought. In this system marks acted as signifiers, signifying an original order that meant, in the case of language, an original Text. But between the signifier and the signified there existed, during the sixteenth century, a middle term connecting those two elements through an endless series of interpretations. Just as the history of nature was an inexhaustible series of stories, the study of language was an infinite commentary of texts: "Scriptual commentary, commentaries on Ancient authors, commentaries on the accounts of travellers, commentaries on legends and fables. . . . Language contains its own inner principle of proliferation."[42]

The discourse on labor followed the same epistemological configuration as the discourses on life and language. Like words and natural beings, money was regarded both as a sign and as a signifier of other signs, although it could only function in this way if it contained precious metal. "And just as words had the same reality as what they said, just as the marks of living beings were inscribed upon their bodies in the manner of visible and positive marks, similarly the signs that indicated wealth and measured it were bound to carry the real mark in themselves."⁴³ The amount of metal in money, though, could not serve as an absolute standard of value, since money was also a commodity whose value fluctuated with changing prices. Foucault believes that the relationship between prices and money dominated sixteenth-century economic thought. But because this relationship was fixed by God, knowledge of the value of things was analogous to knowledge of the order of things. Thus, what "the *soothsayers* were to the undefined interplay of resemblances and signs, the *merchants* are to the interplay, also forever open, of exchange and money."⁴⁴

The ternary system of signs, as well as the resemblances that made this system possible, suddenly collapsed in the middle of the seventeenth century, to be replaced by a binary system based on an analysis of representation. While words and things in the sixteenth century were joined together through resemblances and linked to a divine order (again through resemblances), during the Classical period words and things separated and resemblance no longer served as a mediating agent. Words became signifiers and things were signified, but no direct connections between them existed. Instead the order of words represented the order of things and these two orders paralleled each other and were not, as before, intertwined with each other. This change, Foucault concludes,

> involved an immense reorganization of culture, a reorganization of which the Classical age was the first and perhaps the most important stage, since it was responsible for the new arrangement in which we are still caught—since it is the Classical age that separates us from a culture in which . . . primitive being shone in an endless dispersion. There is nothing now, either in our knowledge or in our reflection, that still recalls the memory of that being. Nothing except perhaps literature.⁴⁵

The Classical Episteme

Just as the "primitive being" of the Renaissance can only be glimpsed through the works of the mad poets of the Modern period (Hölderlin, Nietzsche, Roussel, and Artaud), so too the break between the Renaissance and Classical periods is best symbolized by a work of literature. For Foucault, Cervantes's *Don Quixote* is suspended between two eras: the Renaissance world of the same and the Classical world of the different. The first half of Cervantes's novel finds Don Quixote living in a realm in which words (the chivalric romances he reads) and things (the objects he encounters in the world) are perceived as the same. In the second half of the text the novel becomes a work representing itself; Don Quixote then stands between the order of words and the order of things. The fabric of resemblances he had earlier perceived disappeared, since it no longer served as a sanctioned form of knowledge and would henceforth be knowledge only for madmen and poets. A new form of knowledge had emerged. "Because of an essential rupture in the Western world, what had become important [was] no longer resemblances but identities and differences."[46]

In this new episteme signs did not function as symbols but as representations of other signs. The power to re-present one order of things by another is most obvious in painting, and Foucault considers Velasquez's *Maids of Honor* an illustration of the Classical episteme. Foucault's complex analysis of this painting is too lengthy to summarize here, but a few points should be mentioned. Velasquez's painting depicted an artist in the process of painting a portrait, not of the princess who occupies the center of the picture, but of the king and queen who are absent. Their presence is nevertheless indicated by their dim reflection in a mirror and by the gaze of the artist who, in regarding his subject (the royal couple), stares out of the painting directly at us, the viewers. Thus the absent subject of the portrait and the real observer of Velasquez's painting are located in the same position: "the observer and the observed take part in a ceaseless exchange. . . . subject and object, the spectator and the model, reverse their roles to infinity."[47] What is represented in Velasquez's painting, then, is more than an image or a series of images; it is the process of representation itself.

Yet Foucault did not merely wish to describe the visible expressions of Classical representation. He wanted to uncover the structures that made this form of knowledge systematic. Consequently, his analysis of the Classical episteme relies more heavily on the logical theories of this period than on painting, and he has drawn particularly on the Port-Royal *Logic, or The Art of Thinking* (1662). This work and its sister volume, the Port-Royal *General Grammar* (1660), were models for epistemological studies throughout the Classical period and into the nineteenth century.[48] They are vital works for

Foucault's analysis because they articulated a theory of signs. Foucault has used this theory to establish the Classical discourses of life, labor, and language as systematic forms of knowledge independent of the mathematical and mechanical models that usually dominate studies of the thought of this period.

According to Foucault, the Classical episteme consisted of three structures which might be visualized as concentric circles: *mathesis*, *taxinomia*, and *genesis*. *Mathesis* refers to "a universal science of measurement and order"[49] in which measurement (based on algebra) analyzed things into units, and order (based on sign systems) arranged nonquantifiable differences into a taxonomic table. The Classical sciences of language, life, and labor were all forms of *taxinomia* and represented their objects on tables, as Linnaeus did in natural history. Although these tables indicated relationships among visible, distinct structures, they also assumed an invisible continuum (a "genesis") that served as a background for, and a limit to, knowledge. It was in this background and on the edges of knowledge that resemblance existed in the Classical period.

The actual configuration of the Classical episteme is described by Foucault in terms of five modifications of the Renaissance thought structure and three variables that defined signs in the Classical period. Although both Bacon (from within the Renaissance episteme) and Descartes (from within the Classical episteme) denounced resemblances as a basis for knowledge, the modifications that characterized the shift between epistemes were more general than the principles articulated by these two thinkers. The major displacements may be summarized as those that substituted analysis for analogy, finite differences for infinite resemblances, certain knowledge for probable relationships, discrimination of differences for the synthesis of similarities, and those that divorced history (what was heard and recounted) from science (what was seen and observed). In Foucault's analysis, the last shift signaled a new arrangement of knowledge that divided *mathesis* (science) from *genesis* (history) and that further distinguished between those disciplines dealing with what were "seen" as self-evident truths (philosophy and mathematics) and taxonomic disciplines based on "observed" relationships (natural history, general grammar, and analysis of wealth). But in Foucault's opinion, the three main categories of Classical thought were not isolated:

It is patent that these three notions—*mathesis, taxinomia, genesis*—designate not so much separate domains as a solid grid of kinships that defines the general configuration of knowledge in the Classical age. *Taxinomia* is not in opposition to mathesis: it resides within it and is distinguished from it; for it too is a science of order—a qualitative mathesis. . . . In relation to mathesis, *taxinomia* functions as an ontology confronted by an apophantics; confronted by genesis, it functions as a semiology confronted by history. It defines, then, the general law of beings, and at the same time the conditions under which it is possible to know them.[50]

Since *taxinomia* functioned in the Classical period as a semiology (a theory of signs) as well as an ontology (a theory of being), Foucault examined the Classical concept of sign before describing particular sign systems. According to the Port-Royal *Logic*, signs were not things but relations that could be classified in three ways. First, instead of the ternary Renaissance system, signs during the Classical period consisted of binary relations between two already known elements. This meant that there was no hidden connection to be uncovered and no need for interpretation (and thus no room for *divinatio* as a form of knowledge). Second, whereas "similitude was able in the sixteenth century to triumph over space and time," the "sign in Classical thought does not erase distances or abolish time."[51] It existed instead on a table of spatial relationships and must have coincided in time with what it signified at least once. For example, a sound could only become a verbal sign of an object for a child if it were heard at the same moment as the object was perceived.[52] The third characteristic of the Classical sign was the significance of conventional (man-made) signs as compared to natural signs. Since conventional signs are arbitrary and therefore easier to combine and analyze, these signs were paradigmatic for Classical thought and all sign systems aimed at becoming a well-constructed "language." This was the inverse of the situation during the sixteenth century, when language was regarded as merely another thing in the world; it is, however, similar to the contemporary theory of signs in which language is primary.

Although the Classical sign system was consciously expressed by Port-Royal logicians (Antoine Arnauld and Pierre Nicole), Foucault obviously believes that this system functioned on an unconscious level in other discourses. He thus does not look to specific theorists for an explanation of the origins of Classical thought but maintains that, "if we question Classical thought at the level of what, archaeologically, made it possible, we perceive that the dissociation of the sign from resemblance in the early seventeenth century caused these new forms—probability, analysis, combination, and universal language system—to emerge . . . as a single network of necessities. And it was this network that made possible the individuals we term Hobbes, Berkeley, Hume, or Condillac."[53] This network also made possible the taxonomic discourses Foucault calls natural history, analysis of wealth, and general grammar, which were all sign systems in an episteme based on representation rather than resemblance. Moreover, these discourses illustrated the permeability of thought between different forms of *taxinomia*. It was not accidental, then, that Classical economists such as Turgot and Adam Smith wrote on language, that grammarians and philosophers such as Condillac and Destutt de Tracy discussed trade and economics, and that naturalists such as Adanson and Linnaeus recognized similar patterns in natural and social forms.[54] Still, such conscious articulations are not Foucault's primary concern. His examination of the Classical discourses of life, labor, and language is situated at the unconscious "archaeological" level, not at the level of doxology where the history of ideas and philosophy of history are located.

Of the three Classical taxonomic discourses Foucault examined, general grammar occupies a privileged position. General grammar was a discourse located between logic (with its aspiration to define universal forms of thought) and grammar (with its focus on the structure of specific languages). Yet general grammar was not equivalent to comparative grammar, since general grammar did not compare changing language elements but sought to compare the way similar elements functioned within different language systems. The Classical analysis of grammatical functions and the concept of grammatical systems has appeared to some contemporary linguists, particularly Noam Chomsky, as a prefiguration of structural linguistics. Although Foucault, like Chomsky, regards Port-Royal general grammar as a philosophy of language, he disagrees with Chomsky's understanding of it as an embryonic form of modern linguistics or as a basis for a universal theory of knowledge. Instead, Foucault believes that general grammar must be regarded as a developed form of knowledge specific to an episteme fundamentally different from our own.[55]

In the Classical period the grammatical functions of articulation, attribution, designation, and derivation were the major categories of the discourse on language and languages were compared on the basis of these functions, not on the basis of their historical development. Consequently, languages that would later be classified together (such as the Romance languages) were not grouped together during the Classical period. Nor were languages classified as they were during the sixteenth century, when Hebrew was taken as the primary language by virtue of its proximity to a hypostatized lost original tongue. Furthermore, since languages were grouped together on the basis of their grammatical functions rather than their relation to an original text, the Renaissance preoccupation with commentary was replaced by the Classical concern with criticism. Classical criticism was simultaneously a critique of form (function) and content (the value of different functions). Thus, questions such as the type of language necessary to construct philosophy and science or the proper methods of exegesis were forms of criticism made possible by the new perception of language as a system of representation.

Although language was only one form of representation, it provided analytic possibilities that other sign systems could not provide. Since language is a temporal series of sounds, it can represent thought by variable linear orders, not merely by fixed images that must be apprehended at once. The spatial and temporal characteristics of language were expressed in the Classical episteme by rhetoric and grammar, the two "sciences" of language during this period. Rhetoric dealt with "the manner in which language is spatialized in verbal signs"; grammar revealed "the order that distributed that spatiality in time."[56] Although Foucault discusses various tropes of rhetoric, he is clearly more interested in the theory of order provided by general grammar. There were, in fact, two theories of general grammar that reflected two perceptions of the nature of nomination. According to one theory, only certain language elements named (and thus represented) things or ideas, and language was built with these basic units. According to the other theory, all language elements represented something and "each word, down to the last of its molecules, had to be a meticulous form of nomination."[57] Nomination, however, was the central grammatical function for both theories of general grammar and indeed for all Classical discourse:

The fundamental task of Classical "discourse" is *to ascribe a name to things, and in that name to name their being.* For two centuries Western discourse was the locus of ontology. When it named the being of representation in general it was philosophy. . . . When it ascribed to each thing represented the name that was fitted to it, and laid out the grid of a well-made language across the whole field of representation, then it was science—nomenclature and taxonomy.[58]

The Classical science most closely identified with taxonomy was natural history. This discourse, Foucault claims, obeyed the same laws as the science of nomenclature (general grammar). The same four functions of attribution, articulation, designation, and derivation existed in natural history and again the nominative function (articulation) predominated. During this period, the study of natural beings was organized around two problems: identifying particular beings and placing them in a relationship with other beings. The first problem was solved by the theory of structure, which combined both the function of verbs (affirming identity) and the function of proper nouns (describing the features of individual entities). The second problem was answered by a theory of characteristics, which established each structure in a larger taxonomy and made it possible to designate relationships and to derive sequences of changes.

Since the theory of structure functioned within the Classical episteme as a way of establishing identities and differences, the relevant variables were those that identified the basic form of an object and those that differentiated entities by the number of elements in each structure as well as by the distribution and size of these elements. These four variables, which Linnaeus termed form, number, situation, and proportion, were used by all naturalists during the Classical period.[59] One should not, therefore, allow the controversies separating figures such as Linnaeus and Buffon to obscure this common grid. Nor should the two Classical procedures for comparing structures, what Foucault called system and method, be regarded as conflicting forms of thought. Method refers to a vertical mode of classification that moves from the general to the specific, such as the modern series: phylum, class, order, family, genus, and species. System refers to the horizontal classifications by which certain elements from diverse groups, such as the leaves of different plants, are compared to each other. Again, both forms of classification reflect the same epistemological configuration in which order is established by an analysis of differences and similarities. And, significantly, both forms of classification parallel the way proper nouns become common nouns—by the use of increasingly general substantives (spaniel, dog, quadruped) or by the use of qualifying adjectives ("narrow" leaves).[60]

The Classical science of natural history did not, in Foucault's view, indicate either a progress in knowledge or an advancement in the scientist's powers of observation. It signified instead a reorganization of knowledge that excluded hearsay, taste, and smell as acceptable sources of information, left little room for touch, and restricted sight to the perception of forms devoid of color.[61] Consequently, one cannot regard Jonston's *Natural History of Quadrupeds* (1657), which symbolized the beginning of natural history, as superior to Aldrovandi's *History of Serpents and Dragons* (1640), which belonged to the Renaissance episteme. The difference between these two works lay not in Jonston's greater erudition (since this was not the case) but in his systematic exclusion of everything that could not be represented. In a similar manner, one cannot say that the Classical science of nature was inferior to nineteenth-century biology because according to Foucault these two discourses are completely different forms of knowledge. It makes no sense to discuss "life" or "evolution" in the Classical period because the modern perception of organism or of the interaction of organisms with an environment did not exist.[62] Even the distinction between animate and inanimate beings was not relevant for Classical taxonomy because natural beings were perceived as various combinations of elements that could be described and ordered on a table of relationships.

Despite the fact that there was no concept of evolutionary change in the seventeenth and eighteenth centuries, there were theories of change. In natural history, as in general grammar, change was understood in spatial, not temporal, terms. Just as the forms of rhetoric represented different spatial relationships, so changes in the natural order were regarded not as internal transformations of beings but as displacements in spatial positions on a table. This was explained in two ways. Either the entire hierarchy of beings shifted upward, so that man moved closer to the angels and apes occupied the slot formerly reserved for man. Or, alternatively, each species occupied every slot in succession so that birds, for example, had once been fish.[63] Evidence that changes did occur in the order of beings was provided by the existence of monsters and fossils. While monsters illustrated the formation of new slots and thus explained the emergence of differences, fossils confirmed the continuity of being by showing that all spaces between current slots had once been filled. The existence of monsters and fossils, however, implied that nature was continuous and that present species were only the visible forms on an invisible continuum of adjacent (not evolving) beings.

This concept of natural history meant that taxonomy, like nomenclature, was a system of signs in which each sign derived its meaning from its relationship to other signs. Like general grammar, natural history was also based on spatial relationships and visible differences while time and resemblances played subordinate roles. But although natural history and general grammar were similar means of organizing knowledge, no direct causal relationship existed between them. It was "not a question of a transference of method from one to the other; nor of a communication of concepts; nor of the prestige of a model. . . . Nor is it a question of a more general rationality imposing identical forms upon grammatical thinking and upon *taxinomia*. Rather it concerns a fundamental arrangement of knowledge, which orders the knowledge of beings so as to make it possible to represent them in a system of names."[64] This "fundamental arrangement of knowledge," this historical a priori, is of course the Classical episteme, which paradoxically represents both the totality of knowledge in the Classical period and the inexplicable cause of this knowledge.

The last example cited by Foucault as an illustration of the Classical episteme was the analysis of wealth, the knowledge of the value of things in a system of exchange. This system, and not the intrinsic value of metals (the sixteenth-century view) or the processes of production (the nineteenth-century view), characterized economic thought during the Classical period. In the system of exchange, money was not itself wealth; it was a representation, a sign, of wealth. Like other signs, money derived its significance from its function, which in this case was to act as a substitute for goods and to serve as a measure of value. The function of money dominated seventeenth- and eighteenth-century mercantilism and assumed a privileged place in the more general analysis of wealth because "all wealth is *coinable*; and it is by this means that it enters into *circulation*—in the same way that any natural being was *characterizable*, and could thereby find its place in a *taxonomy*; that any individual was *nameable* and could find its place in an *articulated language*; that any representation was *signifiable* and could find its place, in order to be *known*, in a *system of identities and differences*."[65] Money, then, functioned in Classical economic thought as the grammatical categories of articulation and designation functioned in the Classical discourses of language and life. Money maintained these functions even within apparently opposing monetary theories. The conflicts between those who regarded money as an arbitrary "token accepted by common consent"[66] (John Law) and those who viewed money as a representation of precious metals (Turgot) were not significant at a deeper archaeological level because both groups were united in the perception of money as a "pledge," a designation of a future exchange of goods.

There were, however, important differences between the monetary system of exchange and grammatical or taxonomic systems. The monetary system was more closely connected to social praxis than the other two systems, and the time during which goods and money circulated introduced a temporal index "not to be found in any other area of the theory of order."[67] Despite these differences, the analysis of wealth followed the same pattern as general grammar and natural history and encompassed all four functions of the "quadrilateral of language." Just as the nominative function was expressed by the concept of monetary exchange and designation was reflected in the notion of a monetary pledge, the remaining functions of attribution and derivation found expression in the Classical theory of value.

In Classical economic thought, to be valuable meant not only to be desired (and thus subject to exchange) but also to have a value previous to the act of exchange. Although these two notions, which corresponded to the grammatical categories of verbs and roots, were not really separable in the analysis of wealth, they were sufficiently distinct to permit two forms of the Classical theory of value to coexist. On the one hand, utilitarians such as Condillac analyzed value from the point of view of need and usefulness; on the other, Physiocrats such as Quesnay saw value as originating in the natural abundance of land. These two schools were not, in Foucault's scheme, opposing structures of knowledge. Rather, they reflected symmetrical forms of thought because one stressed a need while the other stressed an abundance, and exchange required both conditions.

Since the Classical theory of value incorporated the function of attribution (being), it is not surprising that Foucault found concealed in this theory a concept that both typified Classical thought and marked the fissure between the Classical and Modern epistemes. Desire, and the possibility of representing the objects of desire in a system of exchange, is a concept of particular importance in Foucault's analysis of the Classical "unconscious." Classicism was synonymous with the perception of the representability of things, and Classicism disappeared when this perception was no longer capable of relating the order of words to the order of things. Its disappearance coincided with Sade's demonstration that objects of desire could not be represented by the order of words. Sade, then, stands halfway between the Classical and Modern periods. As Foucault noted, "possibly *Justine* and *Juliette* are in the same position on the threshold of modern culture as that occupied by *Don Quixote* between the Renaissance and Classicism. . . . It is no longer the ironic triumph of representation over resemblance; it is the obscure and repeated violence of desire battering at the limits of representation."[68] After Sade, desire was no longer contained within the limits of representation and a new perception was born. The Modern form of knowledge restructured the discourses of life, labor, and language and reoriented the axis of thought from the space of representation to the time of desire (sexuality) and violence (life and death).

The Modern Episteme

The rupture that divided the Classical from the Modern episteme occurred at the turn of the eighteenth century and included two distinct phases. The first phase, roughly from 1775 to 1795, was marked by the sudden dominance of temporal concepts in the discourses on life, labor, and language. According to Foucault, Lamarck's concept of organic structure, Adam Smith's theory of labor, and William Jones's study of the inflections of words all reflected the new historical dimension that was to shatter the spatial "table" of Classical thought. Yet these figures were not revolutionary thinkers, since they still depicted the order of things by the order of words and were thus tied to Classical representation as a mode of knowledge. The real break came during the second phase, from 1795 to 1825, when David Ricardo (1772–1823), Georges Cuvier (1769–1832), and Franz Bopp (1791–1867) removed the concepts of labor, organic structure, and word inflection from the Classical thought structure and reorganized their disciplines into totally new discourses.

Foucault's conception of a radical break in thought preceded by the development of concepts still tied to an earlier perceptual structure is analogous to current interpretations of revolutions in the physical sciences. As Einstein himself noted, the special theory of relativity consisted largely of extricating Maxwell's conception of the electromagnetic field from the Newtonian system and of restructuring scientific knowledge around new principles. Also, for revolutions in both the empirical and physical sciences, there is the implicit assumption that changes are determined by factors internal to the discipline or by a larger collective unconscious and that these changes have little relation to specific external social and political events. Einstein, for example, did not even discuss the pressures of prewar or wartime politics in his history of physics, and Foucault has described a revolution in the empirical sciences without reference to the French Revolution that occurred simultaneously. Yet Foucault, who examined unconscious rather than hyperconscious forms of change, posed the essential and unanswerable question: "What event, what law do they obey, these mutations that suddenly decide that things are no longer perceived, described, expressed, characterized, classified and known in the same way?"[69]

In the absence of known external determinants (events) or internal determinants (laws), Foucault turned again to a description of the "mutations" themselves and the patterns formed by these transformations. Typically, Foucault examined the phases of the mutation from Classical to Modern thought synchronically rather than diachronically, that is, he stressed the relations between simultaneous transformations more than those between successive transformations. He also refused to explain the "mutation of Order into History" in terms of conventional categories such as vitalism and romanticism because he insisted that these concepts are themselves merely the "surface effects" of deeper archaeological shifts.[70]

On the archaeological level, the shift from the visible, static order of the Classical table of knowledge to the hidden life processes of the Modern episteme signaled more than the birth of history as an "empirical science of events"; it announced the emergence of history as a new "mode of being."[71] This shift, however, occurred only in the second phase of the "mutation." During the first phase "the fundamental mode of being of the positivities does not change; men's riches, the species of nature, and the words with which languages are peopled, still remain what they were in the Classical age: double representations."[72] With Adam Smith, for example, the concept of labor still functioned within a system of representation. But as soon as wealth represented labor rather than objects of desire, time displaced things as the basis of exchange. The analysis of wealth thus shifted from a spatial to a temporal orientation and this led to two new forms of thought: an economics based on production rather than exchange, and an "anthropology" that defined man in terms of his alienated relation to time.

A similar displacement occurred in natural history. With Lamarck, Jussieu, and Vicq d'Azyr, natural beings were still classified on the basis of structures, but these structures were no longer external, visible, and unchanging forms. The principal structures were now organs concealed deep within the body that were significant not because the same organ recurred in different beings but because organs perform vital functions. It became difficult, then, to identify natural beings by describing (naming) their appearance. "The parallelism between classification and nomenclature is thus, by this very fact, dissolved. . . . language and nature cease to be automatically interlocked. The order of words and the order of beings no longer intersect except along an artificially defined line."[73] Moreover, as organic structures became the basis for classification, a new discontinuity was introduced into the perceptions of natural beings—that between organic and inorganic beings. With the perception of life as a basic category, "something resembling a biology became possible" while at the same time Bichat's anatomical studies marked the emergence of the modern perception of death.[74]

A parallel shift also occurred, although somewhat more slowly, in language analysis. As with the concepts of labor and organic structure, word inflections were known before the late eighteenth century, but they had not previously served as a basis for ordering knowledge. With William Jones and his contemporaries, analysis turned from an examination of the way language systems were articulated (nominative function) to a comparison of changes in different language systems, in particular, to a comparison of root changes. According to Classical language theory, there were a small number of unvarying roots that designated primitive cries or gestures. As Jones demonstrated, however, if one compared the conjugations of verbs in Sanskrit, Greek, and Latin, it became apparent that the roots varied while the inflectional systems were analogous.[75]

In all three discourses, then, temporal processes displaced spatial relationships in the classificatory systems that ordered knowledge. As Foucault explained, "what came into being with Adam Smith, with the first philologists, with Jussieu, Vicq d'Azyr, or Lamarck, is a minuscule but absolutely essential displacement, which toppled the whole of Western thought: representation has lost the power to provide a foundation."[76] Words could no longer represent things because things had "escaped from the space of the table" and turned toward "an *internal* space" that could not be re-presented.[77] Consequently, instead of naming things, words began to function, as they had during the sixteenth century, as signs that signified interpretations of things rather than the things themselves. In the Modern episteme, however, words interpreted the meaning of things for man rather than for God, and thought emerged from and turned back on man.

This shift from representation to self-representation was evident in philosophy as well as in the empirical sciences and can best be seen by comparing Ideology (Destutt de Tracy) to critical philosophy (Kant). Ideology was an attempt to make philosophy scientific by representing sensation by words. It was therefore still within the Classical system of representation, although Foucault considers Ideology "the last of the Classical philosophies."[78] The Kantian critique, which was developed at the same time, belonged instead to the first phase of the formation of the Modern episteme. Kant had not attempted to represent thought; he set out to discover the a priori conditions for thought itself. Between these two philosophies emerged a widening gap that divided philosophy into the poles of formalization (science) and interpretation (metaphysics) and that separated the philosophical "field" from the epistemological "field," thereby shattering the unity of the Classical *mathesis* (see fig. 1). Significantly, these divisions, which characterize the Modern episteme, are the very divisions that Foucault's "archaeology" seeks to bridge by making philosophy both scientific and critical and by reconnecting the metaphysical and epistemological "fields."

Within the new metaphyiscal space of interpretation, another split occurred, separating the transcendental subject (the source of meaning) from transcendental objects such as Life, Labor, and Language. This split, indicated on Foucault's diagram in figure 1 by the terms "meaning" and "history," coincided with the second phase of the mutation in Western thought that gave birth to the Modern episteme. According to Foucault, "what changed at the turn of the century, and underwent an irremediable modification, was knowledge itself as an anterior and indivisible mode of being between the knowing subject and the object of knowledge. . . . Production, life, language—we must not seek to construct these as objects that imposed themselves from the outside. . . . They are fundamental modes of knowledge."[79]

Production, for example, signified both the subjective activity of the producer and the objects produced. This new form of knowledge was incompatible with the older analysis of wealth, which was based on the circulation of objective things within a closed system. With Ricardo the "circular and surface causality" of circulation was replaced by the perception of a "great linear, homogeneous series which is that of production."[80] Moreover, since political economy severed the connection between labor and wealth (labor and wealth no longer represented each other, as they had with Adam Smith), a new theory of value emerged. For Ricardo labor did not represent goods; it represented the value of goods, a value that varied with historical processes. These processes needed to be made intelligible, and, according to Foucault, Ricardo and Marx provided the two interpretations possible within the assumptions of the new discourse of political economy. Both interpretations were based on the perception that biological need (consumption necessary for life) determined scarcity and that nature was not infinitely abundant but was rapidly being depleted. These perceptions were themselves reducible to a single perception: the death of man and nature. Both Ricardo and Marx structured their theories around the threat of death, but in Ricardo's view time moved inexorably toward death, whereas Marx believed that History would stop and Man would live. For Foucault, however, these two theorists were not themselves important. "What is essential is that at the beginning of the nineteenth century a new arrangement of knowledge was constituted, which accommodated simultaneously the historicity of economics (in relation to the forms of production), the finitude of human existence (in relation to scarcity and labor), and the fulfilment of an end to History—whether in the form of an indefinite deceleration or in that of a radical reversal."[81]

The replacement of the analysis of wealth by political economy was paralleled by an analogous displacement of natural history by biology. Just as economics indicated the primacy of production over circulation, biology reflected the dominance of function over structure. The flat and immobile space of Classical taxonomy was thus replaced, beginning with Cuvier, by an analysis that included both depth and time. This meant that the previous "grid" of knowledge, which classified beings in terms of visible identities and differences (form, number, situation, and proportion), was superseded by a new mode of classification based on a series of oppositions. In this classificatory system, primary organs which controlled vital functions such as respiration, circulation, and digestion were opposed to secondary organs; the spatial location of organs in the body was opposed to temporal organic processes; and visible differences between species were opposed by hidden, but fundamental, similarities.[82]

Cuvier's works, in particular his *Lessons in Comparative Anatomy* (1800), were important not merely as an indication of a new way of perceiving individual beings but also as a new way of perceiving the "spaces" between beings. In Classical taxonomy individual beings and the relationships between beings could be represented on a table. Moreover, the space between beings on the taxonomic table was homogeneous. These two features, which Foucault called the "representability" and the "continuity of being" (see fig. 1), constituted the metaphysical dimension of the Classical episteme. It was precisely "this fabric, ontological and representative at the same time, that is definitely torn apart by Cuvier."[83] Comparative anatomy located continuity within the organism and established a fundamental discontinuity between different organisms. It was no longer possible to visualize a filled taxonomic table as a series of adjacent beings, because life itself established an absolute division between beings. Moreover, the concept of life set up a new continuity that could not be represented on a table at all, the continuity between living beings and the environment necessary to sustain life.

Seen in this light, within the epistemological configuration of the Modern episteme, the traditional assessments of Cuvier and Lamarck are reversed. According to Foucault, Lamarck's "transformist intuitions" were not really prefigurations of evolutionary thought because Lamarck was still a Classical thinker. Nor was Cuvier's so-called fixism an indication of regressive thought; on the contrary, it was Cuvier who made the new discourse of biology possible.[84] Cuvier, then, cannot be compared to Lamarck, but he can be seen as an inverted image of Ricardo, since political economy was based on a new perception of death whereas biology reflected a new perception of life.

Cuvier can also be compared to Bopp, whose *Comparative Gram-*

mar (1833) represents the same epistemological shift as Cuvier's *Comparative Anatomy*. The parallel between these two disciplines was recognized by a few astute thinkers of the time such as Friedrich von Schlegel, who noted in 1808 that "the structure of comparative grammar of languages furnishes as certain a key of their genealogy as the study of comparative anatomy has done to the loftiest branch of natural science."[85] Just as natural beings were suddenly viewed as organisms that changed through time, languages were perceived as living forms that could be classified on the basis of their shared genealogies. Bopp's research was particularly significant for the new philology because his grammatical analysis of Sanskrit suggested a common ancestry for the Indo-European languages. Moreover, Bopp's diachronic study of languages introduced the same discontinuity into the "space" of Classical representation as Cuvier had introduced into Classical taxonomy. Since languages were now viewed as organisms, each language was isolated within its own identity and all the "spaces" between languages could never be filled.

The Classical concept of derivation (language changes) was not the only aspect of the "quadrilateral of language" to be altered as general grammar was replaced by comparative grammar. Designation, which had previously been expressed in a theory of the roots of nouns, was now expressed in a theory of inflection and in the study of verb roots that "designate not 'things' but actions, processes, desires, wills."[86] Likewise, articulation no longer described fixed elements within written language systems. It expressed the internal variations of spoken languages and phonetics then became a major area of study. Finally, attribution no longer meant that a language derived its identity from its capacity to represent things; it owed its identity to the unique way representative elements (words) and nonrepresentative elements (sounds and syllables such as those necessary for inflection) united syntactically to endow each language with life. Consequently, Classical criticism, which evaluated languages in terms of presumed differences in their ability to represent thought, was replaced by a new perception in which "all languages have an equal value" and "primitive" languages began to be studied seriously.[87]

With the emergence of philology as a new science, language ceased to be a representation of thought in general and became merely another historical object. It could no longer serve as a model for other discourses, as it had during the Classical period, and was instead dispersed throughout the fabric of the Modern episteme. Yet this very dispersal carried with it important consequences. Within the philosophical "field," now polarized between formalization and interpretation, language played various roles. The attempt to formalize language (to make it scientific) led to efforts to create both a value-free language and a nonverbal language (symbolic logic). The attempt to discover in language the cultural traditions of the past led to the major interpretive efforts of the nineteenth century. According to Foucault, "the first book of *Das Kapital* is an exegesis of 'value'; all Nietzsche is an exegesis of a few Greek words; Freud, the exegesis of all those unspoken phrases that support and at the same time undermine our apparent discourse, our fantasies, our dreams, our bodies."[88]

More significant than even these interpretive and scientific efforts was the birth of modern literature. Literature, which Foucault defines as the mode of being of language when it takes itself as its object, was born under circumstances of almost cosmic intensity. As Foucault describes this event, "at the beginning of the nineteenth century, at a time when language was burying itself within its own density as an object . . . it was also reconstituting itself elsewhere, in an independent form, difficult of access, folded back upon the enigma of its own origin and existing wholly in reference to the pure act of writing."[89] Modern literature, in Foucault's imagery, is the "singularity" that remains after the the collapse and dispersion of the previously unified being of language. Instead of representing thought in general or specific things in the world, modern literature represents man conscious of himself as a verbal being. Consequently, literature has become a form of self-representation and "there is nothing for it to do but to curve back in a perpetual return upon itself."[90]

Nineteenth-century literature was not the only "human science" that reflected the emergence of a new perception of man. Like modern literature, the discourses of psychology and sociology could not have existed if the empirical sciences had not made life, labor, and language historical. Once the perceptions of organic life, economic production, and historical languages took shape, it was possible to develop a concept of man as a species being (psychology), a producing being (sociology), and a verbal being (literature). Man had now become that being which existed as both the conscious subject of knowledge and the unconscious object of historical processes. Such a perception would have been impossible during the Classical period because man was then perceived merely as a knowing subject.

For Foucault, then, Man is "a quite recent creature . . . but he has grown old so quickly that it has been only too easy to imagine that he has been waiting for thousands of years in the darkness for that moment of illumination in which he would finally be known."[91]

This Modern perception of man forms the basis for all those humanistic philosophies which Foucault refers to pejoratively as "anthropology." From Kant to Sartre philosophy has interpreted the being of man, and it is this discourse that most concerns Foucault. As before, Foucault describes the discursive "field" of Modern thought in terms of a quadrilateral, but in his philosophical quadrilateral new categories are introduced. Instead of attribution, Foucault refers to "the analytic of finitude"; in place of articulation, he discusses an "empirico-transcendental doublet"; instead of designation, he examines the "unthought"; and, finally, in place of derivation, he analyzes "the retreat and return of the origin." These concepts, which resemble the more traditional philosophical problems of determinism (finitude), subject-object (empirico-transcendental), unconscious (unthought), and past-present (origin), have specific functions in the Modern episteme.

In the Classical episteme, attribution was expressed in philosophical discourse merely by asserting being ("I think therefore I am"). In the Modern episteme existence became historical and was thus both predetermined and finite. It was no longer possible to equate thought and being because "in one sense, man is governed by labor, life, and language: his concrete existence finds its determinations in them; it is possible to have access to him only through his words, his organism, the objects he makes."[92] To know man would now require reflecting on a being whose physical, social, and cultural essence preceded his existence. Man had become a creature whose body died, whose desires directed his activity, and whose words were formed before his birth.

Knowledge of man in the Modern period could not, therefore, be acquired by "articulating" a table of similarities and differences among natural beings and placing man on it. It could only be acquired by making man an object for a consciousness capable of transcending historical determinisms. This, Foucault believes, resulted in two kinds of analysis: one that studied man as a physical entity and one that studied man as a social being. Both types of analysis are necessary and complementary forms of thought made possible by the Modern episteme. According to Foucault, however, the requirement that man be an "empirico-transcendental doublet" may be an impossible demand, and the question then arises whether man as a unified being really exists. Nietzsche suspected, and Foucault obviously agrees, "that our modern thought about man, our concern for him, our humanism, were all sleeping serenely over the threatening rumble of his non-existence."[93]

Man's nonexistence is "designated" in Foucault's quadrilateral by the presence of man's "double." This double, which Foucault calls the "Other" or the "unthought," refers not to a personal unconscious but to a collective unconscious. Both the concept of Man and the concept of the Other emerged simultaneously with the Modern episteme. Neither concept would have been possible in the Classical episteme, since man was then an individual, thinking subject rather than the shifting locus of collective and unconscious determinisms. Both concepts, however, have so dominated Modern philosophy that whenever a philosophy of man emerged, his double also appeared. For Hegel the "unthought" was the *an sich*; for Marx it was alienated man; for Schopenhauer it was *das Unbewusste*; and for Husserl it was the "inactual."[94] In every case an effort was made to reconcile man to his double, that is, to integrate thought with being. According to Foucault, "the whole of modern thought is imbued with the necessity of thinking the unthought—of reflecting the contents of the *In-itself* in the form of the *For-itself*, of ending man's alienation by reconciling him with his own essence . . . of lifting the veil of the Unconscious, of becoming absorbed in its silence, or of straining to catch its endless murmur."[95]

The last segment of the quadrilateral (derivation) refers to the Modern conception of the past. In the Classical period the past was understood in terms of an "ideal genesis," an irreducible moment in an irretrievable past. For natural history this meant a full "table"; for the analysis of wealth it meant the original form of exchange (barter); and for general grammar it meant an archaic body language.[96] In the Modern period, such a perception of the past was replaced by a new conception of "origin." Although the origin of things such as species, products, or words now receded indefinitely into the past, it could still break through to the present (a notion that is called the return of the repressed in Freudian thought). Man in the Modern period, then, possesses an origin but not a beginning. As Foucault explains, "origin, for man, is much more the way in which man in general, any man, articulates himself upon the already-begun of labor, life, and language. . . . The original, as modern thought has never ceased to describe it since *the phenomenology of mind*, is thus very different from that ideal genesis that the Classical age had attempted to reconstitute."[97] Since Hegel, Modern philosophy has been faced with the impossibility of locating a genesis (a beginning) for man and the necessity to see man as infinitely repeating himself against the "already-begun" of the Other. Foucault believes that this explains the failed attempts of Hegel, Marx, and Spengler to annihilate time by postulating a completion, cessation, or regression of History. It also explains the opposite efforts of Hölderlin, Nietzsche, and Heidegger not to withdraw toward the sameness of a beginning but to open themselves to the retreat and return of the origin.[98]

These four sides of the philosophical quadrilateral no longer represent the order of things. They represent man's representation of his own "mode of being," a self-representation that divorces words from things and throws thought back on the words in which thought is expressed. In attempting to define his own being, man has thus reintroduced the being of language. Contemporary philosophy, Foucault concludes, must awaken thought from its "anthropological sleep" and examine, without returning to Classical discourse, language itself and the way the order of words represents other words rather than nature or man. This, obviously, is Foucault's own project and he sees himself somewhere between the Modern episteme and a new, yet unformed, epistemological structure: "In attempting to reconstitute the lost unity of language, is one carrying to its conclusion a thought which is that of the nineteenth century, or is one pursuing forms that are already incompatible with it? . . . I do not know what to reply to such questions. . . . Nevertheless, I now know why I am able, like everyone else, to ask them."[99]

The Contemporary Episteme

Since Foucault regards the present as a transition period, he has not described the "shape" of knowledge in our time. What he has done instead is to locate the human sciences in the nineteenth-century "field" and to suggest how the twentieth-century counterhuman sciences are altering the basic configuration of Modern thought. When one examines Foucault's diagram (fig. 1), it becomes immediately apparent that the human sciences are missing. They are not located at either pole of the philosophical field, nor are they present in the epistemological field where biology, political economy, and philology have been placed. They exist, rather, in the "space" behind these fields and maintain a precarious balance between the formalized discourses (mathematics and analytic philosophy), the interpretive discourses (history and metaphysics), and the empirical sciences. In language simultaneously poetic and scientific Foucault reflected that "it is perhaps this cloudy distribution within a three-dimensional space that renders the human sciences so difficult to situate, that gives their localization in the epistemological domain its irreducible precariousness, that makes them appear at once perilous and in peril."[100] Although the human sciences cannot be precisely located, they lie on the same "plane" as the empirical sciences and have similar "forms." But they did not evolve from the empirical sciences and should not be confused with them. Biology, economics, and philology examine life, labor, and language, but do not interpret these activities in terms of what they mean for man; they attempt to examine these processes in themselves. By contrast, psychology, sociology, and literature-myth address themselves directly to the question of what it means for man to represent himself as a being who lives, works, and speaks.

In spite of the distance separating the empirical and the human sciences, Foucault implies that a causal relationship exists because the human sciences established their "positivity" on the basis of concepts borrowed from the empirical sciences. What has been transferred, however, are not mathematical models or images, such as organic metaphors in sociolgy or energy metaphors (Janet) and geometrical metaphors (Lewin) in psychology, since Foucault claims that these have no "operational efficacy."[101] Instead, Foucault has isolated three pairs of "constituent models" which were formed in the empirical sciences and function as categories of thought in the human sciences. These constituent models are the biological concepts of function and norm, the economic concepts of conflict and rule, and the linguistic concepts of signification and sign system. Biology studies organisms (including man) in terms of their vital functions and their ability to adjust to the norms of their environment. Economics perceives men coming into conflict in their efforts to satisfy desires and being forced to establish rules to limit such conflicts. Language analysis includes both a study of the meanings (significations) of human expressions and a study of the sign systems that make these expressions coherent.[102] Although each of the human sciences uses all six of these concepts, Foucault believes that the associations between psychology and the study of man in terms of functions and norms, sociology and the study of human conflicts and rules, and linguistics and the study of significations and systems identify each of these discourses as distinct entities.

The relative importance of these pairs of constituent models, as well as the relative importance of each component in these three pairs, shifted over the course of the nineteenth century. The biological model dominated the human sciences during the early part of the century when man, society, and language were viewed by the Romantics as living organisms. The economic model predominated at mid-century when Comte and Marx developed their sociological theories. By the end of the century, the philological model was preeminent as Nietzsche the philologian sought hidden significations in value-loaded words and Freud uncovered fundamental sign systems in his patients' verbal and nonverbal expressions.[103] While the human sciences were shifting "from a form more dense in living models to another more saturated with models borrowed from language,"[104] another shift occurred within each pair of models. At the beginning of the century processes (function, conflict, signification) were stressed; by the turn of the century structures (norm, rule, system) predominated. This shift, which can be seen by comparing the sociologies of Durkheim and Mauss or the psychologies of Janet and Goldstein, meant that "it was no longer possible to speak of 'morbid consciousness' (even referring to the sick), of 'primitive mentalities' (even with reference to societies left behind by history), or of 'insignificant discourse' (even when referring to absurd stories, or to apparently incoherent legends). Everything may be thought within the order of the system, the rule, and the norm."[105]

The relation between each term of the three pairs of constituent models has an internal as well as a historical significance. The first term of each pair (function, conflict, signification) refers to processes accessible to consciousness. The second term (norm, rule, system) refers to structures that are not conscious. Consequently, the human sciences can only approach the realm of the unconscious by using the concepts of function, conflict, and signification to represent the unconscious. Such a project would have been inconceivable in the Classical period when representation and consciousness were inseparable. Yet, since the human sciences do attempt to represent thought, they are closer to the Classical episteme than either the empirical sciences or the counterhuman sciences. The effort to represent the unconscious has also led to the repeated process of self-examination, which distinguishes the human sciences from other sciences. As Foucault explains, the human sciences "seek not so much to generalize themselves or make themselves more precise as to be constantly demystifying themselves. . . . We shall say, therefore, that a 'human science' exists, not wherever man is in question, but wherever there is analysis—within the dimension proper to the unconscious—of norms, rules, and signifying totalities which unveil to consciousness the conditions of its forms and contents."[106] This definition of the human sciences has two controversial implications. First, the human sciences are not, according to Foucault, sciences of "man"; they are explorations of the unconscious. Second, the human sciences are not "sciences" at all. There can be no science of man, not because man is too complex for systematic analysis but because it is impossible for man to be simultaneously a knowing subject and an object of knowledge.[107]

If the human sciences are not sciences and cannot be securely placed among either the formalized discourses or the empirical sciences, what then is their relation to the interpretive pole of the philosophical field? In particular, what is their relation to history? According to Foucault, the historicity of the empirical sciences did not emerge as a result of bourgeois man attempting to project his own evolution onto the order of things. On the contrary, man's self-image as a historical being came only after the formation of a new perception of the historicity of organic forms, economic processes, and spoken languages.[108] Moreover, the historicity of men as well as of economic, social, and linguistic forms implied the perception of a diversity of historical processes incompatible with earlier conceptions of history as a single "stream, uniform in each of its points, drawing with it in one and the same current . . . men . . . things and animals."[109] This Modern perception of multiple historical forms means that the human sciences must themselves be viewed as historical discourses and that they are bound, like history proper, to confine themselves to relating one historical form to another.[110]

While the human sciences lie "behind" Foucault's image of the epistemological and philosophical "fields," filling the "spaces" between the interpretive, formal, and empirical disciplines, the contemporary counterhuman sciences are diffused throughout the philosophical field. They have, indeed, largely replaced traditional philosophical discourse and are attempting to reintegrate the poles of formalization and interpretation. On the one hand, contemporary structural psychoanalysis (Lacan), structural ethnology (Lévi-Strauss), and structural linguistics (Dumézil, Greimas, and Martinet, for example) aim to uncover the deep structures that make it possible for the human sciences to represent norms, rules, and systems to consciousness. On the other hand, these same discourses hope to gain access to more fundamental forms of the unconscious without the intermediary process of representation. This latter effort presupposes that beyond the unconscious norms represented in life functions lies an even more fundamental experience of death. Likewise, beyond the unconscious rules regulating social conflicts lies the explosive force of desire; and beyond the unconscious systems determining the meanings of words lies a basic law of all language.

Death, desire, law, and the being of language are the four figures of Contemporary thought that are replacing the philosophical quadrilateral of the Modern period. To think today means to affirm the being of language, to articulate the form of death, to designate the reality of desire, and to derive the laws of one's own thought. None of these functions requires a concept of man. In fact, all of the structuralist sciences "dissolve man"; they are *counter*-human sciences which undermine the very attempt to create a science of man.[111] It appears, then, that "man is in the process of perishing as the being of language continues to shine ever brighter."[112]

The Disorder of Things

Foucault's "archaeology" is an unclassifiable discourse that functions simultaneously as philosophy, history, science, and literature, yet cannot be identified with any of these disciplines. It is recognizable as philosophy because it raises the two most fundamental questions posed in philosophical discourse: what does it mean *to be* and *to know*? But archaeology is not philosophy in any conventional sense. Foucault does not believe that ontological and epistemological questions can receive lasting answers but that each culture answers these questions in its own way. Since there are no transcendent truths, the philosopher today must become a historian and move from the study into the "archive."

But archaeology is not history in any conventional sense either. The historical periods Foucault has identified are not moments in a continuous historical process. They are distinct entities, unique in their own right, and isolated from each other. Yet they are not life forms that grow and die; they are systems that emerge fully formed and disappear abruptly. Since Foucault maintains that each culture represents a systematic (if unconscious) form of knowledge, he thinks that the past can only be understood by developing a "science" capable of decoding these unconscious systems. Foucault's archaeology claims to be such a science. It has attempted to confront the relativity of knowledge with a methodology based on the principles and imaginative vision of contemporary relativity theory. It aims to make philosophical reflection and historical analysis systematic by incorporating new concepts of space and time, by dissolving both subject and object, by introducing discontinuous changes, and by holding in suspension the irresolvable problem of causality. However, archaeology cannot be considered a science properly speaking because it possesses no procedures for verifying or rejecting its statements and has no established community of "archaeological" scholars to examine its propositions and apply its methods.

Since archaeology aspires to be a science of thought, it is committed to examining the relation between thought and language rather than that between thought and external "reality." Foucault does not claim to discuss "things"; he only studies words and the different ways in which words have represented things and other words. In fact, Foucault has concluded that things, and man in particular, cannot be known in our time. We can only know what language is, a knowledge that is itself determined by language. Consequently, language both "is" and "thinks" and man is merely its medium. Such an assessment may convince those theorists who are prepared to accept Foucault's "quadrilaterals" as deep structures which generate all the "discourses" characteristic of any cultural "language." It will be harder to persuade more empirical scholars, or just plain skeptics, that Foucault's linguistic structures are anything other than elaborate and artificial inventions.

The test (if there is one) of Foucault's method will be the plausibility of his reclassifications of major categories of thought and the possibility of applying his archaeological method to a wide range of issues. Thus far Foucault's methods have appealed primarily to literary critics, who welcome his unification of the categories of form and content and who assent to his apotheosis of language. Literary critics have also been dazzled by Foucault's brilliant metaphors and awed by his ability to make words radiate connotations and thus reveal multiple and unexpected meanings. Leading structuralist critics, here as well as in France, already regard *The Order of Things* and many of Foucault's literary essays as creative accomplishments of major importance.[113]

Foucault's bitterest critics, on the other hand, have come from the established schools of French thought. Existentialists, Marxists, and humanists from diverse disciplines refuse to accept Foucault's theory of a "positive unconscious" or his radical conception of discontinuous change. They are especially hostile to his rejection of man as both a knowing subject and a knowable object endowed with a universal human nature, a concept that they do not believe to be a recent invention dating only from the beginning of the nineteenth century. In leading French journals Foucault has been accused of "killing" history, dehumanizing man, and undermining rational thought.[114] One critic has even claimed that Foucault's nihilism is similar to Hitler's and that Foucault's archaeology expresses a rejection of the paternalistic authority of the present and a desire to return to the maternal womb of an irretrievable past.[115]

Although such criticism may raise important moral and political questions and throw some light on the psychosocial motivation of Foucault's analysis, it does not deal with the value of archaeology as a historical methodology. Foucault has broken with the usual classifications of social thought by which supposedly true modes of thought are opposed to apparently false or fictional modes (science-magic, rational-irrational, positivist-romantic, and normal-abnormal). But the question remains whether these oppositions can be replaced by other categories of thought and whether Foucault's categories can provide coherent explanations of cultural phenomena. Can the sixteenth century, for example, be better understood by erasing the distinction between science and magic that informs our own thought? Even if one grants that Foucault is correct in regarding sixteenth-century conceptions of money, natural beings, and words as "isomorphic" expressions of the same perception of "resemblances," can one really say that resemblances determined *all* thought during this period? To do so would make it impossible to regard Galileo or Kepler as "scientists" engaged in pursuits similar to those undertaken by modern scientists and would consequently make it impossible to write the history of science (or any history) from an evolutionary viewpoint.

Similarly, can one regard the Classical period in terms other than those that oppose rationalism to irrationalism? In Foucault's archaeologies, Classical thought was ordered but was neither rational nor irrational. It was representational and only that which could be represented was "seen." Those confined in the general hospitals were not only physically invisible; they did not "exist" at all, since their perceptions of reality did not fit into the Classical grid of knowledge. In their case, out of sight really did mean out of mind. Perhaps Foucault is also correct in claiming that the Classical discourses of life, labor, and language were based on a similar perception that excluded everything not visible and "orderable." But how far can one extend this analysis? Where, for example, does religion fit into the Classical system of representation?

Foucault's conception of the nineteenth century is even more complicated. He has replaced the usual "isms" with three main categories of thought: formal, interpretive, and epistemological. Furthermore, he asserts that all forms of knowledge in the nineteenth century can be located in relation to these basic categories. None of these categories, however, is representational, that is, none relates thought to things. In his scheme even the empirical sciences represented historical processes rather than objects. Likewise, the human sciences did not represent man as either a natural or a historical object. They represented man as a thinking being attempting to understand himself as a historical being, a task Foucault regards as inherently contradictory. Again, one wonders just how far such an analysis can be applied. Where, for instance, would Foucault place the physical sciences in the nineteenth century? Did they not represent "things" in the world?

Foucault's view of the Modern period has another relevant implication. Since Foucault regards nineteenth-century thought as interpretive rather than representational, he considers the distinctions between positivism and romanticism largely artificial. Foucault alluded to this earlier in *The Birth of the Clinic*, when he asserted that positivism and romanticism were born together in the new perception of death that emerged with Bichat's clinical anatomy and Sade's literary creations. Foucault is himself an example of the conflation of these two seemingly incompatible categories. Although he calls himself a positivist, others have termed him a romantic. Gilles Deleuze once referred to him as a "romantic positivist," and this label appears accurate. If one focuses on Foucault's glorification of madness, death, and desire, his admiration for the mad poets of the nineteenth and twentieth centuries, his literary and pictorial imagination, or his moral nihilism and political anarchism, then one recognizes the archetypical romantic. If, however, one attends to his highly structured arguments, his formal systems, his detailed descriptions, and his encyclopedic scholarship, then he appears to be a modern positivist.

Of all the oppositions Foucault has attempted to undermine, one in particular runs consistently (if opaquely) through his works. The opposition between normal and abnormal made it possible to view the mad as mentally ill, to identify diseases with pathological reactions, and to regard criminals as deviants. Without this opposition modern psychology and sociology could hardly exist, since these human sciences require a notion of normalcy that did not exist before the nineteenth century and that seems to be in the process of disappearing with the twentieth-century counter-human sciences. Although Foucault does not discuss the unitary perception that might replace the normal-abnormal polarity, one can guess that it would be a perception of value-free differences. This would satisfy both the romantic impulse to cherish the uniqueness of each being and the structuralist requirement that systems be defined by the differences between their elements.

It is ironic that while trying to collapse binary categories within each of his epistemes Foucault seems to have set up binary relations between epistemes. Although he would claim that his four epistemes are merely different, the sixteenth and nineteenth centuries appear to represent interpretive modes of knowledge, whereas the Classical and Contemporary epistemes appear to be formalist systems. Foucault's history of Western thought may then be regarded not as a series of unconnected ruptures between periods, but as an endless oscillation between two modes of thought. And these modes resemble those very categories that Foucault attempts to reconcile by combining romanticism and positivism.

However, Foucault is not really attempting to determine whether the "history" of Western thought oscillates between binary forms, jumps erratically between an indeterminate number of unique forms, or progresses through stages as in Hegel's or Vico's philosophy of history. Foucault's primary intention is to demolish our conventional categories of thought and to render unbelievable the science-myths that organize our perception of the past. He is likely to be more successful as a destroyer than as a creator. The new science-myths he offers for our reflection are too complex to persuade by their imaginative power and too unprovable to persuade by their systematic rigor. If they are believable, it is because traditional evolutionary history no longer appears convincing and because archaeology seems to fit in with other assumptions of contemporary thought. One of these assumptions is that order is imposed upon a fundamental disorder. Thus is does not really matter if Foucault's epistemes are only formal structures. All thought, including scientific thought, is an invention superimposed on an essential chaos. Archaeology and modern physics can be viewed as "isomorphic" forms of thought which both present "a view of chaos *beneath* order—or what is the same thing, of order imposed on a deeper and more fundamental chaos. This is in startling contrast to the view developed and solidified in the three centuries from Kepler to Einstein, a view of order beneath chaos."[116]

EPILOGUE:

BEYOND ARCHAEOLOGY

Since completing *The Archaeology of Knowledge*, Foucault appears to be engaged in yet another methodological experiment. In contrast to his earlier "archaeologies," Foucault refers to his recent books as "genealogies." By this Nietzschean term, Foucault signals a shift in emphasis from unconscious perceptual structures to concrete power relations. Given this new stress on "nondiscursive" (institutional) change, Foucault's study of the French penal system resembles historical analysis, although it is still too speculative to be regarded as conventional history. His most recent study of sexuality (the first volume of a projected six-volume work) is even more difficult to classify. This study appears to combine archaeological and genealogical analyses to expose the relations between knowledge, power, and truth in the history of sexuality since the Middle Ages.

In various articles and interviews, Foucault has acknowledged that his recent works are to some degree a result of the revolutionary events of May 1968. His more tentative earlier efforts to develop a theory of power were frustrated by a lack of support from French leftist intellectuals still tied to Marxist dogma. The 1968 uprising seriously discredited the established parties and created an atmosphere more conducive to an independent analysis of power. Although Foucault uses concepts taken from Marx, he does not regard power as a substance "possessed" by a class or by the state, nor does he view economic change as the sole determinant of social change or a totalizing ideology as an adequate interpretation of complex social phenomena. Moreover, his criticism of socialism is as harsh as his critique of capitalism, and for similar reasons. While none of this may seem remarkable to an Anglo-American audience, it has proved quite disturbing to French intellectuals and accounts for much of the current French debate on Foucault's work.

In a thematic if not methodological sense, *Discipline and Punish: The Birth of the Prison* and *The History of Sexuality, Volume I: An Introduction* can be viewed as a continuation of Foucault's earlier studies. Foucault had previously argued that psychiatry, medicine, and the human sciences all developed classifications that justified the rejection and confinement of "abnormal" or "deviant" individuals. He traced this process of exclusion to modes of thought formulated during the eighteenth century, an age usually praised for its rationalism and humanitarianism. But in these earlier works Foucault had not analyzed how the process of normalization and exclusion functioned, and he had focused his attention on only two institutions, the asylum and the hospital. In *Discipline and Punish*, however, he examines a number of confining institutions, primarily prisons, but also schools, barracks, and factories. And his current history of sexuality extends the study of normalization to children, women, perverts, and races.

Foucault's study of the birth of the prison bears a curious relationship to his earlier study of the birth of the clinic. Both works cover the same chronological and geographical ground—the period between 1750 and 1850 in France. Both works also deal with a radical new perception of the body, and both explore the relationship between "scientific" knowledge and confinement. Yet these two works represent the extremes of Foucault's methodological approaches. *The Birth of the Clinic*, Foucault's first "archaeology" and the one most closely tied to structural analysis, is concerned almost exclusively with spatial relationships and unconscious forms of perception. One has to struggle to orient oneself in time, there are few references to known historical figures or events, and the argument proceeds at a high level of abstraction. *Discipline and Punish*, by contrast, makes explicit references to dates, places, and sources and combines abstract analysis with direct exposition and imagery. Although it too is concerned with spatial relationships, there is a clear narrative line, making this the most readable of Foucault's works.

Discipline and Punish begins with a grisly description of the execution of Damiens, who was condemned for regicide in 1757. The punitive process followed the established judicial pattern: a secret interrogation modeled on the principles of the Inquisition; judicial torture designed to extract a confession and assure conviction; and public punishment, in this case death by slow and meticulous physical torture. Torture was essential to this system because "it revealed truth and showed the operation of power. It assured the articulation of the written on the oral, the secret on the public, the procedure of investigation on the operation of the confession; it made it possible to reproduce the crime on the visible body of the criminal; in the same horror, the crime had to be manifested and annulled. It also made the body of the condemned man the place where the vengeance of the sovereign was applied, the anchoring point for a manifestation of power, an opportunity of affirming the dissymmetry of forces."[1]

By the end of the century, a large number of lawyers and magistrates demanded a reform of the judicial system. Their motives were more pragmatic than humanitarian. These groups represented the interests of the rising middle class, which resented the privileges of the upper classes and regarded the variety of royal, religious, and secular courts as inefficient. They were also concerned with the rise in crimes against property and the vulnerability of capital investments such as factories, ports, and warehouses. Their goal was "not to punish less, but to punish better; to punish with an attenuated severity perhaps, but in order to punish with more universality and necessity; to insert the power to punish more deeply into the social body."[2] These reforming jurists proposed a major reclassification of crime and planned to draw up a "taxonomy" of crimes comparable to the Linnaean classification of species. They also sought to justify punishment not in terms of the vengeance of a sovereign king betrayed by his subject, but in terms of a violation of the "social contract" by one of the community of citizens.

For the reformers, the purpose of punishment was to transform, not eliminate, the criminal and to reincorporate him into society. This required altering his soul as well as controlling his body. To effect this change, the reformers proposed a number of measures: establish a fitness between crime and punishment that would make the pain of the punishment just greater than the pleasure of the crime; make the judicial process public and institute new rituals of shame and mourning to impress both the criminal and the public; modify the duration of the penalty to the change in the behavior of the criminal; and include confinement as one form of punishment. In general, these late eighteenth-century reformers were skeptical of the value of confinement. They regarded prisons as costly, secretive, and more likely to encourage criminal behavior than to eliminate it. But they accepted imprisonment as appropriate for certain offenses and were attracted to the model of the Walnut Street Prison, which opened in Philadelphia in 1790. In this Quaker-inspired prison, inmates were required to work and were regulated by a strict timetable of activities. They were carefully supervised, their behavior was recorded, and they were allowed very little social interaction.[3]

With the proposals of the reformers, there were three "technologies of power" available at the end of the eighteenth century: "the sovereign and his force, the social body and the administrative apparatus; mark, sign, trace; ceremony, representation, exercise; the vanquished enemy, the juridical subject in the process of requalification, the individual subjected to immediate coercion; the tortured body, the soul with its manipulated representations, the body subjected to training."[4] After the French Revolution, only one form of power remained. The monarchical system was destroyed and the reformers' proposals failed to find institutional expression, but the "administrative apparatus" became an entrenched reality. For the penal system, this meant that imprisonment became the dominant, almost exclusive, form of punishment. Despite the immediate recognition that prisons failed to reform criminals, confinement was accepted as an integral part of modern society. Moreover, the prison was only one of several examples of what Foucault calls a new "political anatomy" and a new "microphysics" of power.

Although prisons, as well as schools, barracks, hospitals, and factories, existed before the nineteenth century, these confining institutions assumed new functions in the industrialized societies of Western Europe. A mechanized, regulated, and impersonal social system requires a high degree of conformity, and all the major institutions reflected the effort to render individuals obedient and productive with a minimum of violence and expense. Soldiers, children, workers, patients, and criminals were all subjected to a disciplinary system that attempted to regulate their bodies and souls, their time and activities. The demographic explosion had created new masses to be divided into groups, subdivided into ranks, assigned fixed spaces, held to a strict timetable, trained to perform according to a precise regimen, supervised, judged, examined, and classified in the institutional records as cases. The process of hierarchical observation, normalizing judgment, and constant examination controlled the education of children, the training of soldiers and workers, and the care of patients. It was particularly obvious in the reformatories, which mirrored the larger society by incorporating within a single institution classrooms, workshops, and infirmaries. The disciplined life was not altogether new to Western societies; the monastic orders provided a model from the past. For Foucault, however, the relevant model for modern societies is the army. "Historians of ideas usually attribute the dream of a perfect society to the philosophers and jurists of the eighteenth century; but there was also a military dream of society; its fundamental reference was not to the state of nature, but to the meticulously subordinated cogs of a machine, not to the primal social contract, but to permanent coercions, not to fundamental rights, but to indefinitely progressive forms of training, not to the general will but to automatic docility."[5]

This military dream was prefigured in the social regulations established during plagues. By the seventeenth century, a city beset by plague quarantined its inhabitants, established a rigid system of surveillance, and carefully recorded the condition of individuals and groups. Surveillance on a wider scale was made possible by new arrangements of social spaces developed during the next century. Military camps and military schools in the early eighteenth century established circular structures with a central observation point, but it was only with Jeremy Bentham's *Panopticon* (1791) that this architectural principle was recognized as a pervasive technique for exercising power. Bentham's system of permanent visibility required a circular arrangement of individual cells walled in on the sides and penetrated front and back by windows, thereby illuminating the cell's occupant. A supervisor in a central tower, constructed with windows surrounding the outer wall only, could then observe each occupant without himself being seen. The occupant was thus effectively isolated from others and subject to constant surveillance. This panoptic principle, which was quickly adopted in prison design, was also applicable to hospitals, classrooms, and factories. The result was a generalized system of surveillance with an enormous expansion of police powers. It represented a political transformation equal to and parallel with the economic changes in the eighteenth century. "If the economic take-off of the West began with the techniques that made possible the accumulation of capital, it might perhaps be said that the methods for administering the accumulation of men made possible a political take-off in relation to the traditional, ritual, costly, violent forms of power, which soon fell into disuse and were superseded by a subtle, calculated technology of subjection. In fact, the two processes—the accumulation of men and the accumulation of capital—cannot be separated. . . . Each makes the other possible and necessary; each provides a model for the other."[6]

Viewed as part of this technology of subjection, the prison system cannot be regarded as a failure. It is only a failure if the purpose of prison is to rehabilitate the prisoner or reduce crime. These purposes have never been accomplished. For almost two centuries prisons have hardened rather than reformed their inmates and have had little success in preventing crime. The prison system persists because it fulfills other functions. One function is to prevent the more dangerous elements of the lower classes from gaining popular support. This became especially important after the French Revolution when workers and peasants resisted the new authority of the bourgeoisie, and it is still an important function today; it is no accident that poor people are the most frequent victims of crime.[7] Another function of the prison system is to separate unacceptable forms of illegality from tolerated illegalities. In effect, this means making "delinquency" a special category of crime and distancing delinquents from upperclass criminals whose activities are tolerated. A third function of the prison system, one closely tied to the other two, is to create a permanent criminal class which can then be used by more powerful social groups as informers, strike breakers, and middlemen in lucrative businesses such as prostitution and drug traffic.

The creation of a hardened criminal population serves yet another important role: it justifies a large police force and the extensive surveillance of the general population. It also justifies, indeed helps to create, our modern categories of normal and abnormal behavior and permits the growth of a whole range of professionals (including judges, lawyers, doctors, criminologists, teachers, psychologists, and social workers) who examine and classify vast segments of the population. This last function of the prison system most closely reflects the intimate connection between power and knowledge as well as the diffusion of power throughout society. The prison is only part of what Foucault calls a "carceral archipelago" and, like the rest of this network of power relations, it has succeeded very well. It has succeeded "in producing delinquency, a specific type, a politically or economically less dangerous—and, on occasion, usable—form of illegality; in producing delinquents, in an apparently marginal, but in fact centrally supervised milieu; in producing the delinquent as a pathologized subject."[8]

Foucault's history of the prison system concludes, as did his earlier works, with a critique of the normal-abnormal polarity central to both our social sciences and our social institutions. While developing this theme, he has combined a number of previously established concepts, such as the mechanization of man and the function of a lumpenproletariat, with a profusion of new insights and forceful images.[9] Perhaps most novel in this work is Foucault's insistence that the processes of normalization cannot be understood merely as a form of repression. Negative theories of repression (Marcuse's, for example) fail to account for the positive functions of knowledge-power in our society. Instead of repression, Foucault prefers the military model of conflict and regards all social interactions as a form of war. His language reflects this new orientation: he now speaks of tactics, strategies, and maneuvers. In attempting to define this new "genealogical" approach, Foucault has suggested applying the term genealogy "to the union of erudite knowledge and local memories which allows us to establish a historical knowledge of struggles and to make use of this knowledge tactically today."[10] He also distinguishes between archaeology as the methodology of the "analysis of local discursivities" and genealogy as "the tactics whereby, on the basis of the descriptions of these local discursivities, the subjected knowledges which were thus released would be brought into play."[11] His ongoing study of sexuality, which promises to be a major genealogical work, returns to the problems arising from the limitations of the theory of repression and develops an analysis based on the positive functions of power within social systems of constantly changing force fields.

The introductory volume of Foucault's history of sexuality, entitled *The Will to Know* in the French edition, outlines the assumptions guiding Foucault's current research. Like *The Archaeology of Knowledge*, this volume is a relatively brief reflection on theory and method. Unlike *The Archaeology of Knowledge*, however, it is not a systematic study of a methodology already applied; it is both a critique of an established theory (of repression) and a preliminary exploration of a new mode of analysis. The issues preoccupying Foucault are the endless fascination in the West with the "truth" of sex and the underlying presumption that this truth defines contemporary man, much as reason defined man's essential nature in the eighteenth century.

When he was writing *Madness and Civilization* over twenty years ago, Foucault had already planned a parallel work on sexuality, but at that time his analysis focused on the process of exclusion. Since then, he has reassessed his view of power and is more interested in the production of pathology than in its repression. Indeed, he now regards theories of sexual repression and their concomitant promise of liberation as part of the same network of power relations that controls the social body by classifying individual bodies in sexual terms.

According to the repressive hypothesis, a radical restriction in the discussion and practice of sex occurred between the seventeenth and twentieth centuries. The rise of the bourgeoisie was accompanied by a curtailment of nonproductive activity and a new moral asceticism, traits that intensified during the nineteenth-century Victorian regime. This repression is considered the cause of our present sexual misery, and we have only to throw off these constraints to rediscover the natural pleasure of sex. Of the flaws in this theory, the most significant is the assumption that the term "sex" refers to a single phenomenon central to our identity. Beyond this assumption, the repressive theory fails to account for the elaboration of a sexual consciousness and the development of a whole technology of sexuality which Foucault believes has taken place since the sixteenth century.

According to Foucault's genealogy, sex, like the body itself, is not a constant but a changing relation, as madness was in his earlier study. During the medieval period, sexual relations were merely one of many subjects discussed in the confessional and emphasis was placed on fulfilling marital obligations, not on illicit relations. In the sixteenth century, there was a sudden elaboration, not a restriction, in the discourse on the body. The Reformation and Counter-Reformation made the "flesh" a focus of new attention, and both Catholicism and Protestantism demanded a stricter examination of conscience that included the requirement to confess desires as well as acts. During the next two centuries, the discourse on "flesh" was replaced by a "science" of sexuality, which was part of a new political anatomy. Foucault contrasts this *scientia sexualis* with *ars erotica*, a form of knowledge largely absent in modern culture. While erotic knowledge is taught by a master to a select group of initiates who preserve a precious secret, the "scientific" knowledge of sexuality is extorted from and imposed on the bodies of vast numbers of people, and its "secret" is considered too base to be acknowledged. To the extent that *ars erotica* persists in our culture, it does so not as a pleasure of direct sensation but rather as an eroticization of the confessional and analytic processes.

During the nineteenth century Foucault claims that there was a second intensification of sexuality and that the modern concept of "sex" was formed. In this view, sex does not refer to a simple physical act but to the redefinition of women and children's sexuality and to the specification of social bodies (population) and abnormal bodies ("degenerate" individuals and races). Far from being a period of repression, the nineteenth century was a period of sexual incitement: the bourgeois family became the locus of rarified sexual relations; psychoanalysis emerged as a "confessional science"; and a new "medicine of sex," blithely ignorant of the science of plant and animal reproduction, established a "pornography of the morbid."[12] According to Foucault, "nineteenth-century 'bourgeois' society— and it is doubtless still with us—was a society of blatant and fragmented perversion. . . . Modern society is perverse, not in spite of its puritanism or as if from a backlash provoked by its hypocrisy; it is in actual fact, and directly, perverse."[13] It is perverse because the essential forms of human relations are all subject to a technology of sexuality that has invented a host of pathological forms and has spread from the bourgeoisie to all elements of society.

The twentieth century is now witnessing the consequences of the "bio-power" developed over the last three centuries. Western societies are no longer tied together by blood relationships and governed by legal prohibitions; they are penetrated by sexualized relationships and ruled by norms. Governments have expanded their powers from repressing transgressors of the law to controlling the life functions of whole populations. The grim result has been that modern conflicts assume the proportion of species struggles and that even genocide is accepted to preserve the "health" and security of a people. We are not in an age of diminishing repression, and Foucault does not believe that the "liberation" of sex will free us. He suggests that freedom is more likely to come from a desexualization of relations than from any of the contemporary forms of hyperconscious sexuality.

Given this overview of the genealogy of Western sexuality, Foucault intends to devote the remaining volumes to five specific forms of knowledge-power crucial to the deployment of sexuality: "the Christian notion of the flesh . . . , the sexualization of children, the hysterization of women, the specification of the perverted, and the regulation of populations—all strategies that went by way of a family which must be viewed, not as an agency of prohibition, but as a major factor of sexualization."[14] His objective is to develop an "analytic" of power that reveals the relationship between power and sex without relying on the older legal model of power relations. According to this older "juridico-discursive" model, power is essentially the power to refuse; it is expressed in rules, prohibitions, and censorship and is exercised uniformly throughout society. Yet Foucault maintains that in modern technological societies power affirms as well as refuses, is more effective in its elaboration than its prohibitions, and is exercised differentially (although extensively) throughout the social body. Moreover, he does not view power as the privileged possession of a sovereign ruler or select groups and institutions. He regards it "as the moving substrate of force relations" which can be coded "either in the form of 'war' or in the form of 'politics.'"[15]

Although Foucault does not develop a rigorous methodology in this slim volume, he does suggest four methodological rules for relating power and sex: the rules of immanence, variation, double conditioning, and polyvalence. By these he means that knowledge-power should be studied from "local centers" (such as the relation between penitents and confessors); that relations within groups change (as in the relations among parents, children, doctors, and teachers); that local and general relations of power condition, without duplicating, each other (as between the family and the state); and that the same discourse may serve as both an instrument of and a resistance to power (for example, homosexuality was established as a negative identity, but was then asserted by some individuals as a positive identity on the basis of the same discourse).[16] The purpose of these four rules is to establish a strategic model of power relations in place of the usual legalistic model.

In sum, this "positive" theory of knowledge-power and these tentative methods provide a sketch of Foucault's coming works. On its own, the introductory volume can hardly be considered more than a suggestive essay. The argument is diffuse and repetitive, and the thesis is presented by assertion and implication without supporting evidence. Foucault himself has called this work a "fabrication" and the entire project a "game."[17] It is obviously a serious game, one he has been planning for years. In many ways, Foucault has always said indirectly what this study promises to say directly: that abnormality is a creation of our culture, that power and knowledge combine to produce the pathological forms that define our bodies and souls, and that these forms are essential to our present social system. His own critique, whether "archaeological" or "genealogical," falls outside established academic disciplines, while touching them all. It is, perhaps, most closely related to the history of the life sciences as practiced by Georges Canguilhem, whose early study, *On the Normal and the Pathological*, deeply influenced Foucault.[18]

Foucault's archaeological works are already recognized as a significant contribution to the history of science, and his archaeological method points the way to a new "science" of history based on twentieth-century scientific models. Whatever the outcome of his current genealogical research, Foucault's status as one of the most paradoxical and provocative writers of our time is by now assured.

NOTES

Chapter 1

1. Foucault, the son of a physician, was born in Poitiers, France, in 1926. He attended the École normale supérieure, received the Licence de Philosophie (1948) and the Licence de Psychologie (1950) from the Sorbonne and the Diplôme de Psycho-Pathologie (1952) from the University of Paris. He was a lecturer at the University of Uppsala for four years and during 1959–60 was director of the Institut Français in Hamburg. During the 1960s he was director of the Institut de Philosophie at the University of Clermont-Ferrand and then professor of philosophy at the University of Vincennes. Since 1970 he has held the Chair of the History of Systems of Thought at the prestigious Collège de France. He is also an editor of the literary journal *Critique*, one of the directors of the leftist paper *Libération*, and a founder of Le Groupe d'Information sur les Prisons.

2. Michel Foucault, *L'Archéologie du savoir* (Paris: Gallimard, 1969), translated by A. M. Sheridan Smith as *The Archaeology of Knowledge* (New York: Harper and Row, 1972), pp. 21–23; hereafter cited in the English translation.

3. Foucault, *Archaeology of Knowledge*, pp. 47, 32, 37.

4. Ibid., pp. 93, 95.

5. Michel Foucault, *Folie et déraison: Histoire de la folie à l'âge classique* (Paris: Plon, 1961; abridged ed., 1964), translated by Richard Howard from the 1964 abridged edition as *Madness and Civilization: A History of Insanity in the Age of Reason* (New York: Random House, 1965); *Naissance de la clinique: Une archéologie du regard médical* (Paris: Presses Universitaires de France, 1963), translated by A. M. Sheridan Smith as *The Birth of the Clinic: An Archaeology of Medical Perception* (New York: Vintage Books, 1973); *Surveiller et punir: Naissance de la prison* (Paris: Gallimard, 1975), translated by Alan Sheridan as *Discipline and Punish: The Birth of the Prison* (New York: Pantheon, 1977); *Histoire de la sexualité, I: La volunté de savoir* (Paris: Gallimard, 1976), translated by Robert Hurley as *The History of Sexuality, Volume 1: An Introduction* (New York: Pantheon, 1978). The English translations will be referred to throughout this book.

6. Michel Foucault, *Les mots et les choses: Une archéologie des sciences humaines* (Paris: Gallimard, 1966), translated by Alan Sheridan-Smith as *The Order of Things: An Archaeology of the Human Sciences* (New York: Random House, 1970).

7. Raymond Bellour (interviewer), "Deuxième entretien avec Michel Foucault" (1967), p. 204.

8. See Suzanne Gillet-Stern, "French Philosophy over the Last Decade," p. 9.

9. Émile Bréhier, *Contemporary Philosophy–since 1850*. More recent studies of French philosophy include: Colin Smith, *Contemporary French Philosophy*; Joseph Chiari, *Twentieth-Century French Thought*; and Jean-Luc Chalumeau, *La pensée en France de Sartre à Foucault*. In *The Obstructed Path* H. Stuart Hughes views the 1930s, the decade with which Bréhier concluded his work, as the beginning of a period of desperation in French social thought. For Hughes the 1930s marked the end of the French classical tradition rooted in Cartesian rationalism and the beginning of a belated attempt to come to terms with the decline of French power and prestige. Hughes thinks that French intellectuals were handicapped by the isolation of France before and during World War II. Moreover, the dominance of Bergsonian and Durkheimian ideas made it difficult for postwar French theorists to assimilate the more radical critiques of rationalism developed by Freud and Max Weber. This provincial cultural environment during Foucault's youth may have motivated, in part, Foucault's own attack on Cartesian rationalism and his critique of social systems. Furthermore, like Foucault himself, Hughes sees a definitive change taking place in the mid-1950s.

10. Bréhier, *Contemporary Philosophy*, p. 243.

11. Gaston Bachelard, *Le nouvel esprit scientifique*, p. 48, as quoted in Bréhier, *Contemporary Philosophy*, p. 248.

12. Bréhier, *Contemporary Philosophy*, p. 249.

13. Eugène Dupréel, *Esquisse d'une philosophie des valeurs*, p. 239, as quoted in Bréhier, *Contemporary Philosophy*, p. 250.

14. Bréhier, *Contemporary Philosophy*, p. 253.

15. Ibid., p. 255. Although he referred briefly to Russell, Bréhier neglected analytic philosophy, which was slow to penetrate French thought and is consequently still being absorbed today. Foucault is clearly indebted to Russell and Wittgenstein in the sense that his own theories owe much to their stress on analysis, language, relational logic, description, criticism of metaphysics, and modern science.

16. See John Heckman, "Hyppolite and the Hegel Revival in France," pp. 128–45, which discusses French philosophical developments from the 1930s to the 1970s and traces the role of Hyppolite and his influence on a whole generation of philosophers that includes Foucault, Deleuze, and

Derrida. Also see Mark Poster, "The Hegel Renaissance," pp. 109–27, as well as that author's *Existential Marxism in Postwar France*, especially pp. 3–35.

17. Gillet-Stern, "French Philosophy," p. 3.

18. Ibid., p. 5. Among the works on Husserl published in the 1960s was a translation of Husserl's *L'origine de la géométrie* by the young philosopher Jacques Derrida.

19. The "groupe d'épistémologie" publishes the *Cahiers pour l'analyse*, a periodical Gillet-Stern describes as "in the Bachelardian line." This group posed a number of theoretical questions to Foucault, which he answered in the important article "Réponse au Cercle d'épistémologie," pp. 9–40.

20. Gillet-Stern, "French Philosophy," p. 6.

21. See Bernard Pingaud's introduction to "Sartre aujourd'hui," which begins as follows: "1945, 1960: pour mesurer le chemin parcouru entre ces deux dates, il suffit d'ouvrir un journal ou une revue et de lire quelques critiques de livres. Non seulement on ne cite plus les mêmes noms, on n'invoque plus les mêmes références, mais on ne prononce plus les mêmes mots. Le langage de la réflexion a changé. . . . On ne parle plus de 'conscience' ou de 'sujet', mais de 'règles', de 'codes', de 'systems' . . . on n'est plus *existentialiste*, mais *structuraliste*" (p. 1).

22. Paolo Caruso (interviewer), "Conversazione con Michel Foucault" (1967), pp. 94–95. I am grateful to my father, Dr. Stephen Major, for a translation of this important text.

23. Kant's *Anthropologie in pragmatischer Hinsicht* (1798) is an effort to define human nature and to develop a science of man. Kant contrasts the pragmatic perspective, the study of what man makes of himself, to the physiological perspective, which would examine what nature makes of man. This is precisely the kind of subjectivist philosophy Foucault rejects and he has referred to all such humanistic philosophies as "anthropology."

24. Foucault was introduced to Hegel through Hyppolite's classes. After Hyppolite's death in 1968, Foucault was among those of Hyppolite's students and friends who contributed essays to a volume entitled *Hommage à Jean Hyppolite* (Paris: Presses Universitaires de France, 1971). When Foucault assumed Hyppolite's chair at the College de France in 1970, he closed his inaugural address with a warm tribute to his predecessor. See Foucault's inaugural address *L'ordre du discours* (Paris: Gallimard, 1971), which has been translated by Robert Swyer as "The Discourse on Language" and published as an appendix to *The Archaeology of Knowledge*, pp. 215–37.

25. Madeleine Chapsal (interviewer), "Entretien: Michel Foucault," pp. 14–15. A further discussion of Foucault's assessment of Sartre (and of phenomenology) may be found in Caruso, "Conversazione con Michel Foucault," pp. 108–16. Foucault believes that philosophy has aspired to

total comprehension only since Hegel and that Husserl was the last philosopher with absolutely universalist claims. Sartre, he says, is a contemporary philosopher because for Sartre today philosophy is reduced to political action.

26. Jean-Paul Sartre, "Replies to Structuralism," p. 110. This is a translation of an interview with Sartre in *L'Arc* (1966).

27. Ibid., p. 112.

28. Ibid., p. 115.

29. Jean-Pierre El Kabbach (interviewer), "Foucault répond à Sartre," pp. 20–22. The original interview was abridged and broadcast on the radio. The interview published by *La Quinzaine littéraire* included portions Foucault had deleted from the broadcast (such as the reference to his association with the Communists and certain comments critical of Sartre). The following issue of *La Quinzaine littéraire* carried a letter by Foucault denouncing the publication of what he called a distorted and unauthorized version of the original interview. Foucault also indicated in this letter the great respect he has for Sartre's work and political action and his reluctance to have his own more modest historical and methodological efforts compared to Sartre's immense accomplishments.

30. Ibid., p. 21.

31. Cited in Caruso, "Conversazione con Michel Foucault," pp. 122–23.

32. Chapsal, "Entretien: Michel Foucault," p. 15.

33. Ibid.

34. Foucault, *Archaeology of Knowledge*, p. 7.

35. Ibid., p. 23.

36. Ibid., p. 24. Nonetheless, Foucault has himself participated in assembling the "complete works" of Nietzsche and Bataille. Foucault and Deleuze were jointly responsible for the French publication of the posthumous fragments of Nietzsche's *Gay Science*; see their introduction to *Le Gai Savoir*. Also see Foucault's foreword to Georges Bataille, *Oeuvres Complètes*, vol. 1, *Premier Écrits, 1922–1940*, for an outline of the chronological and thematic choices made in the collected works. Foucault regards Bataille, who died in 1962, as "un des écrivains les plus importants de son siècle." Besides his other literary works, Bataille founded the journal *Critique*, for which Foucault has been an editor for several years.

37. Foucault, *Archaeology of Knowledge*, p. 22.

38. Ibid., p. 21.   39. Ibid.

40. Ibid., pp. 21–22.   41. Ibid., p. 22.

42. Ibid., pp. 4–5. Foucault continued this discussion by noting that "the most radical discontinuities are the breaks effected by a work of theoretical transformation 'which establishes a science by detaching it from the ideology of its past and by revealing this past as ideological.' To this should be added, of course, literary analysis, which now takes as its unity,

not the . . . sensibility of a period, nor 'groups,' 'schools,' 'generations,' or 'movements,' nor even the personality of the author . . . but the particular structure of a given *oeuvre*, book, or text" (p. 5).

43. Traian Stoianovich, *French Historical Method.*

44. See Fernand Braudel's foreword to Stoianovich, *French Historical Method*, p. 10.

45. Martin Siegel, "Henri Berr's *Revue de synthèse historique*," p. 324. Also see Hughes, *Obstructed Path*, pp. 19–64.

46. Stoianovich, *French Historical Method*, p. 38.

47. See J. H. M. Salmon's review of *Écrits sur l'histoire*, by Fernand Braudel, p. 347.

48. Stoianovich, *French Historical Method*, pp. 78–82.

49. Salmon, review of Braudel's *Écrits sur l'histoire*, p. 348.

50. Stoianovich, *French Historical Method*, p. 121.

51. Ibid., pp. 118–19.

52. Ibid., pp. 158–59.

53. Ibid., pp. 159, 160–64.

54. See the article by Jacques Revel and Raymond Bellour entitled "Foucault et les historiens," pp. 10–13. Here Revel discusses what he believes to be fairly typical reactions of historians to Foucault. Despite Foucault's own statements that historians have recognized his works as historical, Revel believes that most French historians have had mixed reactions. *Annales* scholars at first mistook *Madness and Civilization* for a work on the "mentality" of past periods, and thought that Foucault was writing psychological history similar to theirs. Subsequently, according to Revel, they were baffled by *The Birth of the Clinic*, regarded *The Order of Things* as metaphysical, and did not read *The Archaeology of Knowledge*. Nevertheless, Revel acknowledges that historians have benefited from Foucault's recognition that historical "objects" are complex, that areas regarded as marginal (sorcery, death, festivals, madness) may indeed reveal how a society functions by indicating social limits, and that historical research must examine the rules by which historical time and space are organized. Revel also believes that Foucault's recent work *Discipline and Punish* has had a great influence on contemporary historians. In the same issue of *Magazine Littéraire*, also see the articles by Bernard-Henri Lévy and Philippe Venault, which discuss Foucault's works.

55. Stoianovich, *French Historical Method*, pp. 205–6.

56. Ibid., p. 215. Also see the comments of Pierre Nora (the editor of Gallimard's new series, Bibliothèque des Histoires) in Foucault, *Histoire de la sexualité*, vol. 1. For a further discussion by Nora of the "nouvelle histoire," see his interview with Jean-Jacques Brochier entitled "L'événement et l'historien du présent," *Magazine Littéraire* 123 (April 1977): 34–37. Also see Philippe Ariès, Michel de Certeau, Jacques Le Goff, Emmanuel

Le Roy Ladurie, and Paul Veyne, "L'histoire, une passion nouvelle: Table ronde," pp. 10–23; this work will hereafter be referred to as Ariès et al., "Table ronde." Refer also to Georges Canguilhem's comment that "malgré ce qu'en ont dit la plupart des critiques de Foucault, le terme d'archéologie dit bien ce qu'il veut dire. C'est la condition d'une *autre histoire* ("Mort de l'homme ou épuisement du *cogito?*" p. 607).

57. Stoianovich, *French Historical Method*, pp. 212–17.

58. Ibid., p. 215.

59. Ibid., pp. 218–22.

60. Foucault, *Archaeology of Knowledge*, pp. 29, 231 (the latter quotation is from Foucault's "Discourse on Language," included as an appendix).

61. Ibid., p. 230.

62. In particular, see his "Réponse au Cercle d'épistémologie," pp. 9–40; and his "Réponse à une question," pp. 850–74, which was translated into English as "History, Discourse and Discontinuity," *Salmagundi* 20 (Summer-Fall 1972): 225–48. The English translation is hereafter cited for the latter work. Also see Bellour, "Deuxième entretien avec Michel Foucault," pp. 189–207.

63. Bellour, "Deuxième entretien avec Michel Foucault," pp. 190, 189.

64. Ibid., p. 191. See also Caruso, "Conversazione con Michel Foucault," pp. 104–6, for a discussion by Foucault of older forms of linear history and his admiration for Braudel. For his part, Braudel also has a high regard for Foucault; see his foreword to Stoianovich, *French Historical Method*, p. 17.

65. Foucault, *Archaeology of Knowledge*, p. 10. Also compare Foucault's distinction between global and general history in "History, Discourse and Discontinuity," pp. 239–40.

66. Bellour, "Deuxième entretien avec Michel Foucault," p. 192.

67. Ibid., p. 197.

68. Ariès et al., "Table ronde," p. 20.

69. Foucault, *Archaeology of Knowledge*, p. 136.

70. Ibid., p. 138.

71. Raymond Bellour (interviewer), "Entretien avec Michel Foucault" (1966), p. 144.

72. Foucault, *The Order of Things*, pp. ix–x.

73. Foucault has referred to archaeology as the science of the "archive"; see Bellour, "Entretien avec Michel Foucault," p. 139. He has also stated that he "never presented archaeology as a science, or even as the beginnings of a future science"; see his *Archaeology of Knowledge*, p. 206. In discussing discursive formations, he once commented that "la distinction du scientifique et non scientifique n'est pas pertinente: elles sont épistémologiquement neutres." See Foucault, "Réponse au Cercle d'épistémologie," p. 32.

74. Jean-Claude Guédon, "Michel Foucault," p. 263.

75. Foucault, *Archaeology of Knowledge*, p. 187.
76. Ibid., p. 190.
77. Ibid., p. 187.
78. Ibid., p. 188.
79. Michel Serres, "Géométrie de l'incommunicable: La folie" (1962), pp. 167–90.
80. Gilles Deleuze, "Un nouvel archiviste," p. 209.
81. Foucault, *Archaeology of Knowledge*, p. 109.
82. Ibid., pp. 91, 87.
83. Ibid., p. 87.
84. See Deleuze, "Un nouvel archiviste," p. 201.
85. Foucault, *Archaeology of Knowledge*, p. 205.
86. Bellour, "Entretien avec Michel Foucault," p. 138.
87. Foucault, "History, Discourse and Discontinuity," pp. 226–27.
88. Foucault, *Archaeology of Knowledge*, pp. 114–15.
89. Foucault, "History, Discourse and Discontinuity," pp. 227–28.
90. Ibid., p. 228.
91. Ibid., p. 230.
92. Ibid., p. 231.
93. Ibid., p. 228. For a further discussion of Foucault's method of relating discourses to each other, see his *Archaeology of Knowledge*, pp. 157–65.
94. Foucault, *Archaeology of Knowledge*, p. 191.
95. Ibid., p. 192.
96. Foucault, "History, Discourse and Discontinuity," p. 228.
97. Foucault, "Discourse on Language," p. 216.
98. Ibid., pp. 216–19.   99. Ibid., p. 220.
100. Ibid., pp. 220–24.   101. Ibid., pp. 224–27.

Chapter 2

1. Jean-Jacques Brochier (interviewer), "Entretien sur la prison," p. 33.
2. Ibid.
3. Michel Foucault, "Nietzsche, Freud, Marx," pp. 183–200.
4. Michel Foucault, *The Order of Things*, p. xi.
5. Lévi-Strauss has been a major influence on Foucault, although Foucault does not consider himself a structuralist. In response to a question regarding his spiritual masters, Foucault once commented that he never fully resolved the conflict between his attraction to literary figures such as Blanchot and Bataille and his respect for the more positivistic studies of men like Lévi-Strauss and Dumézil. See Paolo Caruso (interviewer), "Conversazione con Michel Foucault," pp. 120–21.

6. Foucault, "Nietzsche, Freud, Marx," p. 183. The following discussion is, for the most part, a summary of this article.

7. Ibid., p. 186.

8. Ibid., p. 187.

9. For a discussion of the problem of origins, see Edward W. Said, *Beginnings*. See particularly *"Abecedarium Culturae"* (chap. 5 of this volume), in which Foucault is discussed. Said has also examined Foucault's works in an excellent article entitled "Michel Foucault as an Intellectual Imagination," pp. 1–36.

10. Foucault, "Nietzsche, Freud, Marx," p. 188.

11. Friedrich Nietzsche, *Beyond Good and Evil*, no. 39, as cited by Foucault in "Nietzsche, Freud, Marx," p. 188.

12. Foucault, "Nietzsche, Freud, Marx," p. 191.

13. Ibid., p. 192.

14. Ibid.

15. Raymond Bellour (interviewer), "Deuxième entretien avec Michel Foucault," p. 206.

16. Brochier, "Entretien sur la prison," p. 33.

17. Michel Foucault, "Nietzsche, la généalogie, l'histoire," English translation entitled "Nietzsche, Genealogy, History," in *Language, Counter-Memory, Practice*, ed. Donald F. Bouchard, pp. 139–64; hereafter cited in the English translation.

18. Ibid., p. 139.

19. Foucault has often referred to himself as an "archivist." When asked to define "archive," he once replied: "J'appellerai *archive*, non pas la totalité des textes qui ont été conservés par une civilisation, ni l'ensemble des traces qu'on a pu sauver de son désastre, mais le jeu des règles qui déterminent dans une culture l'apparition et la disparition des énoncés, leurs rémanence et leur effacement, leur existence paradoxale *d'événements* et de *choses* ("Réponse au Cercle d'épistémologie," p. 19).

20. Foucault, "Nietzsche, Genealogy, History," p. 139.

21. Ibid., p. 140. The similarity of Foucault's archaeological perception to theatrical and cinematic structure has occasionally been noted. Foucault himself once presented a lecture that he divided into five "acts." See Foucault's "Cérémonie, Théâtre et Politique au XVIIe siècle," pp. 22–23.

22. Foucault, "Nietzsche, Genealogy, History," p. 150.

23. Ibid., p. 151.   24. Ibid., p. 153.

25. Ibid., p. 154.   26. Ibid., p. 155.

27. Ibid., p. 157.   28. Ibid., p. 160.

29. Ibid.   30. Ibid.

31. Ibid., p. 161.   32. Ibid.

33. Ibid.   34. Ibid., p. 164.

35. Note, for example, the following passage: "Here we see clearly how

necessary a third way of looking at the past is to man, beside the other two. This is the 'critical' way, which is also in the service of life. Man must have the strength to break up the past, and apply it, too, in order to live. . . . The process is always dangerous, even for life; and the men or the times that serve life in this way, by judging and annihilating the past, are always dangerous to themselves and others" (Friedrich Nietzsche, *The Use and Abuse of History*, pp. 20–21).

36. Foucault, "Nietzsche, Genealogy, History," p. 162.

37. Ibid., p. 163. This passage is from Nietzsche's *The Dawn*, no. 429.

38. Friedrich Nietzsche, *The Genealogy of Morals*, p. 157. Nietzsche was here referring to *Zarathustra*, although this description applies to his other works as well.

39. Michel Foucault, "Résumés des cours donnés au Collège de France [Années 1970–74]," English translation of 1970–71 résumé entitled "History of Systems of Thought," in *Language, Counter-Memory, Practice*, ed. Donald F. Bouchard, p. 199; English translation cited hereafter unless otherwise noted.

40. The English translation does not indicate this distinction. The French reads: "distinction entre savoir et connaissance; différence entre volonté de savoir et volonté de vérité" (Foucault, "Résumés des cours," in Angèle Kremer-Marietti, *Foucault et l'archéologie du savoir*, p. 197). Foucault's course résumés from 1970 to 1974 have been included in an appendix to this work.

41. Foucault, "History of Systems of Thought," p. 201.

42. Ibid., p. 204.

43. Michel Foucault, ed., *Moi, Pierre Rivière, ayant égorgé ma mère, ma soeur et mon frère*. . . . (Paris: Gallimard, 1973), translated by Frank Jellinek as *I, Pierre Rivière, having slaughtered my mother, my sister, and my brother . . . : A Case of Parricide in the 19th Century* (New York: Pantheon Books, 1975).

44. Foucault defined these terms for the English translation of *The Archaeology of Knowledge* as follows: "By *connaissance* I mean the relation of the subject to the object and the formal rules that govern it. *Savoir* refers to the conditions that are necessary in a particular period for this or that type of object to be given to *connaissance* and for this or that enunciation to be formulated." See his *Archaeology of Knowledge*, p. 15n.

45. This quotation, presumably by Nietzsche, is cited in Albert Camus, *The Rebel*, p. 67.

46. After the appearance of *The Birth of the Prison*, the French newspaper *Le Monde* ran a full two-page coverage of the book, including an interview with Foucault and a discussion of his other works. At that time Foucault commented: "Mon discours est évidemment un discours d'intellectuel, et comme tel il fonctionne dans les réseaux de pouvoir en place.

Mais un livre est fait pour servir à des usages non définis par celui qui
l'a écrit. Plus il y aura d'usages nouveaux possibles imprévus, plus je serais
content. Tous mes livres . . . sont, si vous voulez, de petites boîtes à outils.
Si les gens veulent bien les ouvrir, se servir de telle phrase, telle idée, telle
analyse . . . pour court-circuiter, disqualifier, casser les systèms de pouvoir,
y compris éventuellement ceux-là mêmes dont mes livres sont issus . . .
eh bien, c'est tant mieux!" (*Le Monde*, 21 February 1975, p. 16).

47. Fons Elders once asked Foucault why he made a problem out of a
personal question, to which Foucault replied: "I'm not making a problem
out of a personal question, I make of a personal question the absence of a
problem." Elders, however, believes that "Foucault's psychology has a lot
to do with his philosophy." See *Reflexive Water: The Basic Concerns of
Mankind*, ed. Fons Elders (London: Souvenir Press, 1974), pp. 161–62
and 289.

48. Bellour, "Deuxième entretien avec Michel Foucault," pp. 201–2.

49. Jean-Louis Ezine (interviewer), "Sur la sellette: Michel Foucault,"
p. 3.

50. Michel Foucault, "Réponse à une question," English translation entitled "History, Discourse and Discontinuity," p. 225.

51. Ibid., p. 236.   52. Ibid., p. 237.

53. Ibid.   54. Ibid.

55. Ibid., p. 239.   56. Ibid., p. 245.

57. See Karl Mannheim, *Ideology and Utopia*, especially pp. 153–64; and
H. Stuart Hughes, "Is the Intellectual Obsolete?" in *An Approach to Peace
and Other Essays*, pp. 157–75.

58. J. P. Nettl, "Ideas, Intellectuals, and Structures of Dissent," in *On
Intellectuals: Theoretical Studies and Case Studies*, ed. Philip Rieff, p. 96.

59. Annie Guédez, *Foucault*, especially chap. 4 and the conclusion.

60. Michel Foucault and Gilles Deleuze, "Les intellectuels et le pouvoir,"
pp. 3–10. This discussion has been translated as "Intellectuals and Power,"
in *Language, Counter-Memory, Practice*, ed. Donald F. Bouchard, pp. 205–
17; English translation cited hereafter.

61. Robert D'Amico, "Introduction to the Foucault-Deleuze Discussion," p. 101.

62. Foucault and Deleuze, "Intellectuals and Power," p. 213.

63. Ibid., p. 212.   64. Ibid., p. 215.

65. Ibid., p. 216.   66. Ibid., p. 205.

67. Ibid., p. 206.   68. Ibid., pp. 207–8.

69. Ibid., p. 212.

70. Daniel and Gabriel Cohn-Bendit, *Obsolete Communism*, p. 250.

71. Marc Kravetz, "Qu'est-ce que le G.I.P.?" p. 13.

72. Serge Livrozet, *De la prison à la révolte* (Paris: Mercure de France,
1973).

73. K. S. Karol (interviewer), "Michel Foucault," abridged English translation entitled "The Politics of Crime," p. 456; hereafter cited in English translation.
74. Ibid., p. 455.
75. Ibid.
76. Claude Mauriac has published the details of this incident in rambling diary form; see his *Les espaces imaginaires*, pp. 274–95.
77. John K. Simon (interviewer), "A Conversation with Michel Foucault," pp. 193, 192, 198.
78. Ibid., p. 201.
79. Ibid., p. 195.
80. Ibid., p. 200.
81. See Michel-Antoine Burnier's introduction to *C'est demain la veille* (Paris: Editions du Seuil, [1973]), pp. 7–17. The interview with Foucault is reprinted in this collection on pp. 21–43.
82. Michel Foucault, "Revolutionary Action: 'Until Now,'" in *Language, Counter-Memory, Practice*, ed. Donald F. Bouchard, p. 223. This is an English translation of the *Actuel* interview with Foucault conducted by Michel-Antoine Burnier and Philippe Graine.
83. Ibid., p. 225.   84. Ibid., pp. 230, 233.
85. Ibid., p. 231.   86. Ibid., p. 221.
87. Ibid., p. 228.   88. Ibid., p. 230.
89. Noam Chomsky and Michel Foucault, "Human Nature: Justice versus Power," pp. 133–97. This was one of four debates between contemporary philosophers televised by the Dutch Broadcasting Foundation in 1971.
90. Ibid., pp. 137, 138.   91. Ibid., p. 149.
92. Ibid., p. 156.   93. Ibid., p. 160.
94. Ibid., p. 167.   95. Ibid., p. 169.
96. Ibid., p. 177.   97. Ibid., p. 181.
98. Ibid., p. 172.
99. Ibid., p. 171. In an interview with Paolo Caruso in 1967, Foucault claimed that a left-wing politics which "does not make use of all those confused humanist myths" was possible. He suggested that such a politics would be based on a definition of "optimal social functioning" arrived at by considering factors like demographic increase, consumption, and individual liberty. It would not, he said, consider human happiness, since "*happiness does not exist*, [and] *the happiness of men exists even less*." Men exist, he asserted, like animals, only to function and for no higher purpose. The fact that men can, to a certain degree, control their functions has given rise to the illusion that this control implies a purpose. Although Foucault claimed that he rejected "technocratic humanism," and even pointed out the interdependence of technology and humanism, his own discussion of

"optimal social functioning" suggests a technological vision stripped of humanism. See Caruso, "Conversazione con Michel Foucault," pp. 123–30.

100. Chomsky and Foucault, "Human Nature: Justice versus Power," p. 174.

101. Ibid., p. 175.

102. Ibid., p. 182.

103. Michel Foucault, "Sur la justice populaire," pp. 335–66.

104. Ibid., p. 337. Foucault was more receptive to intervention by the Red Army during what the Maoists called the "proletarian" revolution in China. He did not regard the Red Army as a third force, or even as a representative of the people; he viewed it as the embodiment of the masses themselves.

105. Ibid., p. 342.

106. Ibid., p. 346.

107. Camus, *The Rebel*, p. 46.

Chapter 3

1. According to Newton, "Absolute space, in its own nature, without relation to anything external, remains always similar and immovable." Cited from Isaac Newton's *Philosophiae Naturalis Principia Mathematica*, as reprinted in Milton Munitz, ed., *Theories of the Universe from Babylonian Myth to Modern Science*, p. 202. A brief discussion of Newton's allusion to relative space and his suggestion that there might be a center to the universe that would serve as a reference point can be found in Leon Cooper, *An Introduction to the Meaning and Structure of Physics*, pp. 357–59.

2. Leibniz and Kant both questioned Newton's concept of absolute space. At the age of twenty-three, in fact, Kant stated that Euclidean space was not the only possibility and that a science of all "possible kinds of space would undoubtedly be the highest enterprise which a finite understanding could undertake in the field of geometry." Quoted from Immanuel Kant's *Thoughts on the True Estimation of Living Forces* (1746), as cited in Lewis White Beck, *Early German Philosophy*, p. 447.

3. The concept of "difference" in modern structuralism is usually based on Saussure's definition of language as a system of distinguishable differences as opposed to the more traditional belief that language is a representation of reality. Foucault's use of the term *entropy* in the sense of systematic differentiation is the theme of his article "Monstrosities in Criticism," pp. 57–60. This article is a response to two critical reviews of *The Order of Things*: George Steiner's "The mandarin of the hour—Michel Foucault,"

pp. 8, 28–31; and Jean-Marc Pelorson's "Michel Foucault et l'Espagne," pp. 88–99. Foucault claimed that Pelorson's review aimed at "increasing entropy," because it tried to "efface whatever can distinguish the book about which he is speaking from any other" until the "maximum of entropy is thus attained." By contrast, Foucault charged Steiner with "decreasing entropy" by inventing so many distinctive features that he created "the most improbable phantasm imaginable of the book." Steiner answered Foucault's criticism in the winter 1971 issue of *Diacritics* (p. 59) and Foucault continued the hostilities by a second reply to Steiner in the same issue of *Diacritics* (p. 60).

4. Although the wave theory of light was fairly well accepted early in the century, experimental confirmation of the theory came in mid-century. One of the conclusive experiments was conducted by the physicist Jean Foucault, who proved that light traveled more slowly in water than in air, as the wave theory had predicted. See Stephen F. Mason, *A History of the Sciences*, p. 473.

5. See William Cecil Dampier, *A History of Science and Its Relation with Philosophy and Religion*, p. 221.

6. Albert Einstein and Leopold Infeld, *Evolution of Physics*, p. 119.

7. Ibid., pp. 146–47.

8. Ibid., p. 151.

9. See Ernst Cassirer, *The Problem of Knowledge: Philosophy, Science, and History since Hegel*, especially chap. 5 ("The Goal and Method of Theoretical Physics"), pp. 81–117.

10. Charles Coulson Gillispie, *The Edge of Objectivity: An Essay in the History of Scientific Ideas*, p. 505.

11. Bertrand Russell, *The ABC of Relativity*, pp. 140, 141.

12. Einstein and Infeld, *Evolution of Physics*, p. 205.

13. Ibid., p. 242.

14. Ibid., pp. 198–99.

15. Cassirer, *The Problem of Knowledge*, p. 34.

16. Jacques Merleau-Ponty and Bruno Morando, *The Rebirth of Cosmology*, p. 176.

17. Albert Einstein, "Considerations on the Universe as a Whole," a selection taken from Einstein's *Relativity: The Special and General Theory*, as reprinted in Munitz, *Theories of the Universe*, pp. 275–79. The Riemannian form of non-Euclidean geometry assumes that space is "positively curved" and thus "spherical." It is also possible to use a different form of non-Euclidean geometry which would assume that space is "negatively curved"; this would mean that space is "hyperbolic" and thus infinite. In contrast to both of these, Euclidean geometry assumes space to be "flat" and infinite. For a discussion of these three possibilities, see William J. Kaufmann III, *Relativity and Cosmology*, especially chap. 10 ("The Shape of the Universe").

18. Einstein and Infeld, *Evolution of Physics*, p. 240.

19. Russell, *The ABC of Relativity*, p. 126.

20. The notion of a creation field was inspired by Mach's principle that matter influences all other matter. As Fred Hoyle explained: "Matter is capable of exerting several types of influence—or fields as they are usually called. There is the nuclear field that binds together the atomic nuclei. There is the electro-magnetic field that enables atoms to absorb light. There is the gravitational field that holds the stars and galaxies together. And according to the new theory there is also a creation field that causes matter to originate. Matter originates in response to the influence of other matter. It is this latter field that causes the expansion of the Universe" (Fred Hoyle, *Frontiers of Astronomy*, p. 303). For a brief discussion of the steady state theory, see that author's "Continuous Creation and the Expanding Universe," excerpted from Hoyle's *The Nature of the Universe*, in Munitz, *Theories of the Universe*, pp. 419–29.

21. Robert Jastrow and Malcolm H. Thompson, *Astronomy: Fundamentals and Frontiers*, p. 264.

22. Ibid.

23. Merleau-Ponty and Morando, *Rebirth of Cosmology*, p. 203.

24. Kaufmann, *Relativity and Cosmology*, p. 45.

25. Ibid., p. 77. The original field equations for black holes were based on the idealized model of a nonrotating collapsing star. In 1963 R. P. Kerr published solutions for a rotating black hole which revealed two event horizons, bridges connecting an infinite number of universes, and many singularities. The Kerr solutions are discussed in Kaufmann, *Relativity and Cosmology*, pp. 61–65; and in Robert M. Wald, *Space, Time and Gravity*, pp. 84–91. The most exciting recent research on black holes is being done by Stephen Hawking, who has suggested that black holes heat up and can explode, and that matter might be created by gravitational fields at the edge of black holes. Hawking's theories may result in a long-awaited combination of thermodynamics, relativity, and quantum mechanics that has staggering implications. A brief and clear discussion of Hawking's theories is provided by Nigel Calder in *The Key to the Universe: A Report on the New Physics*, pp. 154–64.

26. Kaufmann, *Relativity and Cosmology*, p. 125.

27. Bohr has been quoted as saying that "when it comes to atoms, language can be used only as in poetry. The poet, too, is not nearly so concerned with describing facts as with creating images and establishing mental connections." And again: "Language is, as it were, a net spread out between people, a net in which our thoughts and knowledge are inextricably enmeshed." Cited by Werner Heisenberg in *Physics and Beyond: Encounters and Conversations*, pp. 41, 138. Heisenberg discussed his own similar views in both this work and his *Physics and Philosophy: The Revolution in Modern*

Science, especially chap. 10 ("Language and Reality in Modern Physics"). For a brief discussion of Schrödinger's position, see Erwin Schrödinger, *My View of the World*, especially pp. 69–82 ("Linguistic information and our common possession of the world").

28. Quoted by Heisenberg in *Physics and Beyond*, p. 36.

29. Calder, *Key to the Universe*, p. 15.

30. Einstein and Infeld, *Evolution of Physics*, p. 254.

31. Kenneth W. Ford, *The World of Elementary Particles*, pp. 213, 214, 215.

32. Mary B. Hesse, *Forces and Fields: The Concept of Action at a Distance in the History of Physics*, p. 272.

33. Einstein and Infeld, *Evolution of Physics*, pp. 284, 287, 289.

34. See, for example, Hilary Putnam's article, "A Philosopher Looks at Quantum Mechanics," in *Beyond the Edge of Certainty*, ed. Robert G. Colodny, pp. 75–101. According to Putnam, "*no* satisfactory interpretation of quantum mechanics exists today" (p. 100). In the first place, Putnam rejects the De Broglie interpretation, which holds that the "waves" of quantum mechanics "do not merely 'represent' the state of the system; they *are* the system" (p. 78). Putnam also rejects the Bohr interpretation, in which the "wave corresponding to a system of particles does *not* represent the state of the system . . . but rather our *knowledge* of the state, which is always incomplete" (p. 80). Putnam would like to modify the Copenhagen interpretation to read "*micro*-observables do not exist unless measured" rather than "observables do not exist unless measured" (p. 93). This modification would enable macro-observables to maintain sharp values. For another view of the Copenhagen interpretation, see Paul K. Feyerabend, "Niels Bohr's Interpretation of the Quantum Theory," in *Current Issues in the Philosophy of Science*, ed. Herbert Feigl and Grover Maxwell, pp. 371–90. For Heisenberg's own explanation, see that author's "The Copenhagen Interpretation of Quantum Theory," in *Physics and Philosophy*, pp. 44–58. The debate over whether quanta are waves or particles has led some scientists to speak humorously of "waveicles"; see Lincoln Barnett, *The Universe and Dr. Einstein*, p. 33. The oddity of the term "waveicles" reminds one of the term "groupuscles," which was used by the Cohn-Bendits and Deleuze in reference to the necessity for militants to merge their individual identities into a group identity.

35. Einstein and Infeld, *Evolution of Physics*, p. 294.

36. Werner Heisenberg, "The Development of Philosophical Ideas since Descartes in Comparison with the New Situation in Quantum Theory," in *Physics and Philosophy*, p. 81. Niels Bohr has also discussed the relation of knowledge and perception. See, for example, that author's *Atomic Physics and Human Knowledge* (New York: John Wiley and Sons, 1958). Schrödinger, too, has discussed this issue in *My View of the World*, pp. 61–67

("Reasons for abandoning the dualism of thought and existence, or mind and matter").

37. Cooper, *Meaning and Structure of Physics*, p. 548.

38. Ford, *Elementary Particles*, pp. 81, 82.

39. Ibid., p. 210.

40. Foucault, *Archaeology of Knowledge*, p. 49. In this passage Foucault was actually referring to the French title (*Les mots et les choses*) of *The Order of Things*, but his discussion focused on the problem of order.

41. J. D. Bernal, *The Natural Sciences in Our Time*, p. 764.

42. Calder, *Key to the Universe*, p. 49.

43. A clear explanation of quarks is given in Calder's *Key to the Universe*. For a brief discussion of "charmed" particles, see Roy F. Schwitters, "Fundamental Particles with Charm," pp. 56–70.

44. Daniel Z. Freedman and Peter van Nieuwenhuizen, "Supergravity and the Unification of the Laws of Physics," p. 126.

45. See, for example, Ernst Cassirer's 1910 study of classical physics and his 1921 work on modern physics, published together as *Substance and Function and Einstein's Theory of Relativity*. Cassirer also did a study of quantum theory in 1937 and subsequently published a work on the significance of modern physics for philosophy entitled *The Problem of Knowledge*.

46. Gaston Bachelard (1884–1962), born into a family of shoemakers, received a degree in the mathematical sciences in 1912 and a degree in philosophy in 1920. After service in World War I, he taught physics and chemistry in his birthplace, Bar-sur-Aûbe, from 1919 to 1930 and philosophy in Dijon during the next ten years. From 1940 to 1954 he taught at the Sorbonne and became director of the Institute of the History of Sciences.

47. Besides written acknowledgments of his intellectual debt to Bachelard, Foucault also expressed his admiration for Bachelard on a special radio broadcast commemorating the tenth anniversary of Bachelard's death. For excerpts of Foucault's appreciation, as well as comments by Georges Canguilhem and others, see *Le Figaro*, 30 September 1972, pp. 13, 16.

48. Gaston Bachelard, *La philosophie du non: Essai d'une philosophie du nouvel esprit scientifique* (1940), pp. 14–15.

49. A short discussion of these themes can be found in Colin Smith, *Contemporary French Philosophy*, chap. 6.

50. Gaston Bachelard, *Le nouvel esprit scientifique* (1934), p. 173, as cited in Dominique Lecourt, *Pour une critique de l'épistémologie: Bachelard, Canguilhem, Foucault* (Paris: Maspero, 1972); English translation entitled *Marxism and Epistemology: Bachelard, Canguilhem, Foucault* (London: New Left Books and Atlantic Highlands, N.J.: Humanities Press, 1975), p. 49; subsequent citations of the Lecourt book are from the English translation.

51. Lecourt, *Marxism and Epistemology*, pp. 41, 70.

52. Gaston Bachelard, *L'activité rationaliste de la physique contemporaine* (1951), p. 16, as cited by Lecourt in *Marxism and Epistemology*, p. 52.

53. Gaston Bachelard, "Noumenon and Micro-physics," in *Recherches Philosophiques* (1933), as quoted in Lecourt, *Marxism and Epistemology*, p. 38.

54. Lecourt, *Marxism and Epistemology*, p. 77.

55. Bachelard, *L'activité rationaliste*, chap. 4, sec. ix, as quoted in Lecourt, *Marxism and Epistemology*, p. 77.

56. Lecourt, *Marxism and Epistemology*, pp. 60–64.

57. According to Lecourt, Bachelard's "concept of dialectic does not coincide with any of the concepts designated by the word dialectic in traditional philosophy." See Lecourt, *Marxism and Epistemology*, p. 75. Lecourt was here referring to Georges Canguilhem's essay on Bachelard entitled "La dialectique et la philosophie du non," in *Études d'histoire et de philosophie des sciences.*

58. Lecourt, *Marxism and Epistemology*, p. 122.

59. Ibid., p. 81.

60. Gaston Bachelard, *Le matérialisme rationnel* (Paris: Presses Universitaires de France, 1953), p. 19, as quoted by Robert Champigny, "Gaston Bachelard," in John K. Simon, ed., *Modern French Criticism: From Proust and Valéry to Structuralism*, p. 176.

61. Bachelard, *Le nouvel esprit scientifique*, p. 75, as quoted in Lecourt, *Marxism and Epistemology*, p. 155.

62. Lecourt, *Marxism and Epistemology*, p. 157. The reference is to Bachelard's *La formation de l'esprit scientifique: Contribution à une psychanalyse de la connaissance objective* (Paris: J. Vrin, 1938).

63. Bachelard, *La formation de l'esprit scientifique*, p. 5, as quoted in Lecourt, *Marxism and Epistemology*, pp. 145–46.

64. Georges Canguilhem (1904–) succeeded Bachelard as director of the Institute of the History of Sciences at the University of Paris. Among Canguilhem's essays on Bachelard, see the following: "L'évolution du concept de méthode de Claude Bernard à Gaston Bachelard," "L'histoire des sciences dans l'oeuvre épistémologique de Gaston Bachelard," "Gaston Bachelard et les philosophes," and "Dialectique et philosophie du non chez Gaston Bachelard." These essays have all been reprinted in Canguilhem's collected essays under the title *Études d'histoire et de philosophie des sciences.*

65. Lecourt, *Marxism and Epistemology*, p. 182.

66. Georges Canguilhem, *Essai sur quelque problèmes concernant le normal et le pathologique* (1943), reprinted with "nouvelles reflexions" as *Le normal et le pathologique.*

67. Georges Canguilhem, "Mort de l'homme ou épuisement du *cogito?*" pp. 617, 618.

68. Lecourt, *Marxism and Epistemology*, pp. 176–77. See Georges Can-

guilhem, *La formation du concept de réflexe aux XVIIe et XVIIIe siècles* (Paris: Presses Universitaires de France, 1955).

69. Lecourt, *Marxism and Epistemology*, p. 175.

70. Canguilhem, "Mort de l'homme," p. 607.

71. Georges Canguilhem, *La connaissance de la vie*, 2d rev. ed. (Paris: J. Vrin, 1965), p. 62, as quoted in Lecourt, *Marxism and Epistemology*, p. 174.

72. Georges Canguilhem, "The Role of Analogies and Models in Biological Discovery," in *Scientific Change*, ed. A. C. Crombie, pp. 507–20. The French language version of this paper is included in Canguilhem's *Études d'histoire et de philosophie des sciences*, pp. 305–18.

73. Canguilhem, "Analogies and Models," p. 510.

74. Ibid., pp. 513–14.

75. Ibid., p. 514.

76. Ibid., p. 517.

77. See Ervin Laszlo, "Systems and Structures—Toward Bio-Social Anthropology," pp. 174–92. Here Laszlo argues that "Systems Theory in America, and Structuralism on the Continent, offer concepts and methods for bridging the gap between the natural and the social sciences. . . . Significant isomorphies obtain between the systems theoretical model of biological phenomena on the one hand, and the structuralist model of societal phenomena on the other" (p. 174). Also see that author's "The Case for Systems Philosophy," pp. 123–41. Another discussion on the relation between general systems theory and structuralism can be found in Willis F. Overton, "General Systems, Structure and Development," in *Structure and Transformation*, edited by Klaus F. Riegel and George C. Rosenwald, pp. 61–81.

78. Ludwig von Bertalanffy, "Chance or Law," in *Beyond Reductionism: New Perspectives in the Life Sciences. The Alpbach Symposium 1968*, ed. Arthur Koestler and J. R. Smythies, pp. 56–76.

79. Ibid., p. 59.   80. Ibid.

81. Ibid., p. 66.   82. Ibid., pp. 69, 70.

83. Ibid., p. 70.   84. Ibid., p. 76.

85. Michel Foucault, "Foucault responds/2," p. 60. This is from Foucault's second reply to George Steiner in the Steiner-Foucault controversy. If Canguilhem did indeed shape and inspire Kuhn's thought, it is not apparent in Kuhn's citations. Kuhn referred to several French works in *The Structure of Scientific Revolutions*, but there was no mention of Canguilhem's publications.

86. Thomas S. Kuhn, *The Structure of Scientific Revolutions*, p. 102. For a similar, briefer discussion of scientific revolutions as changes in thought structure, see Werner Heisenberg, "Changes in Thought Pattern in the Progress of Science" (originally delivered in 1969 as a lecture before the Association of German Scientists in Munich), in *Across the Frontiers*, pp. 154–65.

87. Kuhn, *Scientific Revolutions*, p. 195.

88. A similar argument was made earlier by Norwood Russell Hanson, whom Kuhn occasionally quotes. Hanson, like Kuhn, draws most of his examples from the history of physics. See his *Pattern of Discovery* and his posthumous work, *Perception and Discovery*.

89. Kuhn, *Scientific Revolutions*, p. 180.

90. In the preface to *The Structure of Scientific Revolutions*, Kuhn listed a number of his writings that discuss the role of external influences on scientific thought (see footnote on page x). For a short summary of the role of internal and external factors, see Thomas S. Kuhn, "The History of Science," in *International Encyclopedia of the Social Sciences*, 14:75–83.

91. Kuhn, *Scientific Revolutions*, pp. 86–88.

92. Ibid., pp. 52, 55.

93. Thomas S. Kuhn, "Second Thoughts on Paradigms," in *The Structure of Scientific Theories*, ed. Frederick Suppe, p. 482.

94. Raymond Bellour (interviewer), "Deuxième entretien avec Michel Foucault," p. 206.

95. Kuhn, *Scientific Revolutions*, p. 121. By "traditional" Kuhn meant the Cartesian-Newtonian philosophical world view.

96. Kuhn, "Second Thoughts on Paradigms," p. 478.

97. See, for example, David Bleich, "The Subjective Paradigm in Science, Psychology and Criticism," pp. 313–34. Bleich, however, does not discuss the systematic features of this new paradigm; he stresses instead the rejection of "objective" knowledge and the adoption of a "subjective" world view that he traces to Einstein, Bohr, Freud, and I. A. Richards.

98. Paolo Caruso (interviewer), "Conversazione con Michel Foucault," p. 117.

99. Quoted by James G. Roy, Jr., in a brochure entitled *Pierre Boulez*.

100. Caruso, "Conversazione con Michel Foucault," pp. 118–19.

101. Michel Foucault, *Ceci n'est pas une pipe: Deux lettres et quatre dessins de René Magritte*. This title is taken from one of Magritte's paintings depicting a large, carefully drawn pipe with an easel underneath it on which a small version of the pipe appears and the inscription "This is not a pipe."

102. When I was first introduced to Escher's works a few years ago, I was under the impression that no one else had noticed the resemblance between Escher and Foucault. Clifford Geertz, however, has recently remarked on this similarity in a review of *Discipline and Punish*, in which he commented that Foucault has become "a kind of impossible object: a nonhistorical historian, an anti-humanist human scientist, and a counter-structural structuralist. If we add to this his tense, impacted prose style, which manages to seem imperious and doubt-ridden at the same time, and a method which supports sweeping summary with eccentric detail, the resemblance of his work to an Escher drawing—stairs rising to platforms

lower than themselves, doors leading outside that bring you back inside—
is complete" (Clifford Geertz, "Stir Crazy," p. 3). For a discussion of
Escher's "structuralism," see G. W. Locher, "Structural Sensation," in *The
World of M. C. Escher*, pp. 41–48. Escher's debt to Gestalt psychology is
chronicled in Marianne L. Teuber's article, "Sources of Ambiguity in the
Prints of Maurits C. Escher," pp. 90–104.

103. See Gardner Murphy's essay "Gestalt and Field Theory," in *Readings in Philosophy of Science*, ed. Philip P. Wiener, pp. 207–19. Wolfgang
Köhler's own comments on his discovery of field theory in physics can be
found in his posthumously published work, *The Task of Gestalt Psychology*,
especially pp. 59–62.

104. See Kurt Lewin, *Field Theory in Social Science*. Also see Gardner
Murphy's comment that as a young man Lewin "began to think of psychological problems more and more in terms of events occurring in a kind of
space which had something in common with physical space, and to think of
psychological activity as a progression from one point to another within
this life space, or psychological space. Here he felt the need for more
adequate mathematical tools. . . . He found what he needed in the branch
of mathematics known as topology, in which one is concerned with regions
and their boundaries and subdivisions, the modes of progression which are
possible within them, and the possibility of transformation of such portions
of space as a result of weakening or strengthening barriers" (Murphy,
"Gestalt and Field Theory," p. 219).

105. Jean Piaget, "The Child and Modern Physics," pp. 46–51. Also see
Jean Piaget, *Structuralism*, chap. 3 ("Physical and Biological Structures").

106. See Piaget's critique of *The Order of Things* in *Structuralism*,
pp. 128–35. According to Piaget, Foucault's epistemes are arbitrary classifications and his structures are "mere diagrams, not transformational systems."

107. Michel Foucault, Introduction to *Le rêve et l'existence*, by Ludwig
Binswanger; and Michel Foucault, *Maladie mentale et psychologie*.

108. Viktor von Weizsaecker, *Der Gestaltkreis* (1939), translated by
Michel Foucault and Daniel Rocher as *Le cycle de la structure*.

109. Foucault does not even recognize the validity of "structuralism" as
a unified concept. He once stated that "Le structuralisme, c'est une catégorie qui existe pour les autres, pour ceux qui ne le sont pas. . . . C'est à
Sartre qu'il faut demander ce que c'est que les structuralistes puisqu'il considère que les structuralistes constituent un group cohérent (Lévi-Strauss,
Althusser, Dumézil, Lacan et moi) . . . mais cette unité, dites-vous bien
que nous, nous ne la percevons pas." See Foucault, "Foucault repond à
Sartre," p. 21. His critics' persistent identification of archaeology with
structuralism led Foucault to protest, in the foreword to the English
edition of *The Order of Things*, that he "used none of the methods, concepts, or key terms that characterize structural analysis" (p. xiv). Not-

withstanding such disclaimers, Foucault continues to be classified as a structuralist. Foucault's relation to structuralism is discussed in Jean-Marie Auzias's essay, "Le non-structuralisme de Michel Foucault," pp. 128–46; and in François Wahl's piece, "Y a-t-il une *épistémè* structuraliste?" pp. 305–90. For a satiric play ridiculing the entire structuralist debate in which the main character is clearly modeled on Foucault, see Roger Crémant, *Les matinées structuralistes*.

110. Ferdinand de Saussure, *Course in General Linguistics*. This volume is based on notes taken from courses that Saussure taught between 1906 and 1911. Saussure's course lectures were first published in 1916.

111. Saussure, *General Linguistics*, p. 30.

112. Ibid., p. 68.
113. Ibid., pp. 22–23.
114. Ibid., pp. 99–100.
115. Ibid., pp. 115–16.
116. Ibid., p. 122.
117. Ibid., p. 118.
118. Ibid., p. 123.
119. Ibid., p. 126.
120. Ibid., p. 131.
121. Ibid., p. 85.
122. Ibid., p. 95.
123. Ibid., p. 139.
124. John Lyons, *Noam Chomsky*, p. 111.

125. Frederic Jameson, *The Prison-House of Language: A Critical Account of Structuralism and Russian Formalism*.

126. For a discussion of Serge Doubrovsky's distinction between "new criticism" and "new, new criticism," see Philip Lewis, "Language and French Critical Debate," pp. 154–65.

127. A summary of the *Tel Quel* "movement" is given in Mary Ann Caws, "*Tel Quel*," pp. 2–8; Jonathan D. Culler, "'Beyond' Structuralism: *Tel Quel*," in *Structuralist Poetics*, pp. 241–55; and Bernard Pingaud, "Où va *Tel Quel*?" pp. 8–9.

128. Besides his articles in *Tel Quel*, Foucault has also participated in discussions organized by *Tel Quel* writers. He directed their colloquium "Débat sur le roman" and was a participant in the "Débat sur la poèsie," both of which were published in *Tel Quel* 17 (Spring 1964).

129. Roland Barthes, *Elements of Semiology; Writing Degree Zero*. Barthes has a different conception of semiology from Saussure's in that Barthes believes "we must now face the possibility of inverting Saussure's declaration: linguistics is not a part of the general system of signs, even a privileged part, it is semiology which is part of linguistics: to be precise, it is that part covering the *great signifying unities* of discourse. By this inversion we may expect to bring to light the unity of the research at present being done in anthropology, sociology, psychoanalysis and stylistics round the concept of signification" (p. 11).

130. Roland Barthes's "Objective Literature," his introduction to *Two Novels by Robbe-Grillet*, p. 24. Barthes's essay was originally published in *Critique* 86–87 (July–August 1954).

131. Barthes, "Objective Literature," p. 22.

132. Ibid., pp. 19–20.

133. Michel Foucault, "Distance, aspect, origine" (1963), pp. 11–24.

134. Ibid., p. 16.

135. "J'effacerais tous les mots contradictoires par quoi facilement on pourrait la dialectiser: affrontement ou abolition du subjectif et de l'objectif, de l'intérieur et de l'extérieur, de la réalité et de l'imaginaire" (ibid., p. 19).

136. Michel Foucault, "Le langage de l'espace" (1964), pp. 378–82.

137. Michel Foucault, "La pensée du dehors" (1966), pp. 523–46.

138. Michel Foucault, "Préface à la transgression" (1963), English translation entitled "A Preface to Transgression," in *Language, Counter-Memory, Practice*, ed. Donald F. Bouchard, pp. 29–52; hereafter cited in the English translation.

139. Foucault, "A Preface to Transgression," p. 30.

140. Michel Foucault, "Le langage à l'infini" (1963), English translation entitled "Language to Infinity," in *Language, Counter-Memory, Practice*, ed. Donald F. Bouchard, pp. 53–67; hereafter cited in the English translation.

141. Foucault, "Language to Infinity," p. 67.

142. Michel Foucault, "Un 'fantastique' de bibliothèque" (1967; revised 1970), English translation entitled "Fantasia of the Library," in *Language, Counter-Memory, Practice*, ed. Donald F. Bouchard, pp. 87–109.

143. Michel Foucault, "L'arrière-fable" (1966), pp. 5–12.

144. Michel Foucault, *Raymond Roussel*. For a brief assessment of Roussel, see Michel Foucault, "Pourquoi réédite-t-on l'oeuvre de Raymond Roussel? Un précurseur de notre littérature moderne" (1964), p. 9.

145. Roussel's works had previously attracted the attention of André Breton, Salvador Dali, Roger Vitrac, and other surrealists. Roussel published numerous plays, poems, and novels, which Foucault has divided into two groups: "descriptive" works such as *La doublure* (1897) and *La vue* (1902, 1904), and "les merveilles" such as *Impressions d'Afrique* (1910) and *Locus solus* (1914).

146. Raymond Roussel, *Comment j'ai écrit certains de mes livres*. This is a reprint of the posthumously published edition of 1935.

147. Foucault, *Raymond Roussel*, p. 100.

148. Ibid., p. 124.

149. Michel Foucault, "Qu'est-ce qu'un auteur?" (1969), English translation entitled "What is an Author?" in *Language, Counter-Memory, Practice*, ed. Donald F. Bouchard, pp. 113–38; hereafter cited in the English translation.

150. Foucault, "What is an Author?" p. 117.

151. Michel Foucault, Introduction to *Rousseau juge de Jean-Jaques*, pp. vii–xxiv.

152. Michel Foucault, "Le 'Non' du père" (1962), English translation

entitled "The Father's 'No,'" in *Language, Counter-Memory, Practice*, ed. Donald F. Bouchard, pp. 68–86; hereafter cited in the English translation. 153. Michel Foucault, "The Father's 'No,'" p. 84.

Chapter 4

1. Michel Foucault, *Maladie mentale et psychologie* (Paris: Presses Universitaires de France, 1954), translated by Alan Sheridan as *Mental Illness and Psychology* (New York: Harper Colophon Books, 1976). All subsequent references will be to the English edition of this work.

2. It did, however, receive a brief favorable review by Roland Caillois in *Critique* 93 (February 1955): 189–90. After it was reprinted in 1966, a short review by P. Huard of "ce livre très dense et vigoureux" appeared in *Revue de synthèse* 45–46 (January–June 1967): 94–95.

3. Foucault, *Mental Illness and Psychology*, p. 86.

4. Ibid., p. 13.   5. Ibid., p. 2.

6. Ibid., p. 17.   7. Ibid., p. 19.

8. Foucault was referring here to John Hughlings Jackson, *The Croonian Lectures on the Evolution and Dissolution of the Nervous System* (London, [1884?], delivered at the Royal College of Physicians in March of 1884; and to Pierre Janet, *L'automatisme psychologique: Essai de psychologie expérimentale sur les formes inférieures de l'activité humaine* (Paris: Félix Alcan, 1889).

9. Foucault, *Mental Illness and Psychology*, pp. 24–25.

10. Ibid., p. 30.

11. The inability to resolve conflict, incidentally, is one of the features of pathological thought that distinguishes it from mythical thought. While Foucault does not refer here to structural studies of myths—most of Lévi-Strauss's major works appeared only after 1954—he does mention cultural anthropologists such as Ruth Benedict.

12. Foucault, *Mental Illness and Psychology*, p. 45.

13. Ibid., p. 46.

14. Ibid., pp. 47–49.

15. See, for example, Thomas S. Szasz, *Ideology and Insanity: Essays on the Psychiatric Dehumanization of Man*. Szasz believes that "mental illness is a myth, whose function it is to disguise and thus render more palatable the bitter pill of moral conflicts in human relations" (p. 24). Also consult R. D. Laing, *The Divided Self: An Existential Study in Sanity and Madness*. In this work, which was first published in 1959, Laing (like Foucault) drew heavily upon the works of Jaspers, Heidegger, and Binswanger. Laing is also an admirer of Foucault and was instrumental in getting Foucault's works translated into English.

16. Foucault was referring to Eugène Minkowski, *Le temps vécu: Études phénoménologiques et psychopathologiques* (Paris: J. L. L. d'Artrey, 1933); and to Ludwig Binswanger, "Ueber Ideenflucht," *Schweizer Archiv für Neurologie und Psychiatrie* 27–30 (1929–33).

17. Foucault, *Mental Illness and Psychology*, pp. 51, 52.

18. Ibid., p. 53.   19. Ibid., p. 80.

20. Ibid., p. 63.   21. Ibid., p. 65.

22. Ibid., p. 67.   23. Ibid., p. 77.

24. Ibid., p. 69.

25. These reformers are generally credited with introducing compassionate treatment of the insane and advancing the scientific study of madness. This was the traditional view when Foucault was writing and is still the established view. See, for example, Franz G. Alexander and Sheldon T. Selesnick, *The History of Psychiatry*.

26. Foucault, *Mental Illness and Psychology*, p. 71.

27. Ibid., p. 73. Jean Esquirol (1772–1840) was a pupil and loyal follower of Pinel who extended Pinel's nosography.

28. Ibid., pp. 80, 81.   29. Ibid., p. 82.

30. Ibid., p. 84.   31. Ibid., p. 75.

32. Ibid., p. 73.

33. Michel Foucault, *Folie et déraison*. A revised edition appeared in 1964 in which half of the original text, the entire bibliography, and most of the footnotes were deleted. This abridged edition was translated by Richard Howard as *Madness and Civilization*.

34. Roland Barthes, "Savoir et folie," English translation entitled "Taking Sides," in *Critical Essays*, p. 164; hereafter cited from the English translation.

35. Foucault, *Madness and Civilization*, p. ix.

36. The romantic features of this work are seldom discussed in the critical literature. Ronald Paulson, however, commented in passing that Foucault's interpretation is "ultimately based on Romantic ideas of liberty and madness"; see Paulson's review in the *Journal of English and Germanic Philology*, p. 165. Peter Gay, in a much harsher review, claims that Foucault's nostalgia is "overwhelming" and that his message "is little more than old-fashioned primitivism refurbished with impressive modern learning"; see Gay's review, "Chains and Couches," p. 96.

37. Other structuralist aspects of Foucault's study are discussed in Annie Guédez, *Foucault*, especially p. 26; and in Barthes, "Taking Sides," pp. 166–67. Reviews that classify *Madness and Civilization* as a "phenomenological" work include: R. D. Laing, "The Invention of Madness," p. 843; and Steven Marcus, "In Praise of Folly," pp. 36–39.

38. In the original text the final chapter was much longer. Since the section on Goya and Sade is all that remains in the abridged version, Fou-

cault must have considered this the most significant portion. In the 1972 reedition of the unabridged text, Foucault added an appendix ("La folie, l'absence d'oeuvre") that elaborated on the theme of madness and non-being. Foucault argued here that madness has ceased to define the border between inclusion and exclusion and that language has assumed this function.

39. Maurice Blanchot, "L'oubli, la déraison," pp. 289–99.

40. Barthes, "Taking Sides," pp. 167, 169.

41. Michel Serres, "Géométrie de l'incommunicable: La folie" (1962), pp. 167–90.

42. Ibid., pp. 188–89.

43. Jacques Derrida, "Cogito et histoire de la folie" (1964), pp. 51–97. Foucault replied to Derrida's critique in the essay "Mon corps, ce papier, ce feu," which he appended to the 1972 edition of *Folie et déraison*, pp. 583–603.

44. Hayden V. White, "Foucault Decoded: Notes from Underground," pp. 23–54. For a critique of White's article, see Jean-Claude Guédon, "Michel Foucault: The Knowledge of Power and the Power of Knowledge," especially pp. 272–74.

45. White, "Foucault Decoded," p. 53.

46. Foucault, *Madness and Civilization*, p. 43.

47. According to Foucault, about 1 percent of the population of Paris was confined within a few months after the creation of the Parisian Hôpital Général. In the original edition Foucault discussed the various types of people confined, but in the abridged version most of this information was deleted, as was a reference to the doubling of the numbers confined between 1690 and 1790.

48. Foucault reduced his discussion of the French Revolution to a few pages in the abridged edition, but in the original text he devoted almost an entire chapter to it.

49. Foucault noted, for example, that economic factors alone could not account for the continuation of confinement. The general hospitals, he believed, never succeeded in combining the dual economic functions of incarcerating the poor during periods of recession and providing forced labor during periods of high labor demand. See *Madness and Civilization*, pp. 51–54.

50. Foucault, *Madness and Civilization*, pp. 47–48.

51. Ibid., pp. 23, 30.

52. Ibid., pp. 15, 18.

53. Ibid., pp. 19, 20, 21.

54. Cervantes and Shakespeare are important exceptions. According to Foucault, "both testify more to a tragic experience of madness appearing in the fifteenth century, than to a critical and moral experience of Unreason

developing in their own epoch" (ibid., p. 36).

55. Foucault cited Georges de Scudéry's novels and the plays of Jean de Rotrou and Tristan l'Hermite as examples.

56. Foucault, *Madness and Civilization*, p. 39.

57. Robert Mandrou believes that Foucault's "très beau livre" is "une mise en question de toute notre culture occidentale"; see his essay "Trois clefs pour comprendre la folie à l'époque classique," *Annales* 4 (July–August 1962): 761–71. Also see Braudel's comment in the same issue of *Annales* (pp. 771–72) that "ce livre magnifique essaie de poursuivre . . . des structures mentales d'une civilisation."

58. Foucault acknowledged his debt to Georges Dumézil, Jean Hyppolite, and Georges Canguilhem in the preface to the unabridged French text. Note particularly his statement: "Il me faut remercier . . . entre tous, M. Georges Canguilhem, qui a lu ce travail encore informe, m'a conseillé quand tout n'était pas simple, m'a épargné bien des erreurs, et montré le prix qu'il peut y avoir à être entendu" (p. x).

59. Foucault, *Madness and Civilization*, p. 75.

60. Ibid., p. 56.
61. Ibid., p. 58.

62. Ibid., pp. 185–88.
63. Ibid., p. 69.

64. Ibid., p. 167.
65. Ibid., p. 171.

66. Ibid., p. 173. Foucault clarified this phrase (in one of the few explanatory footnotes retained in the abridged edition) by distinguishing between "two temporal structures: that which is proper to the experience of Unreason and to the knowledge it envelops; that which is proper to the knowledge of madness, and to the science it authorizes" (ibid., p. 237, n. 9).

67. Ibid., p. 178.

68. Ibid., pp. 114, 110.

69. Ibid., pp. 72–82, 101–15, and 126–31.

70. Ibid., p. 131.
71. Ibid., p. 84.

72. Ibid., p. 91.
73. Ibid., pp. 151–61.

74. Ibid., p. 223.

75. For examples of enthusiastic reactions in sociological circles, see David Matza's comments in the *American Sociological Review* 31 (August 1966): 551–52; and Michael Peters's assessment in *Sociological Review* 19 (November 1971): 634–38. These men regard Foucault's history of madness as "brilliant," a "masterpiece," and profoundly sociological. Matza believes it is the most important contribution to the study of madness since Freud, and Peters regards Foucault as "a Weberian, rendering intelligible what would otherwise be incoherent and achieving *understanding* by the use of elaborate, but essentially heuristic, typificatory constructs and interpretive schemas" (pp. 637–38).

76. Michel Foucault, *The Birth of the Clinic: An Archaeology of Medical Perception*, p. ix.

77. Foucault, *Birth of the Clinic*, p. 38.

78. Ibid., p. 3.   79. Ibid., p. 105.
80. Ibid., p. 97.   81. Ibid., p. 167.
82. Ibid., p. 163.   83. Ibid., p. 142.

84. Foucault returned to this important point in *The Archaeology of Knowledge*. There, referring specifically to *The Birth of the Clinic*, he stressed that "discourse is not the majestically unfolding manifestation of a thinking, knowing, speaking subject, but, on the contrary, a totality, in which the dispersion of the subject and his discontinuity with himself may be determined" (p. 55). This has been a controversial issue. Consult, for example, David Oldman's review of *The Birth of the Clinic* (*Sociology* 9 [May 1975]: 360), in which Oldman poses the question: "What is it that is supposed to constitute the link between the preconditions and the form of knowledge? What else could it be but the consciousness of men?"

85. Foucault, *Birth of the Clinic*, p. 137.

86. Ibid., pp. xv–xvi. French reviewers occasionally comment on the Kantian aspects of Foucault's archaeology. See, for example, François Dagognet's review, "Archéologie ou histoire de la médecine," pp. 436–47. American reviewers seldom discuss the philosophical significance of this work, although there are rare references to the phenomenological features of Foucault's archaeology. For example, Peter Caws's review, "Medical Change," pp. 28–30, mentions the similarity between Foucault and Husserl and claims that Foucault is "a cultural historian-philosopher of major importance."

87. Foucault, *Birth of the Clinic*, p. xvii. A number of reviewers have commented on the structuralist methodology of this work. See, for example, Jean Starobinski's excellent review, "Gazing at Death," pp. 18, 20–22. Foucault himself later regretted his use of structural methods, as evidenced by his comment in *The Archaeology of Knowledge* that "the frequent recourse to structural analysis threatened to bypass the specificity of the problem presented, and the level proper to archaeology" (p. 16).

88. Foucault, *Birth of the Clinic*, p. 199.

89. Ibid., p. 35.

90. Foucault was referring to works such as François Sauvage's *Nosologie* (1761) and Philippe Pinel's *Nosographie* (1798).

91. Foucault, *Birth of the Clinic*, pp. 31–32.

92. Ibid., p. 52.   93. Ibid., p. 79.
94. Ibid., p. 62.   95. Ibid., p. 54.

96. Pierre Cabanis's works are representative of this early stage of clinical medicine. Foucault cites in particular Cabanis's *Du degré de certitude de la médecine*, 3d ed. (Paris, 1819).

97. As an example of this arithmetical method of making medical decisions, Foucault cited the physician C.-A. Brulley, who opposed an operation because there were four unfavorable probabilities and only two favor-

able ones. See Foucault, *Birth of the Clinic*, p. 104.

98. Ibid., p. xviii.   99. Ibid., p. 121.

100. Ibid., pp. 121, 122.   101. Ibid., p. 122.

102. Predictably, this thesis has not been accepted by most historians of medicine, especially in England and America. As one commentator noted in a thoughtful review of *The Birth of the Clinic*: "Anglo-Saxon historiography of science and medicine remains liberal and empirical. . . . It is not surprising, therefore, that a continental author who insists that empiricism in medicine is a problematical creation of a new theoretical structure, that influences of ideas are unintelligible, and that there are no subjects of history . . . has not achieved widespread recognition in British history of science and medicine" (Karl Figlio in *British Journal for the History of Science* 10 [July 1977]: 165). Even those historians of science who are receptive to revisions in the history of medicine are often resistant to Foucault's inversions. See, for example, Alfred Lars Aronson, "Medicine: History and Theory," pp. 473–76. Aronson insisted that "it is the application of scientific method which enabled the new 'perceptions', and not vice versa" (p. 475). Also note Theodore Zeldin's review, "An Archeologist of Knowledge." Zeldin praises Foucault's attempt to "create a new method of historical analysis and a new framework for the study of the human sciences" but doubts that physicians at the end of the eighteenth century really changed their ideas very radically (p. 861). For an outright hostile reaction, see Donald M. Kaplan's review in *The Village Voice* 18 (22 November 1973): 29, 31. Kaplan claims that *The Birth of the Clinic* is "a typical patch of current Parisian fungus" and "is worse than provincial: it is virtually autistic" (p. 29).

103. Foucault, *Birth of the Clinic*, p. 125.

104. Ibid., p. 126.

105. Xavier Bichat, *Anatomie générale appliquée à la physiologie et à médecine*, 3 vols. (Paris, 1801).

106. Foucault, *Birth of the Clinic*, p. 140.

107. Ibid., p. 144.   108. Ibid., p. 162.

109. Ibid., p. 164.   110. Ibid., p. 166.

111. This, at least, is the opinion of J. B. Loudon, who complained that Foucault omitted major figures but included second-rate ones like Broussais. Still, Loudon admired Foucault as "a writer of originality and wide scholarship." See Loudon's review of *The Birth of the Clinic* in *Man* 9 (June 1974): 319–20.

112. Foucault, *Birth of the Clinic*, p. 191.

113. White, "Foucault Decoded," p. 26.

Chapter 5

1. Foucault selected this title to avoid confusion with other English works entitled *Words and Things*.

2. Foucault's use of this term has aroused considerable controversy. See, for example, Sylvie Le Bon's critical review, "Un positiviste désespéré: Michel Foucault," pp. 1299–1319; and the unsigned article, "The Contented Positivist: M. Foucault and the Death of Man," pp. 697–98.

3. Foucault, *The Order of Things*, p. 307.

4. Ibid., p. xv. Foucault's theoretical system is itself based on a unique method for classifying material. In the words of one commentator, "les analyses de Foucault sont d'une telle maîtrise, d'un ton si nouveau que le lecteur sent l'approche d'une nouvelle manière de penser dans cette réflexion apparente sur l'histoire" (Gilles Deleuze, "L'homme, une existence douteuse," p. 32). Richard Howard, the translator of *Madness and Civilization*, made a similar assessment in a review of *The Order of Things*. He compared Foucault to John Maynard Keynes and William Empson because these thinkers also broke with conventional ways of thinking; all three are important "not because we have mastered them but because they have mastered us: they change our minds by changing the kind of questions we ask rather than by providing new answers" (Richard Howard, "Our Sense of Where We Are," p. 21).

5. According to McLuhan, in preliterate, multisensorial societies touch and sound are as important as sight. With the invention of printing, McLuhan claims, sight began to dominate Western consciousness. In the twentieth century, however, the electronic media transformed visual perception from an apprehension of linear relations to the perception of "configurations." Moreover, electronic media have brought sound and touch (a sense of being in immediate contact with a large part of the world) back into Western sensibility. McLuhan's interest in various structures of perception and his spatial metaphors resemble Foucault's theoretical concerns and literary images, although Foucault is a far more systematic thinker. On McLuhan's views, see his *Gutenberg Galaxy* and *Understanding Media*. For a brief, clear discussion of McLuhan, see Richard Kostelanetz, "Understanding McLuhan (in Part)," in *Molders of Modern Thought*, ed. Ben B. Seligman, pp. 298–312.

6. See Ian Hacking, *Why Does Language Matter to Philosophy?*, pp. 26–33, for his comments on sight in the seventeenth and eighteenth centuries. Hacking also noted Lucien Febvre's 1942 thesis that perceptual structures vary and that thirteenth-century French culture was an "auditory, olfactory universe in which objects of sight have hardly come into consciousness" (p. 32).

7. Foucault, *The Order of Things*, p. xxiv.

8. Ibid., p. xxiii.

9. Foucault's repeated prediction of the "end of man" has provoked widespread reaction: see Michel de Certeau, "Les sciences humaines et la mort de l'homme," pp. 344–360; Jean Lacroix, "Fin de l'humanisme?" p. 13; and Jean Langlois, "Michel Foucault et la mort de l'homme," pp. 209–30. For details on the commercial success of *The Order of Things*, see Pierre Wurms, "Un best-seller," pp. 561–64.

10. Georges Canguilhem, for example, has questioned Foucault's theory of discontinuity since it "interdit toute ambition de reconstitution du passé dépassé" (Canguilhem, "Mort de l'homme," p. 606).

11. Foucault, *The Order of Things*, p. 111. Curiologics, like synecdoche, uses a part to represent the whole. Thus, the curiological writing of the Egyptians represented the word for battle with the image of a bow. Hieroglyphics, like metonymy, is based on a coincidence of qualities or circumstances. For example, since God sees everything he can be represented by an eye. Symbolic writing, like the trope of metaphor, relies on analogy and the resemblances are often remote. Thus, the rising sun may be represented by the head of a crocodile, since the crocodile's eyes are just level with the surface of the water. (These are all examples cited by Foucault.)

12. According to White, Foucault's archaeology is based on the same theory of tropes as Vico's philosophy of history. Consequently, both Foucault and Vico construct a four-stage cycle beginning with metaphor (Foucault's Renaissance and Vico's age of the gods), continuing through metonymy (Foucault's Classical episteme and Vico's age of heroes) to synecdoche (Foucault's Modern episteme and Vico's age of men), and ending with irony (Foucault's Contemporary episteme and Vico's age of decadence). Hence White concludes that "Foucault *does* have both a system of explanation and a theory of the transformation of reason, or science, or consciousness, whether he knows it or will admit it or not." See Hayden V. White, "Foucault Decoded," pp. 47–48. White expanded his discussion of the relation between tropes and historical consciousness in *Metahistory*, especially pt. 1.

13. Foucault, *The Order of Things*, p. 207.

14. This diagram is my own and does not always follow Foucault's categories exactly. Foucault does not, for example, provide an initial date for the Renaissance, although he often equates the Renaissance with the sixteenth century. Nor has Foucault indicated a terminal point for the Modern period; the date 1950 is taken from a comment Foucault made in an interview after *The Order of Things* appeared. The terms *self-representation* and *self-reflection*, as well as the same-other and space-time divisions and this charting of grammatical functions, are all simplifications of Foucault's more complex categories.

15. Although Foucault has not specified the Renaissance "positivities,"

his general discussion suggested the categories indicated in figure 2.

16. Foucault, *The Order of Things*, p. 54.

17. Ibid., p. 56. According to Foucault, mechanism provided a theoretical model for some fields (for example, medicine), but only during the last half of the seventeenth century, and mathematics affected a few areas of thought (astronomy and physics) throughout the Classical period, but had a limited impact on other disciplines.

18. Ibid., p. 345.

19. Ibid., pp. 261, 262.

20. Ibid., p. 262.

21. Foucault included some relevant comments on method in the foreword to the English edition of *The Order of Things*, and in 1969 he published his methodological study *The Archaeology of Knowledge*.

22. Foucault, *The Order of Things*, pp. 346–47.

23. Ibid., p. 382.   24. Ibid., p. xii.

25. Ibid., p. 168.   26. Ibid., p. xiii.

27. Although the quark model cannot offer ultimate explanations, it is explanatory in the sense that the atomic model "explains" the periodic chart, whereas previously the pattern of changes could only be described, not explained.

28. Foucault, *The Order of Things*, p. x.

29. Ibid., p. 375.

30. Ibid., p. xiv.

31. For a discussion of speaking, writing, and lying, see Foucault's essay, "La pensée du dehors," pp. 523–46. A discussion of the role of the "author" is given in his essay, "What Is an Author?" pp. 113–38.

32. Foucault, *The Order of Things*, p. xx.

33. Ibid., p. 18.   34. Ibid., p. 19.

35. Ibid., p. 21.   36. Ibid., p. 23.

37. Ibid., p. 24.   38. Ibid., p. 27.

39. Not surprisingly, Foucault's interpretation of the Renaissance has met with criticism. See, for example, George Huppert, "*Divinatio et Eruditio*: Thoughts on Foucault," pp. 191–207. Huppert, who defends the conventional distinction between magic and science, claims that "there was in the sixteenth century, in France, a tradition of humanist learning which scoffed at magic, at the hermetic doctrines, at Paracelsus, signatures, correspondences, astrology, and all the other faces of the 'system' glorified by Foucault as the *episteme* of the age, and that this tradition was the dominant and respectable one" (p. 204).

40. Foucault, *The Order of Things*, p. 22. As Foucault explained, Belon's work was not comparative anatomy "except to an eye armed with nineteenth-century knowledge. It is merely that the grid through which we permit the figures of resemblance to enter our knowledge happens to

coincide at this point (and at almost no other) with that which sixteenth-century learning laid over things" (ibid.).

41. Ibid., p. 35.   42. Ibid., p. 40.
43. Ibid., p. 169.   44. Ibid., p. 173.
45. Ibid., p. 43.   46. Ibid., p. 50.
47. Ibid., pp. 4–5.

48. According to Ian Hacking, whose analysis was heavily influenced by Foucault, the Port-Royal *Logic* was fundamental for Locke and even Berkeley and was the "prescribed logic text at Oxford and Edinburgh quite late in the nineteenth century" (Hacking, *Why Does Language Matter to Philosophy?*, p. 26). For Foucault's explicit assessment of the significance of the Port-Royal *General Grammar*, see his preface to a recent French edition of Antoine Arnauld and Claude Lancelot, *Grammaire générale et raisonnée, contenant les fondements de l'art de parler*, pp. iii–xxvii.

49. Foucault, *The Order of Things*, p. 56.

50. Ibid., p. 74.   51. Ibid., pp. 60, 61.
52. Ibid., p. 60.   53. Ibid., p. 63.
54. Ibid., p. 76.

55. As Foucault put it in his preface to *Grammaire générale et raisonnée*: "La grammaire générale n'est pas une quasi-linguistique, appréhendée de façon encore obscure; et la linguistique moderne n'est pas une nouvelle forme plus positive donnée à la vieille idée de grammaire générale. Il s'agit en fait de deux configurations épistémologiques différentes" (p. iv).

56. Foucault, *The Order of Things*, p. 84.

57. Ibid., p. 103. In the first theory the basic elements were words, particularly those words that functioned as subjects, verbs, and objects. In the second theory even vowels and consonants represented something, which explained why Jean-Jacques Rousseau could equate vowels with passion and consonants with needs.

58. Ibid., p. 120.

59. Ibid., p. 134.

60. Ibid., p. 97. Foucault's distinction between method and system has a further implication that he did not discuss here. Speculative philosophers have generally tried to formulate a single all-encompassing method by deducing a total order. Foucault's "archaeology" is a system, one of many possible systems that establishes lateral relationships among different structures (discourses) through detailed description.

61. Ibid., pp. 132–33.

62. Ibid., p. 156. Foucault based his assessment of "the non-existence of the biological notion of the 'environment' in the eighteenth century" on Georges Canguilhem's *La Connaissance de la vie*. See Foucault's citation in *The Order of Things*, p. 164, n. 58.

63. Ibid., pp. 151–53. Despite its apparent similarity to evolutionary

theory, the Classical idea referred not to a modification of being but to a series of preordained events.

64. Ibid., p. 157. ʹ
65. Ibid., p. 175.
66. Ibid., p. 181.
67. Ibid., p. 189.
68. Ibid., p. 210.
69. Ibid., p. 217.
70. Ibid., pp. 220, 232, 238.
71. Ibid., p. 219.
72. Ibid., p. 221.
73. Ibid., pp. 229, 230.
74. Ibid., p. 232.

75. Ibid., p. 234. However, the example Foucault cites is the verb "to be," which is irregular.

76. Ibid., p. 238.
77. Ibid., p. 239.
78. Ibid., p. 242.
79. Ibid., pp. 252, 253.
80. Ibid., p. 255.
81. Ibid., p. 262.

82. Ibid., pp. 268–69. For a discussion of eighteenth- and nineteenth-century biological classifications by an admirer of Foucault, see Vernon Pratt, "Foucault and the History of Classification Theory," pp. 163–71. Pratt maintains that Foucault's "brilliant, theatrical, bewildering" study is a significant contribution to both the history and the philosophy of science (p. 163).

83. Ibid., p. 272.

84. Ibid., pp. 274–76. Although this interpretation has not persuaded all historians of science, it has generated considerable interest and won over many specialists. Those who agree with Foucault include Georges Canguilhem and Vernon Pratt, who have already been cited. For critical reactions, see John C. Greene, "Les mots et les choses," pp. 132–38; and Vincent Labeyrie, "Remarques sur l'évolution du concept de biologie," pp. 125–37.

85. Friedrich von Schlegel, *On the Language and Philosophy of the Indians* (1808), in *Aesthetic and Miscellaneous Works* (London, 1849), p. 439. Cited by Foucault in *The Order of Things*, p. 280.

86. Foucault, *The Order of Things*, p. 289.

87. Ibid., p. 285.
88. Ibid., p. 298.
89. Ibid., p. 300.
90. Ibid.
91. Ibid., p. 308.
92. Ibid., p. 313.
93. Ibid., p. 322.
94. Ibid., p. 327.
95. Ibid.
96. Ibid., p. 329.
97. Ibid., pp. 330, 331.
98. Ibid., p. 334.
99. Ibid., p. 307.
100. Ibid., pp. 347–48.
101. Ibid., p. 356.
102. Ibid., pp. 357, 358.
103. Ibid., p. 359.
104. Ibid., p. 360.
105. Ibid.
106. Ibid., p. 364.
107. Ibid., pp. 366–67.
108. Ibid., p. 368.
109. Ibid., p. 367.
110. Ibid., p. 371.

111. Ibid., p. 379.   112. Ibid., p. 386.
113. See, for example, the following articles by Edward Said: *"Abece-darium Culturae"*; "Michel Foucault as an Intellectual Imagination"; and "Linguistics and the Archeology of Mind," pp. 104–34. Also consult Jonathan Culler, "Words and Things," pp. 104–5; and Peter Caws, "Language as the Human Reality," pp. 28, 32–34. For a French "structuralist" response, see Roland Barthes, "Taking Sides," pp. 163–70.
114. Existentialist and humanist critiques include the following: Michel Amiot, "Le relativisme culturaliste de Michel Foucault," pp. 1271–98; Sylvie Le Bon, "Un positiviste désespéré: Michel Foucault," pp. 1299–1319; Pierre Burgelin, "L'archéologie du savoir," pp. 843–61; and Mikel Dufrenne, "L'épistémologie archéologique," pp. 37–47. A Marxist critique is given by Roger Garaudy in "Structuralisme et 'mort de l'homme,'" pp. 107–24. Also see Olivier Revault D'Allonnes's piece "Michel Foucault: Les mots contre les choses," pp. 13–37. French academic philosophers have also been critical of *The Order of Things*. See, for example, Jeanne Parain-Vial, "Les mots et les choses," pp. 176–95; Jean Wahl's comments in *Revue de Metaphysique et de Morale* 74 (April–June 1967): pp. 250–51; and the published conversations of a faculty seminar devoted to a discussion of *The Order of Things* entitled "Trois entretiens sur Foucault," pp. 3–37.
115. Gérard Mendel, "Les mots sans les choses," pp. 288–336.
116. Kenneth W. Ford, *The World of Elementary Particles*, p. 210.

Epilogue

1. Michel Foucault, *Discipline and Punish: The Birth of the Clinic*, p. 55.
2. Ibid., p. 82.   3. Ibid., p. 124.
4. Ibid., p. 131.   5. Ibid., p. 169.
6. Ibid., pp. 220–21.
7. In the United States, this function of the prison system is closely tied to racism. After a visit to Attica in 1972, Foucault commented on the size of the U.S. prison population compared to that of France (more than one million compared to thirty thousand, a figure roughly ten times as great relative to total population). The proportion of black men in prison is significant: approximately one out of thirty-five black American males is imprisoned. See John K. Simon (interviewer), "Michel Foucault on Attica: An Interview" (1974), pp. 154–61.
8. Foucault, *Discipline and Punish*, p. 277.
9. Spatial images are particularly striking and have caught the attention of several commentators. See, for example, Gilles Deleuze, "Ecrivain non: Un nouveau cartographe," pp. 1207–27; and a 1976 interview with Fou-

cault by the editors of the Marxist journal *Hérodote*, "Questions à Michel Foucault sur la géographie," which has been translated as "Questions on Geography," in Michel Foucault, *Power/Knowledge*, ed. Colin Gordon, pp. 63–77.

10. Michel Foucault, "Two Lectures," in *Power/Knowledge*, ed. Colin Gordon, p. 83.

11. Ibid., p. 85.

12. Michel Foucault, *The History of Sexuality, Volume 1: An Introduction*, p. 54.

13. Ibid., p. 47.   14. Ibid., p. 114.

15. Ibid., p. 93.   16. Ibid., pp. 98–101.

17. Michel Foucault, "Le Jeu de Michel Foucault," English translation entitled "The Confession of the Flesh," in *Power/Knowledge*, ed. Colin Gordon, pp. 212, 209.

18. See Foucault's introduction to the English translation of Georges Canguilhem's *Essai sur quelque problèmes concernant le normal et le pathologique*, entitled *On the Normal and the Pathological*. In this important article, Foucault outlines the significance of Canguilhem's study and traces the influence Canguilhem exerted on his generation of French intellectuals.

BIBLIOGRAPHY

Works by Michel Foucault

BOOKS (IN CHRONOLOGICAL ORDER)

Foucault, Michel. *Maladie mentale et psychologie* (1954). 2d rev. ed. Paris: Presses Universitaires de France, 1962. Translated by Alan Sheridan as *Mental Illness and Psychology.* New York: Harper Colophon Books, 1976.

———. *Folie et déraison: Histoire de la folie à l'âge classique.* Paris: Plon, 1961; abridged ed., 1964. Translated by Richard Howard from the 1964 abridged edition as *Madness and Civilization: A History of Insanity in the Age of Reason.* New York: Mentor Books, 1965. Reissued from the 1961 edition as *Histoire de la folie à l'âge classique,* with two appendixes: "Mon corps, ce papier, ce feu" and "La folie, l'absence, d'oeuvre." Paris: Gallimard, 1972.

———. *Naissance de la clinique: Une Archéologie du regard médical.* Paris: Presses Universitaires de France, 1963. Translated by A. M. Sheridan Smith as *The Birth of the Clinic: An Archaeology of Medical Perception.* New York: Vintage Books, 1973.

———. *Raymond Roussel.* Paris: Gallimard, 1963.

———. *Les Mots et les choses: Une Archéologie des sciences humaines.* Paris: Gallimard, 1966. Translated by Alan Sheridan-Smith as *The Order of Things: An Archaeology of the Human Sciences.* New York: Random House, 1970.

———. *L'Archéologie du savoir.* Paris: Gallimard, 1969. Translated by A. M. Sheridan Smith as *The Archaeology of Knowledge.* New York: Harper and Row, 1972.

———. *L'Ordre du discours: Leçon inaugurale au Collège de France prononcée le 2 décembre 1970.* Paris: Gallimard, 1971. Translated by Robert Swyer as "The Discourse on Language," appendix to *The Archaeology of Knowledge.* New York: Harper and Row, 1972.

———. *Ceci n'est pas une pipe: Deux lettres et quatre dessins de René Magritte.* Paris: Fata Morgana, 1973.

Foucault, Michel, ed. *Moi, Pierre Rivière, ayant égorgé ma mère, ma soeur et*

mon frère . . . : Un cas de parricide au XIXe siècle. In collaboration with
Blandine Barret-Kriegel et al. Paris: Gallimard, 1973. Translated by
Frank Jellinek as *I, Pierre Rivière, having slaughtered my mother, my sister,
and my brother . . . : A Case of Parricide in the 19th Century.* New York:
Pantheon, 1975.

Foucault, Michel. *Surveiller et punir: Naissance de la prison.* Paris: Gallimard,
1975. Translated by Alan Sheridan as *Discipline and Punish: The Birth of
the Prison.* New York: Pantheon, 1977.

————. *Histoire de la sexualité, I: La Volonté de savoir.* Paris: Gallimard,
1976. Translated by Robert Hurley as *The History of Sexuality, Volume 1:
An Introduction.* New York: Pantheon, 1978.

Foucault, Michel, et al. *Les Machines à guérir (aux origines de l'hôpital
moderne).* Paris: Institut de l'Environnement, 1976.

Foucault, Michel. *Language, Counter-Memory, Practice: Selected Essays and
Interviews.* Edited, with an introduction, by Donald F. Bouchard. Translated by Donald F. Bouchard and Sherry Simon. Ithaca: Cornell University Press, 1977.

————. *Power/Knowledge: Selected Interviews and Other Writings, 1972–
1977.* Edited, with a preface, by Colin Gordon. Translated by Colin
Gordon, Leo Marshall, John Mepham, and Kate Soper. Brighton, Sussex: The Harvester Press, 1980.

TRANSLATIONS (IN CHRONOLOGICAL ORDER)

Weizsaecker, Viktor von. *Le Cycle de la structure.* Translated from the
German by Michel Foucault and Daniel Rocher. [Paris]: Desclée de
Brouwer, 1958.

Kant, Emmanuel. *Anthropologie du point de vue pragmatique.* Translated
from the German by Michel Foucault. 2d ed. Paris: J. Vrin, 1970.

Spitzer, Leo. *Études de style.* Translated from the English and German by
Éliane Kaufholz, Alain Coulon, and Michel Foucault. Paris: Gallimard,
1970.

INTRODUCTIONS AND PREFACES
(IN CHRONOLOGICAL ORDER)

Foucault, Michel. Introduction and notes to *Le Rêve et l'Existence,* by Ludwig
Binswanger. Translated from the German by Jacqueline Verdeaux.
[Paris]: Desclée de Brouwer, 1954.

————. Introduction to *Rousseau: Juge de Jean Jaques [sic]. Dialogues,* by
Jean-Jacques Rousseau. Paris: Armand Colin, 1962.

Foucault, Michel, and Deleuze, Gilles. Introduction to *Le Gai Savoir:
Fragments posthumes (1881–1882),* by Friedrich Nietzsche. Translated by

Pierre Klossowski. Paris: Gallimard, 1967.

Foucault, Michel. Preface to *Grammaire générale et raisonnée* (1660), by Antoine Arnauld and Claude Lancelot. New ed. Paris: Republications Paulet, 1969.

———. Foreword to *Oeuvres complètes*, vol. 1: *Premier écrits, 1922–1940*, by Georges Bataille. Paris: Gallimard, 1970.

———. "7 propos sur le 7e ange." Preface to *La Grammaire logique* and *La Science de Dieu*, by Jean-Pierre Brisset. Paris: Claude Tchou, 1970.

———. Preface to *De la prison à la révolte*, by Serge Livrozet. Paris: Mercure de France, 1973.

———. Introduction to *Le désir est partout* (Gérard Fromanger). Exhibition catalogue. Paris: Galerie Jeanne Bucher, 1975.

———. Preface to *Les Juges kaki*, by Mireille Debard and Jean-Luc Hennig. Paris: Moreau, 1977.

———. Preface to *Anti-Oedipe: Le capitalisme et la schizophrénie*, by Gilles Deleuze and Felix Guattari. Translated by Robert Hurley, Helen Lane, and Mark Seem as *Anti-Oedipus: Capitalism and Schizophrenia*. New York: Viking Press, 1977.

———. Introduction to *Herculine Barbin dite Alexina B.* (1978). Translated by Richard McDougall as *Herculine Barbin: Being the Recently Discovered Memoirs of a Nineteenth-Century French Hermaphrodite*. New York: Pantheon, 1980.

———. Introduction to *On the Normal and the Pathological*, by Georges Canguilhem. Translated by Carolyn R. Fawcett. Boston: D. Reidel, 1978.

ARTICLES AND REVIEWS (IN CHRONOLOGICAL ORDER)

Foucault, Michel. "Le 'Non' du père" (on Friedrich Hölderlin). *Critique* 178 (March 1962): 195–209. Translated as "The Father's 'No.'" In *Language, Counter-Memory, Practice: Selected Essays and Interviews*, edited by Donald F. Bouchard, pp. 68–86. Ithaca: Cornell University Press, 1977.

———. "Un si cruel savoir." *Critique* 182 (July 1962): 597–611.

———. "Le langage à l'infini." *Tel Quel* 15 (Autumn 1963): 44–53. Translated as "Language to Infinity." In *Language, Counter-Memory, Practice: Selected Essays and Interviews*, edited by Donald F. Bouchard, pp. 53–67. Ithaca: Cornell University Press, 1977.

———. "Préface à la transgression" (on Georges Bataille). *Critique* 195–96 (August-September 1963): 751–69. Translated as "A Preface to Transgression." In *Language, Counter-Memory, Practice: Selected Essays and Interviews*, edited by Donald F. Bouchard, pp. 29–52. Ithaca: Cornell University Press, 1977.

———. "Distance, aspect, origine" (1963). In *Théorie d'ensemble*, edited by Philippe Sollers, pp. 11–24. Paris: Editions du Seuil, 1968.

———. "Guetter le jour qui vient" (on Roger Laporte). *La nouvelle revue française* 130 (October 1963): 709–16.

———. "La prose d'Actéon" (on Pierre Klossowski). *La nouvelle revue française* 135 (March 1964): 444–59.

———. "Le langage de l'espace." *Critique* 203 (April 1964): 378–82.

———. "Nietzsche, Freud, Marx." In *Nietzsche*, pp. 183–200. Proceedings of the Seventh International Philosophical Colloquium of the Cahiers de Royaumont, 4–8 July 1964. Paris: Editions de Minuit, 1967.

———. "Pourquoi réédite-t-on l'oeuvre de Raymond Roussel? Un précurseur de notre littérature moderne." *Le Monde*, 22 August 1964, p. 9.

———. "Le Mallarmé de J.-P. Richard." *Annales* 5 (September–October 1964): 996–1004.

———. "La pensée du dehors" (on Maurice Blanchot). *Critique* 229 (June 1966): 523–46.

———. "L'arrière-fable" (on Jules Verne). *L'Arc* 29 (1966): 5–12.

———. "Un 'fantastique' de bibliothèque" (on Gustave Flaubert). *Cahiers Renaud-Barrault* 59 (March 1967): 7–30. Revised as "La Bibliothèque fantastique." In *Flaubert*, edited by Raymonde Debray-Genette, pp. 171–90. Paris: Marcel Didier, 1970. Translated from the 1967 version as "Fantasia of the Library." In *Language, Counter-Memory, Practice: Selected Essays and Interviews*, edited by Donald F. Bouchard, pp. 87–109. Ithaca: Cornell University Press, 1977.

———. "Une mise au point de Michel Foucault." *La Quinzaine littéraire* 46 (15–31 March 1968): 21.

———. "Réponse à une question." *Esprit* 371 (May 1968): 850–74. Translated by Anthony M. Nazzaro as "History, Discourse and Discontinuity." *Salmagundi* 20 (Summer–Fall 1972): 225–48.

———. "À propos des 'Entretiens sur Foucault.'" *La Pensée* 139 (1968): 114–19.

———. "Réponse au Cercle d' épistémologie." *Cahiers pour l'analyse* 9 (Summer 1968): 9–40.

———. "Les déviations religieuses et le savoir médical." In *Hérésies et sociétés*, edited by Jacques Le Goff, pp. 19–29. Paris: Mouton, 1968.

———. "Ariane s'est pendue" (on Gilles Deleuze). *Le Nouvel Observateur* 229 (31 March 1969): 36–37.

———. "Qu'est-ce qu'un auteur?" *Bulletin de la Société française de Philosophie* 63 (1969): 73–104. Translated as "What Is an Author?" In *Language, Counter-Memory, Practice: Selected Essays and Interviews*, edited by Donald F. Bouchard, pp. 113–38. Ithaca: Cornell University Press, 1977.

Foucault, Michel, and Canguilhem, Georges. "Hommage à Jean Hyppolite." *Revue de Métaphysique et de Morale* 74 (1969): 129–36.

Foucault, Michel. "Il y aura scandale, mais. . . ." (on Pierre Guyotat). *Le Nouvel Observateur* 304 (7 September 1970): 40.

———. "La situation de Cuvier dans l'histoire de la biologie." *Revue d'histoire des sciences et de leurs applications* 23 (1970): 64–92.

———. "Croître et multiplier" (on François Jacob). *Le Monde*, 15–16 November 1970, p. 13.

———. "Theatrum Philosophicum" (on Gilles Deleuze). *Critique* 282 (November 1970): 885–908. Translated under the same title in *Language, Counter-Memory, Practice: Selected Essays and Interviews*, edited by Donald F. Bouchard, pp. 165–96. Ithaca: Cornell University Press, 1977.

———. "Résumés des cours donnés au Collège de France sous le titre général: Histoire des systèmes de pensée [Années 1970–74]." In appendix to *Foucault et l'archéologie du savoir*, by Angèle Kremer-Marietti, pp. 195–234. Paris: Seghers, 1974. Résumé for 1970–71 translated as "History of Systems of Thought." In *Language, Counter-Memory, Practice: Selected Essays and Interviews*, edited by Donald F. Bouchard, pp. 199–204. Ithaca: Cornell University Press, 1977.

———. "Nietzsche, la généalogie, l'histoire." In *Hommage à Jean Hyppolite*, by Suzanne Bachelard et al., pp. 145–72. Paris: Presses Universitaires de France, 1971. Translated as "Nietzsche, Genealogy, History." In *Language, Counter-Memory, Practice: Selected Essays and Interviews*, edited by Donald F. Bouchard, pp. 139–64. Ithaca: Cornell University Press, 1977.

———. "Monstrosities in Criticism." Translated by Robert Matthews. *Diacritics* 1 (Fall 1971): 57–60.

———. "Foucault responds/2." *Diacritics* 1 (Winter 1971): 60.

———. "Le discours de Toul." *Le Nouvel Observateur* 372 (27 December 1971): 15.

———. "Cérémonie, Théâtre et Politique au XVIIe siècle." Summarized in English by Stephen Davidson. In *Proceedings of the Fourth Annual Conference of XVIIth Century French Literature*, pp. 22–23. Minneapolis: University of Minnesota Press, 1972.

———. "Piéger sa propre culture" (on Gaston Bachelard). *Le Figaro littéraire*, 30 September 1972, p. 16.

———. "Les deux morts de Pompidou." *Le Nouvel Observateur* 421 (4 December 1972): 56–57. Translated in abridged form by Paul Auster as "The Guillotine Lives." *The New York Times*, 8 April 1973, sec. 4, p. 15.

———. "En guise de conclusion." *Le Nouvel Observateur* 435 (13 March 1973): 92.

Foucault, Michel; Landau, A.; and Petit, J.-Y. "Convoqués à la P. J." *Le Nouvel Observateur* 468 (29 October 1973): 53.

Foucault, Michel. "Les Rayons noirs de Byzantios." *Le Nouvel Observateur* 483 (11 February 1974): 56–57.

———. "La Naissance des prisons." *Le Nouvel Observateur* 536 (17 February 1975): 69–86.

———. "Two Lectures" (Collège de France, 7 and 14 January 1976). Translated by Kate Soper. In *Power/Knowledge: Selected Interviews and Other Writings, 1972–1977*, edited by Colin Gordon, pp. 78–108. Brighton, Sussex: The Harvester Press, 1980.

———. "L'Occident et la vérité du sexe." *Le Monde*, 5 November 1976. Translated by Lawrence Winters as "The West and the Truth of Sex." *Sub-Stance* 20 (1978): 5–8.

———. "La politique de la santé au XVIIIe siècle." In *Les Machines à guérir (aux origines de l'hôpital moderne)*, by Michel Foucault et al. Paris: Institut de l'Environnement, 1976. Translated by Colin Gordon as "The Politics of Health in the Eighteenth Century." In *Power/Knowledge: Selected Interviews and Other Writings, 1972–1977*, edited by Colin Gordon, pp. 166–82. Brighton, Sussex: The Harvester Press, 1980.

———. "La Vie des hommes infâmes." *Les Cahiers du Chemin* 29 (15 January 1977): 12–29.

———. "Le Citron et le Lait." *Le Monde*, 21 October 1978, p. 14.

———. "Inutile de se soulever?" *Le Monde*, 11 May 1979, pp. 1–2.

CONVERSATIONS AND INTERVIEWS
(IN CHRONOLOGICAL ORDER)

Foucault, Michel. "Débat sur le roman." With Philippe Sollers et al. *Tel Quel* 17 (Spring 1964): 12–54.

———. "Débat sur la poésie." With Philippe Sollers et al. *Tel Quel* 17 (Spring 1964): 69–82.

Chapsal, Madeleine, interviewer. "Entretien: Michel Foucault." *La Quinzaine littéraire* 5 (15 May 1966): 14–15.

Bellour, Raymond, interviewer. "Entretien avec Michel Foucault" (1966). In *Le Livre des autres*, by Raymond Bellour, pp. 135–44. Paris: Editions de l'Herne, 1971.

———. "Deuxième entretien avec Michel Foucault" (1967). In *Le Livre des autres*, by Raymond Bellour, pp. 189–207. Paris: Editions de l'Herne, 1971.

Caruso, Paolo, interviewer. "Conversazione con Michel Foucault" (1967). In *Conversazioni con Claude Lévi-Strauss, Michel Foucault, Jacques Lacan*, by Paolo Caruso, pp. 91–131. Milan: Mursia, 1969.

El Kabbach, Jean-Pierre, interviewer. "Foucault répond à Sartre." *La Quinzaine littéraire* 46 (1–15 March 1968): 20–22.

Brochier, Jean-Jacques, interviewer. "Michel Foucault explique son dernier livre." *Magazine Littéraire* 28 (April–May 1969): 23–25.

Palmier, Jean-Michel, interviewer. "La naissance d'un monde." *Le Monde*, 3 May 1969, p. viii.

Loriot, Patrick, interviewer. "La piège de Vincennes." *Le Nouvel Observateur* 274 (9 February 1970): 33–35.

Simon, John K., interviewer. "A Conversation with Michel Foucault." *Partisan Review* 38 (1971): 193–201.

Chomsky, Noam, and Foucault, Michel. "Human Nature: Justice versus Power" (1971). In *Reflexive Water: The Basic Concerns of Mankind*, edited by Fons Elders, pp. 133–97. London: Souvenir Press, 1974.

Burnier, Michel-Antoine, and Graine, Philippe, interviewers. Untitled 1971 interview with Michel Foucault conducted under the auspices of *Actuel*. Reprinted in *C'est demain la veille*, edited, with an introduction, by Michel-Antoine Burnier, pp. 19–43. Paris: Editions du Seuil, [1973]. Translated as "Revolutionary Action: 'Until Now.'" In *Language, Counter-Memory, Practice: Selected Essays and Interviews*, edited by Donald F. Bouchard, pp. 218–33. Ithaca: Cornell University Press, 1977.

Foucault, Michel. "Sur la justice populaire: Débat avec les Maos." *Les Temps Modernes* 310 BIS (1972): 335–66. Translated by John Mepham as "On Popular Justice: A Discussion with Maoists." In *Power/Knowledge: Selected Interviews and Other Writings, 1972–1977*, edited by Colin Gordon, pp. 1–36. Brighton, Sussex: The Harvester Press, 1980.

Foucault, Michel, and Deleuze, Gilles. "Les intellectuels et le pouvoir." *L'Arc* 49 (March 1972): 3–10. Translated as "Intellectuals and Power." In *Language, Counter-Memory, Practice: Selected Essays and Interviews*, edited by Donald F. Bouchard, pp. 205–17. Ithaca: Cornell University Press, 1977.

Foucault, Michel. "Table ronde." With J.-M. Domenach et al. *Esprit* 413 (April–May 1972): 678–703.

Simon, John K., interviewer. "Michel Foucault on Attica: An Interview." *Telos* 19 (Spring 1974): 154–61.

Bonitzer, Pascal, and Toubidna, Serge, interviewers. "Anti-rétro: Entretien avec Michel Foucault." *Cahiers du Cinéma* 251–52 (July–August 1974): 5–15.

Foucault, Michel, and Cixous, Hélène. "À propos de Marguerite Duras." *Cahiers de la Compagnie Renaud-Barrault* 89 (1975): 8–22.

Droit, Roger-Pol, interviewer. "Des supplices aux cellules." *Le Monde*, 21 February 1975, p. 16. Excerpts translated by Leonard Mayhew as "Michel Foucault on the Role of Prisons." *The New York Times*, 5 August 1975, p. 31.

Ezine, Jean-Louis, interviewer. "Sur la sellette: Michel Foucault." *Les Nouvelles littéraires* 2477 (17 March 1975): 3.

Brochier, Jean-Jacques, interviewer. "Entretien sur la prison: le livre et sa méthode." *Magazine Littéraire* 101 (June 1975): 27–33. Translated by Colin Gordon as "Prison Talk." In *Power/Knowledge: Selected Interviews and Other Writings, 1972–1977*, edited by Colin Gordon, pp. 37–54. Brighton, Sussex: The Harvester Press, 1980.

Foucault, Michel. "Pouvoir et Corps" (1975). Translated by Colin Gordon as "Body/Power." In *Power/Knowledge: Selected Interviews and Other Writings, 1972–1977*, edited by Colin Gordon, pp. 55–62. Brighton, Sussex: The Harvester Press, 1980.

——. "Questions à Michel Foucault sur la géographie" (1976). Translated by Colin Gordon as "Questions on Geography." In *Power/Knowledge: Selected Interviews and Other Writings, 1972–1977*, edited by Colin Gordon, pp. 63–77. Brighton, Sussex: The Harvester Press, 1980.

Feret, René, interviewer. "Sur *Histoire de Paul*." *Cahiers du Cinéma* 262–63 (January 1976): 62–65.

Karol, K. S., interviewer. "Michel Foucault: Crimes et châtiments en U.S.S.R. et ailleurs. . . ." *Le Nouvel Observateur* 585 (26 January 1976): 34–37. Translated in abridged form by Mollie Horwitz as "The Politics of Crime." *Partisan Review* 43 (1976): 453–59.

Jaccard, Roland, interviewer. "Sorcellerie et folie." *Le Monde*, 23 April 1976, p. 18.

Kané, Pascal, interviewer. "Entretien avec Michel Foucault." *Cahiers du Cinéma* 271 (November 1976): 52–53.

Fontana, Alessandro, and Pasquino, Pasquale, interviewers. "Intervista a Michel Foucault" (1977). Translated by Colin Gordon as "Truth and Power." In *Power/Knowledge: Selected Interviews and Other Writings, 1972–1977*, edited by Colin Gordon, pp. 109–33. Brighton, Sussex: The Harvester Press, 1980.

Finas, Lucette, interviewer. "Les rapports de pouvoir passent à l'intérieur des corps." *La Quinzaine littéraire* 247 (1–15 January 1977): 4–6. Translated by Leo Marshall as "The History of Sexuality." In *Power/Knowledge: Selected Interviews and Other Writings, 1972–1977*, edited by Colin Gordon, pp. 183–93. Brighton, Sussex: The Harvester Press, 1980.

Foucault, Michel. "Pouvoirs et Stratégies." *Les Révoltes Logiques* 4 (1977): 89–97. Translated by Colin Gordon as "Powers and Strategies." In *Power/Knowledge: Selected Interviews and Other Writings, 1972–1977*, edited by Colin Gordon, pp. 134–45. Brighton, Sussex: The Harvester Press, 1980.

Barou, Jean-Pierre, and Perrot, Michelle, interviewers. "Un entretien avec Michel Foucault: L'oeil du pouvoir." *Nouvelles littéraires* 2578 (April 1977): 6–7. Translated by Colin Gordon as "The Eye of Power." In

Power/Knowledge: Selected Interviews and Other Writings, 1972–1977, edited by Colin Gordon, pp. 146–65. Brighton, Sussex: The Harvester Press, 1980.

Lévy, Bernard-Henri, interviewer. "Foucault: Non au sexe roi." *Le Nouvelle Observateur* 644 (March 1977): 92 ff. Translated by David J. Parent as "Power and Sex: An Interview with Michel Foucault." *Telos* 32 (Summer 1977): 152–61.

Foucault, Michel. "Le Jeu de Michel Foucault" (1977). Translated by Colin Gordon as "The Confession of the Flesh." In *Power/Knowledge: Selected Interviews and Other Writings, 1972–1977,* edited by Colin Gordon, pp. 194–228. Brighton, Sussex: The Harvester Press, 1980.

Works on Michel Foucault

BOOKS

Cotesta, Vittorio. *Linguaggio, Potere, Individuo: Saggio su Michel Foucault.* Bari: Dedalio Libri, 1979.

Guédez, Annie. *Foucault.* Paris: Editions Universitaires, 1972.

Kremer-Marietti, Angèle. *Foucault et l'archéologie du savoir.* Paris: Seghers, 1974.

Sheridan, Alan. *Michel Foucault: The Will to Truth.* London: Tavistock Publications, 1980.

ARTICLES AND SELECTIONS

Alterieri, Charles F. "Northrup Frye and the Problem of Spiritual Authority." *PMLA* 87 (October 1972): 964–75.

Arac, Jonathan. "The Function of Foucault at the Present Time." *Humanities in Society* 3 (Winter 1980): 73–86.

Aron, Harry. "Wittgenstein's Impact on Foucault." In *Wittgenstein and his Impact on Contemporary Thought,* pp. 58–60. Proceedings of the Second International Wittgenstein Symposium, 29 August–4 September 1977. Vienna: Hölder-Pichler-Tempsky, 1978.

Auzias, Jean-Marie. "Le non-structuralisme de Michel Foucault." In *Le structuralisme,* pp. 128–46. 3d ed. Paris: Seghers, 1975.

Baudrillard, Jean. "Forgetting Foucault." Translated by Nicole Dufresne. *Humanities in Society* 3 (Winter 1980): 87–111.

Bellour, Raymond. "L'homme, les mots." *Magazine Littéraire* 101 (June 1975): 20–23.

Bertherat, Yves. "La pensée folle." *Esprit* 35 (May 1967): 862–81.

Bové, Paul A. "The End of Humanism: Michel Foucault and the Power of

Disciplines." *Humanities in Society* 3 (Winter 1980): 23–40.

Boyers, Robert. "Politics and History: Pathways in European Film." *Salmagundi* 38–39 (Summer–Fall 1977): 50–79.

Brodeur, Jean-Paul. "McDonell on Foucault: Supplementary Remarks." *Canadian Journal of Philosophy* 7 (September 1977): 555–68.

Brown, P. L. "Epistemology and Method: Althusser, Foucault, Derrida." *Cultural Hermeneutics* 3 (August 1975): 147–63.

Carroll, David. "The Subject of Archeology or the Sovereignty of the Episteme." *Modern Language Notes* 93 (May 1978): 695–722.

Cavallari, Héctor Mario. "*Savoir* and *Pouvoir*: Michel Foucault's Theory of Discursive Practice." *Humanities in Society* 3 (Winter 1980): 55–72.

Le Cercle d'épistémologie. "A Michel Foucault." *Cahiers pour l'analyse* 9 (Summer 1968): 5–8.

_____. "Nouvelles questions." *Cahiers pour l'analyse* 9 (Summer 1968): 41–44.

Chalumeau, Jean-Luc. "L'archéologie des sciences humaines." In *La pensée en France de Sartre à Foucault*, pp. 47–64. Paris: Fernand Nathan-Alliance Française, 1974.

Cranston, Maurice. "Michel Foucault." *Encounter* 30 (June 1968): 34–42. Translated into French as "Les 'périodes' de Michel Foucault." *Preuves* 209–10 (August–September 1968): 65–75.

Daix, Pierre. "Structure du structuralisme (II)—Althusser et Foucault." *Les Léttres françaises* 1239 (3–9 July 1968): 7, 11.

D'Amico, Robert. "Introduction to the Foucault-Deleuze Discussion." *Telos* 16 (Summer 1973): 101–2.

_____. "Four Books on or by Michel Foucault." *Telos* 36 (Summer 1978): 169–83.

El Kordi, Mohamed. "L'Archéologie de la pensée classique selon Michel Foucault." *Revue d'histoire économique et sociale* 51 (1973): 309–35.

Felman, Shoshana. "De Foucault à Nerval: *Aurélia* ou 'Le livre infaisable.'" In *La folie et la chose littéraire*, pp. 61–77. Paris: Editions du Seuil, [1978].

_____. "Foucault/Derrida: Folie et logos." In *La folie et la chose littéraire*, pp. 35–55. Paris: Editions du Seuil, [1978].

Griset, Antoine. "Foucault, un projet historique." *Magazine Littéraire* 123 (April 1977): 24–26.

Hattiangadi, J. N. "Language Philosophy: Hacking and Foucault." *Dialogue* 17 (September 1978): 513–28.

Hayman, Ronald. "Cartography of Discourse? On Foucault." *Encounter* 47 (December 1976): 72–75.

Jambet, Christian. "Une interrogation sur les pouvoirs." *Le Monde*, 21 February 1975, p. 17.

Lecourt, Dominique. "On Archaeology and Knowledge (Michel Foucault)"

(1970; revised 1972). In *Pour une critique de l'épistémologie (Bachelard, Canguilhem, Foucault)*, pp. 98–133. Paris: Maspero, 1972. Translated by Ben Brewster as *Marxism and Epistemology: Bachelard, Canguilhem, Foucault*, pp. 187–213. London: New Left Books and Atlantic Highlands, N.J.: Humanities Press, 1975.

Lévy, Bernard-Henri. "Le système Foucault." *Magazine Littéraire* 101 (June 1975): 7–9.

McDonell, Donald J. "On Foucault's Philosophical Method." *Canadian Journal of Philosophy* 7 (September 1977): 537–53.

McMullen, Roy. "Michel Foucault." *Horizon* 11 (Autumn 1969): 36–39.

Margolin, Jean-Claude. "L'homme de Michel Foucault." *Revue des Sciences Humaines* 128 (1967): 497–521.

————. "Tribut d'un antihumaniste aux études d'humanisme et renaissance: Note sur l'oeuvre de Michel Foucault." *Bibliothèque D'Humanisme et Renaissance* 29 (1967): 701–11.

Miguelez, Roberto. "Théorie du discours et théorie de l'histoire." *Dialogue* 13 (March 1974): 53–70.

Millet, Louis, and Varin d'Ainvelle, Madeleine. "La mort de l'humanisme." In *Le structuralisme*, pp. 69–79. 2d ed. Paris: Editions Universitaires, 1972.

Nemo, Philippe. "D'une prison à l'autre." *Le Nouvel Observateur* 374 (10–16 January 1972): 40–41.

Pelorson, Jean-Marc. "Michel Foucault et l'Espagne." *Pensée* 152 (August 1970): 88–99.

Racevskis, Karlis. "The Discourse of Michel Foucault: A Case of an Absent and Forgettable Subject." *Humanities in Society* 3 (Winter 1980): 41–53.

Revel, Jacques, and Bellour, Raymond. "Foucault et les historiens." *Magazine Littéraire* 101 (June 1975): 10–13.

Said, Edward W. "*Abecedarium Culturae*: Absence, Writing, Statement, Discourse, Archeology, Structuralism" (1971). In *Beginnings: Intention and Method*, pp. 277–343. New York: Basic Books, 1975.

————. "Linguistics and the Archeology of Mind." *International Philosophical Quarterly* 11 (March 1971): 104–34.

————. "Michel Foucault as an Intellectual Imagination." *Boundary 2* 1 (Fall 1972): 1–36.

————. "The Problem of Textuality: Two Exemplary Positions." *Critical Inquiry* 4 (Summer 1978): 673–714.

Sprinker, Michael. "The Use and Abuse of Foucault." *Humanities in Society* 3 (Winter 1980): 1–21.

Venault, Philippe. "Histoires de. . . ." *Magazine Littéraire* 101 (June 1975): 14–19.

Wahl, François. "Y a-t-il une *épistémè* structuraliste? Ou d'une philosophie en deça du structuralisme: Michel Foucault." In *Qu'est-ce que le struc-*

turalisme? by Oswald Ducrot et al., pp. 305–90. Paris: Editions du Seuil, 1968.

White, Hayden V. "Foucault Decoded: Notes from Underground." *History and Theory* 12 (1973): 23–54.

Ysmal, Colette. "Histoire et archéologie. Note sur la recherche de Michel Foucault." *Revue Française de Science Politique* 22 (August 1972): 775–804.

ESSAYS AND REVIEWS OF SPECIFIC WORKS

Mental Illness and Psychology (1954)

Caillois, Roland. Review. *Critique* 93 (February 1955): 189–90.

Huard, P. Review. *Revue de Synthèse* 45–46 (January–June 1967): 94–95.

Madness and Civilization (1961)

Barthes, Roland. "Savoir et folie." *Critique* 174 (November 1961): 915–22. Translated by Richard Howard as "Taking Sides." In *Critical Essays*, pp. 163–70. Evanston: Northwestern University Press, 1972.

Blanchot, Maurice. "L'oubli, la déraison." In *L'Entretien infini*, pp. 289–99. Paris: Gallimard, 1969.

Derrida, Jacques. "Cogito et histoire de la folie" (1963). In *L'écriture et la différence*, pp. 51–97. Paris: Editions du Seuil, 1967.

———. "A propos de 'Cogito et histoire de la folie.'" *Revue de Métaphysique et de Morale* 69 (1964): 116–19.

Gay, Peter. "Chains and Couches." *Commentary* 40 (October 1965): 93–94, 96.

Laing, R. D. "The Invention of Madness." *The New Statesman* 73 (16 June 1967): 843.

Mandrou, Robert. "Trois clefs pour comprendre la folie à l'époque classique." *Annales* 4 (July–August 1962): 761–71.

Marcus, Steven. "In Praise of Folly." *The New York Review of Books*, 17 November 1966, pp. 36–39.

Matza, David. Review. *American Sociological Review* 31 (August 1966): 551–52.

Nemo, Philippe. Review. *Le Nouvel Observateur* 404 (7–13 August 1972): 39.

Paulson, Ronald. Review. *Journal of English and Germanic Philology* 67 (January 1968): 161–65.

Peters, Michael. Review. *Sociological Review* 19 (November 1971): 634–38.

Rousseau, G. S. Review. *Eighteenth-Century Studies* 4 (Fall 1970): 90–95.

Serres, Michel. "Géométrie de l'incommunicable: La Folie" (1962). In *Hermes I: La Communication*, pp. 167–90. Paris: Editions de Minuit, 1968.

Simon, John K. Review. *Modern Language Notes* 78 (January 1963): 85–88.

The Birth of the Clinic (1963)
Aronson, Alfred Lars. "Medicine: History and Theory." *The Yale Review* 63 (March 1974): 473–76.
Caws, Peter. "Medical Change." *The New Republic* 169 (10 November 1973): 28–30.
Dagognet, François. "Archéologie ou histoire de la médecine?" *Critique* 216 (May 1965): 436–47.
Figlio, Karl. Review. *British Journal for the History of Science* 10 (July 1977): 164–67.
Hahn, Roger. Review. *American Journal of Sociology* 80 (May 1975): 1503–4.
Kaplan, Donald M. Review. *The Village Voice* 18 (22 November 1973): 29, 31.
Kupers, Terry A. Review. *Science and Society* 39 (Summer 1975): 235–38.
Lasch, Christopher. "After the church the doctors, after the doctors utopia." *The New York Times Book Review*, 24 February 1974, p. 6.
Loudon, J. B. Review. *Man* 9 (June 1974): 319–20.
"The New Medicine of Organs." *The Times Literary Supplement*, 1 February 1974, pp. 107–8.
Oldman, David. Review. *Sociology* 9 (May 1975): 359–60.
Poynter, F. N. L. Review. *History of Science* 3 (1964): 140–43.
Starobinski, Jean. "Gazing at Death." *The New York Review of Books*, 22 January 1976, pp. 18, 20–22.
Zeldin, Theodore. "An Archeologist of Knowledge." *The New Statesman* 86 (7 December 1973): 861–62.

Raymond Roussel (1963)
André, Robert. "Le trésor de Raymond Roussel." *La nouvelle revue française* 129 (1 September 1963): 489–94.
Bertherat, Yves. Review. *Esprit* 333 (January 1965): 284–86.
Blanchot, Maurice. "Roussel." In *L'Entretien infini*, pp. 493–97. Paris: Gallimard, 1969.
David, Catherine. "L'Ange du bizarre." *Le Nouvel Observateur* 434 (6–12 March 1973): 60–61.
Hahn, Otto. "Interprétations de Raymond Roussel." *Les Temps Modernes* 218 (July 1964): 163–71.
"Revival of a Writer." *The Times Literary Supplement*, 9 January 1964, pp. 17–18.
Robbe-Grillet, Alain. "Énigmes et transparence chez Raymond Roussel." *Critique* 199 (December 1963): 1027–33.
Sollers, Philippe. "Logicus solus." *Tel Quel* 14 (Summer 1963): 46–50.

Sorin, Raphaël. "Le pendule de Foucault ou le critique dans le labyrinthe." *Bizarre* 34–35 (1964): 75–76.

The Order of Things (1966)

Amiot, Michel. "Le relativisme culturaliste de Michel Foucault." *Les Temps Modernes* 248 (January 1967): 1271–98.

Askenazi, Joël. "Michel Foucault et les lendemains de l'homme." *Nouveaux Cahiers* 9 (Spring 1967): 16–19.

Burgelin, Pierre. "L'archéologie du savoir." *Esprit* 360 (May 1967): 843–61.

Canguilhem, Georges. "Mort de l'homme ou épuisement du *cogito?*" *Critique* 242 (July 1967): 599–618.

Caws, Peter. "Language as the Human Reality." *The New Republic* 164 (27 March 1971): 28–34.

Certeau, Michel de. "Les sciences humaines et la mort de l'homme." *Etudes* 326 (March 1967): 344–60. Reprinted as "Le noir soleil du langage: Michel Foucault." In *L'Absent de l'histoire*, pp. 115–34. Paris: Mame, 1973.

Chapsal, Madeleine. "Is Man Dead?" *Atlas* 12 (September 1966): 58–59.

Châtelet, François. "L'homme, ce Narcisse incertain." *La Quinzaine littéraire* 2 (1 April 1966): 19–20.

Colombel, Jeanette. "Les mots de Foucault et les choses." *La Nouvelle Critique* 4 (185), new ser. (May 1967): 8–13.

Corvez, Maurice. "Le structuralisme de Michel Foucault." *Revue Thomiste* 68 (January–March 1968): 101–24.

Cranston, Maurice. "He's Got the Whole World in His Head." *The Washington Post Book World*, 14 February 1971, p. 5.

Culler, Jonathan. "Words and Things: Michel Foucault." *Cambridge Review* 92 (29 January 1971): 104–5.

Deleuze, Gilles. "L'homme, une existence douteuse." *Le Nouvel Observateur* 81 (1 June 1966): 32–34.

D'Ormesson, Jean. "Passage de l'homme ou les avatars du savoir." *La Nouvelle Revue Française* 29 (March 1967): 477–90.

Dufrenne, Mikel. "L'épistémologie archéologique." In *Pour l'homme*, pp. 37–47. Paris: Editions du Seuil, 1968.

Garaudy, Roger. "Structuralisme et 'mort de l'homme.'" *La Pensée* 135 (October 1967): 107–24.

Girardin, Benoît. Review. *Freiburger Zeitschrift für Philosophie und Theologie* 16 (1969): 92–99.

Greene, John C. "Les mots and les choses." *Social Science Information* 6 (August 1967): 131–38.

Harding, D. W. "Good-by Man." *The New York Review of Books*, 12 August 1971, pp. 21–22.

Howard, Richard. "Our Sense of Where We Are." *The Nation* 213 (5 July 1971): 21–22.

Huppert, George. "*Divinatio et Eruditio*: Thoughts on Foucault." *History and Theory* 13 (1974): 191–207.

Labeyrie, Vincent. "Remarques sur l'évolution du concept de biologie." *La Pensée* 135 (October 1967): 125–37.

Lacharité, Normand. "Archéologie du savoir et structures du langage scientifique." *Dialogue* 9 (1970): 35–53.

————. "Les conditions de possibilité du savoir: Deux versions structuralistes de ce problème." *Dialogue* 7 (1968): 359–73.

Lacroix, Jean. "Fin de l'humanisme?" *Le Monde*, 9 June 1966, p. 13.

Langlois, Jean. "Michel Foucault et la mort de l'homme." *Science et Esprit* 21 (1969): 209–30.

Larson, James L. Review. *Isis* 64 (1973): 246–47.

Lavers, Annette. "Man, Meaning and Subject: A Current Reappraisal." *Journal of the British Society for Phenomenology* 1 (October 1970): 44–49.

Le Bon, Sylvie. "Un positiviste désespéré: Michel Foucault." *Les Temps Modernes* 248 (January 1967): 1299–1319.

Leland, Dorothy. "On Reading and Writing the World: Foucault's History of Thought." *Clio* 4 (1975): 225–43.

Lemaigre, B. "Michel Foucault ou les malheurs de la raison et les prospérités du langage." *Revue des Sciences Philosophiques et Théologiques* 51 (1967): 440–60.

Mendel, Gérard. "Les mots sans les choses." In *La révolte contre le père: Une introduction à la sociopsychanalyse*, pp. 288–336. Paris: Payot, 1968.

Miel, Jan. "Ideas or Epistemes: Hazard versus Foucault." *Yale French Studies* 49 (1973): 231–45.

Moore, John Hartwell. Review. *Science and Society* 35 (Winter 1971): 490–94.

Parain-Vial, Jeanne. "Les mots et les choses." In *Analyses structurales et idéologies structuralistes*, pp. 176–95. Toulouse: Edouard Privat, 1969.

Piaget, Jean. "Structuralism without Structures." In *Structuralism*, translated and edited by Chaninah Maschler. pp. 128–35. New York: Harper and Row, 1970.

Pratt, Vernon. "Foucault and the History of Classification Theory." *Studies in History and Philosophy of Science* 8 (1977): 163–71.

Puglisi, Gianni. "La fondazione esistenziale nell'analisi strutturale." In *Che cosa è lo strutturalismo*, pp. 117–60. Rome: Ubaldini, 1970.

Revault D'Allonnes, Olivier. "Michel Foucault: Les mots contre les choses." In *Structuralisme et Marxisme*, by Jean-Marie Auzias et al., pp. 13–37. Paris: Union Générale d'Edition, 1970.

Rousseau, G. S. "Whose Enlightenment? Not Man's: The Case of Michel Foucault." *Eighteenth-Century Studies* 6 (Winter 1972–73): 238–56.

Serres, Michel. "Le retour de la Nef." In *Hermes I: La Communication*, pp. 191–205. Paris: Editions de Minuit, 1968.

Sharratt, Bernard. "Notes after Foucault." *New Blackfriars* 53 (1972): 251–64.

Steiner, George. "The Mandarin of the Hour—Michel Foucault." *The New York Times Book Review*, 28 February 1971, pp. 8, 28–31.

———. "Steiner responds to Foucault." *Diacritics* 1 (Winter 1971): 59.

Testa, Aldo. "The Resurrection of Man and the Extinction of the *Cogito* (Reply to Foucault)." In *The Dialogic Structure of Language*, pp. 133–38. Bologna: Cappelli, 1970.

"Trois entretiens sur Foucault." With B. Balan, G. Dulac, G. Marcy, J.-P. Ponthus, J. Proust, J. Stefanini, and E. Verley. *La Pensée* 137 (January–February 1968): 3–37.

Wahl, Jean. Review. *Revue de Métaphysique et de Morale* 74 (April–June 1967): 250–51.

Wurms, Pierre. "Un best-seller: Michel Foucault: *Les Mots et les Choses*." *Die Neueren Sprachen* 67 (November 1968): 561–64.

The Archaeology of Knowledge (1969)

Caws, Peter. Review. *The New York Times Book Review*, 22 October 1972, pp. 6, 22, 24.

"The Contented Positivist: M. Foucault and the Death of Man." *The Times Literary Supplement*, 2 July 1970, pp. 697–98.

Culler, Jonathan. "Language and Knowledge." *The Yale Review* 62 (Winter 1973): 290–96.

Deleuze, Gilles. "Un nouvel archiviste." *Critique* 274 (March 1970): 195–209.

Guédon, Jean-Claude. "Michel Foucault: The Knowledge of Power and the Power of Knowledge." *Bulletin of the History of Medicine* 51 (Summer 1977): 245–77.

Hacking, Ian. "The Archeology of Knowledge." *Cambridge Review* 93 (2 June 1972): 166–70.

Hector, Josette. "Michel Foucault et l'histoire." *Synthèses* 309–10 (March–April 1972): 86–88.

Hussain, Athar. "A Brief Resumé of the Archaeology of Knowledge." *Theoretical Practice* 3–4 (1971): 104–7.

Kermode, Frank. "Crisis Critic." *The New York Review of Books*, 17 May 1973, pp. 37–39.

Kremer-Marietti, Angèle. "L'archéologie du savoir." *Revue de Métaphysique et de Morale* 75 (1970): 355–60.

Lecourt, Dominique. "On Archaeology and Knowledge (Michel Foucault)" (1970; revised 1972). In *Pour une critique de l'épistémologie (Bachelard, Canguilhem, Foucault)*, pp. 98–133. Paris: Maspero, 1972. Translated by

Ben Brewster as *Marxism and Epistemology: Bachelard, Canguilhem, Foucault*, pp. 187–213. London: New Left Books and Atlantic Highlands, N.J.: Humanities Press, 1975.
Russo, François. Review. *Archives de Philosophie* 36 (January–March 1973): 69–105.
Said, Edward. "An Ethics of Language." *Diacritics* 4 (Summer 1974): 28–37.
Shaffer, E. S. Review. *Studies in History and Philosophy of Science* 7 (1976): 269–75.
Williams, Karel. "Unproblematic Archeology." *Economy and Society* 3 (February 1974): 41–68.

The Discourse on Language (1971)
Daix, Pierre. "Michel Foucault et Georges Duby au Collège de France." *Les Lettres françaises* 1263 (5–9 December 1970): 3–4.
Lacouture, Jean. "Le cours inaugural de M. Michel Foucault: Éloge du discours interdit." *Le Monde*, 4 December 1970, p. 8.
Seem, Mark D. "Liberation of Difference: Toward a Theory of Antiliterature." *New Literary History* 5 (Autumn 1973): 119–33.
W. V. E. Review. *The Review of Metaphysics* 26 (March 1973): 534–35.

I, Pierre Rivière, . . . (1973)
Bittner, Egon. Review. *American Journal of Sociology* 82 (July 1976): 256–58.
Cobb, Richard. "A Triple Murder." *New Society* 44 (8 June 1978): 550–52.
Delany, Paul. Review. *The New York Times Book Review*, 18 May 1975, pp. 31–32.
Fco, Ronald de. "Anatomy of a Murder." *National Review* 27 (29 August 1975): 950–51.
Ferro, Marc. "Au croisement de l'Histoire et du crime." *La Quinzaine littéraire* 176 (1–15 December 1973): 25–26.
Galey, Matthieu. "L'intelligence de l'idiot." *Realités* 336 (January 1974): 82.
Gallo, Max. "Histoire d'une folie." *L'Express* 1162 (15–21 October 1973): 59–60.
Le Roy Ladurie, Emmanuel. "Pierre Rivière, un parricide du XIXe siècle." *Le Monde*, 18 October 1973, pp. 19, 25.
Ménard, Jacques. Review. *Les cahiers du chemin* 20 (15 January 1974): 159–64.
Orgogoso, Isabelle. Review. *Esprit* 3 (March 1974): 532–33.
Roudinesco, Elisabeth. "Le Schreber du pauvre." *Action Poétique* 57 (1974): 64–69.

Discipline and Punish (1975)
Blot, Jean. Review. *La Nouvelle Revue Française* 276 (December 1975): 89–92.
Deleuze, Gilles. "Ecrivain non: Un nouveau cartographe." *Critique* 31 (December 1975): 1207–27.
Di Piero, W. S. "Discipline and Punish: The Birth of the Prison." *Commonweal* 105 (12 May 1978): 313–15.
Enthoven, Jean-Paul. "Crimes et châtiments." *Le Nouvel Observateur* 538 (3–9 March 1975): 58–59.
Ewald, François. "Anatomie et corps politique." *Critique* 31 (December 1975): 1228–65.
Gallo, Max. "La prison selon Michel Foucault." *L'Express* 1233 (24 February–2 March 1975): 31–32.
Geertz, Clifford. "Stir Crazy." *The New York Review of Books*, 26 January 1978, pp. 3–4, 6.
Harding, D. W. "Towards Total Control of Man." *The Listener* 98 (15 December 1977): 802–3.
Kurzweil, Edith. "Law and Disorder." *Partisan Review* 44 (1977): 293–97.
Laslett, Peter. "Under Observation." *New Society* 42 (1 December 1977): 474–75.
Lucas, Colin. "Power and the Panopticon." *The Times Literary Supplement*, 26 August 1975, p. 1090.
McConnell, Frank. Review. *The New Republic* 178 (1 April 1978): 32–34.
Poirier, Richard. "Of Inhuman Bondage." *The Washington Post Book World*, 29 January 1978, pp. 1, 4.
Rothman, David J. "Society and Its Prisons." *The New York Times Book Review*, 19 February 1978, pp. 1, 26–27.
Roustang, François. "La visibilité est un piège." *Les Temps Modernes* 356 (March 1976): 1567–79.
White, Hayden. Review. *American Historical Review* 82 (June 1977): 605–6.
Wright, Gordon. "Foucault in Prison." *Stanford French Review* 1 (Spring 1977): 71–78.
Zoila, Adolfo Fernandez. "La machine à fabriquer des délinquants." *La Quinzaine littéraire* 206 (16–31 March 1975): 3, 5.
Zysberg, A. "Michel Foucault: Surveiller et punir." *Annales* 31 (January–February 1976): 168–73.

The History of Sexuality, Volume I (1976)
Brincourt, André. "Le goulag du sexe." *Figaro Littéraire*, 15–16 January 1977, p. 17.
Burguière, André. Review. *Le Nouvel Observateur* 638 (31 January 1977): 65–66.

Droit, Roger-Pol. "Le pouvoir et le sexe." *Le Monde,* 16 February 1977, pp. 1, 18.

Feldman, Jacqueline. Review. *Cahiers Internationaux de Sociologie* 63 (July–December 1977): 370–73.

Harkness, James. "Rear-guard Mutterings about Michel Foucault." *The New Republic* 179 (25 November 1978): 3, 39.

Poirier, Richard. "The Powerful Secret." *The New York Times Book Review,* 14 January 1979, pp. 1, 28–29.

Robinson, Paul. Review. *The New Republic* 179 (28 October 1978): 29–32.

"Six volumes de Michel Foucault: Une histoire de la sexualité." *Le Monde,* 5 November 1976, p. 1.

Tenner, Edward. "A Valiant Attempt to Forge a Scholarship of Sexuality." *The Chronicle of Higher Education Review,* 8 January 1979, p. 10.

White, Hayden. "The Archaeology of Sex." *The Times Literary Supplement,* 6 May 1977, p. 565.

Zinner, Jacqueline. Review. *Telos* 36 (Summer 1978): 215–25.

Other Works Consulted

BOOKS

Alexander, Franz G., and Selesnick, Sheldon T. *The History of Psychiatry: An Evaluation of Psychiatric Thought and Practice From Prehistoric Times to the Present.* New York: Mentor Books, 1966.

Ardagh, John. *The New French Revolution.* New York: Harper Colophon Books, 1969.

Asimov, Isaac. *Asimov on Astronomy.* Garden City: Doubleday Anchor Books, 1975.

Bachelard, Gaston. *L'activité rationaliste de la physique contemporaine.* Paris: Presses Universitaires de France, 1951.

———. *L'expérience de l'espace dans la physique contemporaine.* Paris: Félix Alcan, 1937.

———. *Le Nouvel esprit scientifique.* Paris: Félix Alcan, 1934; 9th ed., 1966.

———. *La Philosophie du non: Essai d'une philosophie du nouvel esprit scientifique.* Paris: Presses Universitaires de France, 1940; 5th ed., 1970. Translated by G. C. Waterston as *The Philosophy of No: Philosophy of the New Scientific Mind.* New York: Orion Press, 1968.

———. *Le Rationalisme appliqué.* Paris: Presses Universitaires de France, 1949; 4th ed., 1970.

Barnett, Lincoln. *The Universe and Dr. Einstein.* Rev. ed. New York: Mentor Books, 1950.

Barthes, Roland. *Critical Essays.* Translated by Richard Howard. Evanston:

Northwestern University Press, 1972.

———. *Elements of Semiology; Writing Degree Zero.* Translated by Annette Lavers and Colin Smith. Boston: Beacon Press, 1967.

Beck, Lewis White. *Early German Philosophy: Kant and His Predecessors.* Cambridge: Harvard University Press, 1969.

Bernal, J. D. *The Natural Sciences in Our Time.* Vol. 3 of *Science in History.* Cambridge: MIT Press, 1969.

Bersani, Jacques; Autrand, Michel; Lecarme, Jacques; and Vercier, Bruno. *La Littérature en France depuis 1945.* Paris: Bordas, 1970.

Binswanger, Ludwig. *Being-in-the-World: Selected Papers of Ludwig Binswanger.* Translated, with a critical introduction to his existential psychoanalysis, by Jacob Needleman. New York: Basic Books, 1963.

Bohr, Niels. *Atomic Physics and Human Knowledge.* New York: John Wiley and Sons, 1958.

Bréhier, Émile. *Contemporary Philosophy—since 1850* (1932). Translated by Wade Baskin. Vol. 7 of *The History of Philosophy.* Chicago: University of Chicago Press, 1969.

Burtt, Edwin Arthur. *The Metaphysical Foundations of Modern Physical Science.* 2d rev. ed. New York: Doubleday Anchor Books, 1954.

Calder, Nigel. *The Key to the Universe: A Report on the New Physics.* New York: Viking Press, 1977.

Camus, Albert. *The Rebel: An Essay on Man in Revolt.* Translated by Anthony Bower. New York: Vintage Books, 1956.

Canguilhem, Georges. *La connaissance de la vie.* 5th ed. Paris: J. Vrin, 1975.

———. *Essai sur quelque problèmes concernant le normal et le pathologique.* Clermont-Ferrand: Publications de la Faculté des Lettres de l'Université de Strasbourg, 1943. Later reissued as *Le Normal et le pathologique.* Paris: Presses Universitaires de France, 1966. Translated by C. R. Fawcett as *On the Normal and the Pathological,* with an introduction by Michel Foucault. Boston: D. Reidel, 1978.

———. *Etudes d'histoire et de philosophie des sciences.* Paris: J. Vrin, 1968.

———. *Idéologie et rationalité dans l'histoire des sciences de la vie.* Paris: Librairie Philosophique, 1977.

Cassirer, Ernst. *The Problem of Knowledge: Philosophy, Science, and History since Hegel.* Translated by W. H. Woglom and C. W. Hendel. New Haven: Yale University Press, 1950.

———. *Substance and Function and Einstein's Theory of Relativity.* Translated by W. C. Swabey and M. C. Swabey. New York: Dover, [1953].

Charbonnier, Georges, ed. *Conversations with Claude Lévi-Strauss.* Translated by John and Doreen Weightman. London: Jonathan Cape, 1969.

Chiari, Joseph. *Twentieth-Century French Thought from Bergson to Lévi-Strauss.* New York: Gordian Press, 1975.

Cohn-Bendit, Daniel, and Cohn-Bendit, Gabriel. *Obsolete Communism: The*

Left-Wing Alternative. Translated by Arnold Pomerans. New York: McGraw-Hill, 1968.

Cohn-Bendit, Daniel, et al. *The French Student Revolt: The Leaders Speak.* Edited by Hervé Bourges. Translated by B. R. Brewster. New York: Hill and Wang, 1968.

Cooper, Leon. *An Introduction to the Meaning and Structure of Physics.* New York: Harper and Row, 1968.

Crémant, Roger. *Les Matinées structuralistes.* Paris: Robert Laffont, 1969.

Culler, Jonathan D. *Structuralist Poetics: Structuralism, Linguistics and the Study of Literature.* Ithaca: Cornell University Press, 1975.

Dampier, William Cecil. *A History of Science and Its Relation with Philosophy and Religion.* 4th ed. Cambridge: Cambridge University Press, 1966.

Einstein, Albert, and Infeld, Leopold. *The Evolution of Physics: From Early Concepts to Relativity and Quanta.* New York: Simon and Schuster, 1938.

Ehrmann, Jacques, ed. *Structuralism.* Garden City: Doubleday Anchor Books, 1970.

Escher, Maurits Cornelis. *The World of M. C. Escher.* Edited by J. L. Locher. New York: Abrams, 1971.

Ford, Kenneth W. *The World of Elementary Particles.* Waltham, Mass.: Xerox College Publishing, 1963.

Fowlie, Wallace. *The French Critic, 1549–1967.* Carbondale and Edwardsville: Southern Illinois University Press, 1968.

Gamow, George. *The Creation of the Universe.* New York: Mentor Books, 1952.

———. *Thirty Years that Shook Physics: The Story of Quantum Theory.* Garden City: Doubleday Anchor Books, 1966.

Gardner, Howard. *The Quest for Mind: Piaget, Lévi-Strauss, and the Structuralist Movement.* New York: Knopf, 1973.

Garvin, Harry R., ed. *Phenomenology, Structuralism, Semiology.* Lewisburg: Bucknell University Press, 1976.

Gillispie, Charles Coulson. *The Edge of Objectivity: An Essay in the History of Scientific Ideas.* Princeton: Princeton University Press, 1960.

Hacking, Ian. *Why Does Language Matter to Philosophy?* Cambridge: Cambridge University Press, 1975.

Hanson, Norwood Russell. *Pattern of Discovery: An Inquiry into the Conceptual Foundations of Science.* Cambridge: Cambridge University Press, 1958.

———. *Perception and Discovery: An Introduction to Scientific Inquiry.* San Francisco: Freeman, Cooper and Company, 1969.

Hayes, E. Nelson, and Hayes, Tanya, eds. *Claude Lévi-Strauss: The Anthropologist as Hero.* Cambridge: MIT Press, 1970.

Heisenberg, Werner. *Across the Frontiers.* Translated by Peter Heath. New York: Harper Torchbooks, 1974.

270 *Bibliography*

————. *Physics and Beyond: Encounters and Conversations.* Translated by Arnold Pomerans. New York: Harper Torchbooks, 1971.

————. *Physics and Philosophy: The Revolution in Modern Science.* New York: Harper and Row, 1958.

Hesse, Mary B. *Forces and Fields: The Concept of Action at a Distance in the History of Physics.* Totowa, N.J.: Littlefield, Adams and Co., 1965.

Hoffmann, Stanley. *Decline or Renewal? France since the 1930s.* New York: Viking Press, 1974.

Hoyle, Fred. *Frontiers of Astronomy.* New York: Harper and Row, 1955.

Hughes, H. Stuart. *An Approach to Peace and Other Essays.* New York: Atheneum, 1962.

————. *The Obstructed Path: French Social Thought in the Years of Desperation, 1930–1960.* New York: Harper Torchbooks, 1969.

Jameson, Frederic. *The Prison-House of Language: A Critical Account of Structuralism and Russian Formalism.* Princeton: Princeton University Press, 1972.

Jastrow, Robert, and Thompson, Malcolm H. *Astronomy: Fundamentals and Frontiers.* 2d ed. New York: John Wiley and Sons, 1974.

Jones, W. T. *A History of Western Philosophy.* Vol. 4, *Kant to Wittgenstein and Sartre.* 2d ed. New York: Harcourt, Brace and World, 1969.

Kaufmann, William J., III. *Relativity and Cosmology.* New York: Harper and Row, 1973.

Köhler, Wolfgang. *The Task of Gestalt Psychology.* Princeton: Princeton University Press, 1969.

Koyré, Alexandre. *From the Closed World to the Infinite Universe.* New York: Harper Torchbooks, 1958.

Kuhn, Thomas S. *The Structure of Scientific Revolutions.* 2d ed., enlarged. Chicago: University of Chicago Press, 1970.

Laing, R. D. *The Divided Self: An Existential Study in Sanity and Madness.* Baltimore: Penguin Books, 1965.

Lane, Michael, ed. *Introduction to Structuralism.* New York: Basic Books, 1970.

Lecourt, Dominique. *Pour une critique de l'épistémologie (Bachelard, Canguilhem, Foucault).* Paris: Maspero, 1972. Translated by Ben Brewster as *Marxism and Epistemology: Bachelard, Canguilhem, Foucault.* London: New Left Books and Atlantic Highlands, N.J.: Humanities Press, 1975.

LeSage, Laurent. *The New French Criticism: An Introduction and a Sampler.* University Park: Pennsylvania State University Press, 1967.

Lévi-Strauss, Claude. *The Elementary Structures of Kinship.* Translated by J. H. Bell, J. R. von Sturmer, and Rodney Needham. Rev. ed. Boston: Beacon Press, 1969.

————. *The Savage Mind.* [No translator given]. Chicago: University of Chicago Press, 1966.

————. *Structural Anthropology.* Translated by Claire Jacobson and B. G.

Schoepf. Garden City: Doubleday Anchor Books, 1963.
———. *Totemism*. Translated by Rodney Needham. Boston: Beacon Press, 1963.
———. *Tristes Tropiques*. Translated by John and Doreen Weightman. New York: Atheneum, 1974.
Lewin, Kurt. *Field Theory in Social Science: Selected Theoretical Papers*. Edited by Darwin Cartwright. New York: Harper and Brothers, 1951.
Lyons, John. *Noam Chomsky*. New York: Viking Press, 1970.
Macksey, Richard, and Donato, Eugenio, eds. *The Structuralist Controversy: The Languages of Criticism and the Sciences of Man*. Baltimore: Johns Hopkins University Press, 1972.
McLuhan, Marshall. *The Gutenberg Galaxy: The Making of Typographic Man*. New York: Signet Books, 1962.
———. *Understanding Media: The Extension of Man*. New York: McGraw-Hill, 1964.
Man, Paul de. *Blindness and Insight: Essays in the Rhetoric of Contemporary Criticism*. New York: Oxford University Press, 1971.
Mannheim, Karl. *Ideology and Utopia: An Introduction to the Sociology of Knowledge*. Translated by Louis Wirth and Edward Shils. Rev. ed. New York: Harcourt, Brace and World, 1936.
Margolin, Jean-Claude. *Bachelard*. Paris: Editions du Seuil, 1974.
Mason, Stephen F. *A History of the Sciences*. New rev. ed. New York: Collier Books, 1962.
Mauriac, Claude. *Les espaces imaginaires*. Paris: Bernard Grasset, 1975.
Merleau-Ponty, Jacques, and Morando, Bruno. *The Rebirth of Cosmology* (1971). Translated by Helen Weaver. New York: Knopf, 1976.
Munitz, Milton, ed. *Theories of the Universe from Babylonian Myth to Modern Science*. New York: Free Press, 1957.
Nietzsche, Friedrich. *The Birth of Tragedy and The Genealogy of Morals*. Translated by Francis Golffing. New York: Doubleday Anchor Books, 1956.
———. *The Portable Nietzsche*. Selected, translated, with an introduction, prefaces, and notes, by Walter Kaufmann. New York: Viking Press, 1968.
———. *The Use and Abuse of History*. Translated by Adrian Collins. Indianapolis: Bobbs-Merrill, 1957.
Piaget, Jean. *The Place of the Sciences of Man in the System of Sciences*. New York: Harper Torchbooks, 1974.
———. *Structuralism*. Translated and edited by Chaninah Maschler. New York: Harper Torchbooks, 1970.
Polanyi, Michael. *Science, Faith and Society*. Chicago: University of Chicago Press, 1964.
Poster, Mark. *Existential Marxism in Postwar France: From Sartre to Althusser*. Princeton: Princeton University Press, 1975.

Rieff, Philip, ed. *On Intellectuals: Theoretical Studies and Case Studies.* New York: Doubleday Anchor Books, 1970.

Riegel, Klaus F., and Rosenwald, George C., eds. *Structure and Transformation: Developmental and Historical Aspects.* New York: John Wiley and Sons, 1975.

Robey, David, ed. *Structuralism: An Introduction.* Wolfson College Lectures, 1972. Oxford: Clarendon Press, 1973.

Roussel, Raymond. *Comment j'ai écrit certains de mes livres.* 1935. Reprint. Paris: J. J. Pauvert, 1963.

Russell, Bertrand. *The ABC of Relativity.* Edited by Felix Pirani. 3d rev. ed. New York: Mentor Books, 1969.

Said, Edward W. *Beginnings: Intention and Method.* New York: Basic Books, 1975.

Saussure, Ferdinand de. *Course in General Linguistics.* Edited by Charles Bally and Albert Sechehaye, in collaboration with Albert Riedlinger. Translated by Wade Baskin. New York: McGraw-Hill, 1959.

Schrödinger, Erwin. *My View of the World* (1961). Translated by Cecily Hastings. Cambridge: Cambridge University Press, 1964.

Seligman, Ben, ed. *Molders of Modern Thought.* Chicago: Quadrangle Books, 1970.

Simon, John K., ed. *Modern French Criticism: From Proust and Valéry to Structuralism.* Chicago: University of Chicago Press, 1972.

Smith, Colin. *Contemporary French Philosophy: A Study in Norms and Values.* New York: Barnes and Noble, 1964.

Spitzer, Leo. *Linguistics and Literary History: Essays in Stylistics.* Princeton: Princeton University Press, 1948.

Stoianovich, Traian. *French Historical Method: The "Annales" Paradigm.* Foreword by Fernand Braudel. Ithaca: Cornell University Press, 1976.

Suppe, Frederick, ed. *The Structure of Scientific Theories.* Urbana: University of Illinois Press, 1974.

Szasz, Thomas S. *Ideology and Insanity: Essays on the Psychiatric Dehumanization of Man.* Garden City: Doubleday Anchor Books, 1970.

Therrien, Vincent. *La Révolution de Gaston Bachelard en critique littéraire: Ses fondements, ses techniques, sa portée.* Paris: Editions Klincksieck, 1970.

Wald, Robert M. *Space, Time and Gravity: The Theory of the Big Bang and Black Holes.* Chicago: University of Chicago Press, 1977.

White, Hayden. *Metahistory: The Historical Imagination in Nineteenth-Century Europe.* Baltimore: Johns Hopkins University Press, 1973.

Whitehead, Alfred North. *Science and Philosophy.* New York: The Wisdom Library, 1948.

Wiener, Philip P., ed. *Readings in Philosophy of Science: Introduction to the Foundations and Cultural Aspects of the Sciences.* New York: Charles Scribner's Sons, 1953.

ARTICLES AND SELECTIONS

Abel, Lionel. "Jacques Derrida: His *'Difference'* with Metaphysics." *Salmagundi* 25 (Winter 1974): 3–21.
Agassi, Joseph. "Sociologism in Philosophy of Science." *Metaphilosophy* 3 (April 1972): 103–22.
Ariès, Philippe; Certeau, Michel de; Le Goff, Jacques; Le Roy Ladurie, Emmanuel; and Veyne, Paul. "L'Histoire, une passion nouvelle: Table ronde." *Magazine Littéraire* 123 (April 1977): 10–23.
Barthes, Roland. "Objective Literature: Alain Robbe-Grillet." Introduction to *Two Novels by Robbe-Grillet: Jealousy and In the Labyrinth*, by Alain Robbe-Grillet. Translated by Richard Howard. New York: Grove Press, 1965.
Benoist, Jean-Marie. "The End of Structuralism." *20th Century Studies* 3 (May 1970): 31–54.
Bersani, Leo. "From Bachelard to Barthes." *Partisan Review* 34 (Spring 1967): 215–32.
Bertalanffy, Ludwig von. "Chance or Law." In *Beyond Reductionism: New Perspectives in the Life Sciences. The Alpbach Symposium 1968*, pp. 56–76. Edited by Arthur Koestler and J. R. Smythies. Boston: Beacon Press, 1969.
———. "The Quest for Systems Philosophy." *Metaphilosophy* 3 (April 1972): 142–45.
Bleich, David. "The Subjective Paradigm in Science, Psychology and Criticism." *New Literary History* 3 (Winter 1976): 313–34.
Brochier, Jean-Jacques. "L'événement et l'historien du présent." Interview with Pierre Nora. *Magazine Littéraire* 123 (April 1977): 34–37.
Canguilhem, Georges. "De la science et de la contre-science." In *Hommage à Jean Hyppolite*, by Suzanne Bachelard et al., pp. 173–80. Paris: Presses Universitaires de France, 1971.
———. "The Role of Analogies and Models in Biological Discovery." In *Scientific Change: Historical Studies in the Intellectual, Social and Technical Conditions for Scientific Discovery and Technical Invention, from Antiquity to the Present*, edited by A. C. Crombie, pp. 507–20. New York: Basic Books, 1963.
Caws, Mary Ann. "*Tel Quel*: Text and Revolution." *Diacritics* 3 (Spring 1973): 2–8.
Caws, Peter. "The Recent Literature of Structuralism, 1965–1970." *Philosophische Rundschau* 18 (1971): 63–78.
———. "What is Structuralism?" *Partisan Review* 35 (Winter 1968): 75–91.
Culler, Jonathan. "Literary History, Allegory, and Semiology." *New Literary History* 7 (Winter 1976): 259–70.

Domenach, J.-M. "Le système et la personne." *Esprit* 360 (May 1967): 771–79.

Donato, Eugenio. "Structuralism: The Aftermath." *Sub-Stance* 7 (Fall 1973): 9–26.

Dufrenne, Mikel. "La philosophie du néo-positivisme." *Esprit* 360 (May 1967): 781–800.

Einstein, Albert. "Considerations on the Universe as a Whole." In *The Theories of the Universe from Babylonian Myth to Modern Science*, edited by Milton Munitz, pp. 275–79. New York: Free Press, 1957.

Feyerabend, Paul K. "Niels Bohr's Interpretation of the Quantum Theory." In *Current Issues in the Philosophy of Science: Proceedings of Section L of the American Association for the Advancement of Science, 1959*, pp. 371–90. Edited by Herbert Feigl and Grover Maxwell. New York: Holt, Rinehart and Winston, 1961.

Freedman, Daniel Z., and Nieuwenhuizen, Peter van. "Supergravity and the Unification of the Laws of Physics." *Scientific American* 238 (February 1978): 126–43.

Funt, David Paul. "The Structuralist Debate." *The Hudson Review* 22 (Winter 1969–70): 623–46.

Furet, François. "Les intellectuels français et le structuralisme." *Preuves* 192 (February 1967): 3–12.

Gillet-Stern, Suzanne. "French Philosophy over the Last Decade." *Journal of the British Society for Phenomenology* 3 (January 1972): 3–10.

Gullón, Ricardo. "On Space in the Novel." *Critical Inquiry* 2 (Autumn 1975): 11–28.

Gutting, Gary. "Conceptual Structures and Scientific Change." *Studies in History and Philosophy of Science* 4 (November 1973): 209–30.

Heckman, John. "Hyppolite and the Hegel Revival in France." *Telos* 16 (Summer 1973): 128–45.

Hoyle, Fred. "Continuous Creation and the Expanding Universe." In *The Theories of the Universe from Babylonian Myth to Modern Science*, edited by Milton Munitz, pp. 419–29. New York: Free Press, 1957.

Kravetz, Marc. "Qu'est-ce que le G. I. P.?" *Magazine Littéraire* 101 (June 1975): 13.

Kuhn, Thomas S. "Science: The History of Science." In *International Encyclopedia of the Social Sciences*, 14:74–83. Edited by David L. Sills. New York: Collier and MacMillan, 1968.

―――. "Second Thoughts on Paradigms." In *The Structure of Scientific Theories*, edited by Frederick Suppe, pp. 459–99. Urbana: University of Illinois Press, 1974.

Kuzminski, Adrian. "The Paradox of Historical Knowledge." *History and Theory* 12 (1973): 269–89.

Laszlo, Ervin. "The Case for Systems Philosophy." *Metaphilosophy* 3 (April 1972): 123–41.

————. "Systems and Structures—Toward Bio-Social Anthropology." *Theory and Decision* 2 (December 1971): 174–92.

Lévi-Strauss, Claude. "Structuralism and Ecology." *Barnard Alumnae* (Spring 1972): 6–14.

Lewis, Philip. "Language and French Critical Debate." *Yale French Studies* 45 (1970): 154–65.

Locher, J. L. "Structural Sensation." In *The World of M. C. Escher*, edited by J. L. Locher, pp. 41–48. New York: Abrams, 1971.

Mouloud, Noël. "La méthode des sciences de structures et les problèmes de la connaissance rationnelle." *La Pensée* 135 (September–October 1967): 3–18.

Murphy, Gardner. "Gestalt and Field Theory." In *Readings in Philosophy of Science: Introduction to the Foundations and Cultural Aspects of the Sciences*, edited by Philip P. Wiener, pp. 207–19. New York: Charles Scribner's Sons, 1953.

Piaget, Jean. "The Child and Modern Physics." *Scientific American* 196 (March 1957): 46–51.

Pingaud, Bernard. Introduction to entire issue of *L'Arc* entitled "Sartre aujourd'hui." *L'Arc* 30 (1966): 1–4.

————. "Où va *Tel Quel?*" *La Quinzaine littéraire* 42 (1–15 January 1968): 8–9.

Poole, Roger. "Structures and Materials." *20th Century Studies* 3 (May 1970): 6–30.

Poster, Mark. "The Hegel Renaissance." *Telos* 16 (Summer 1973): 109–27.

"Problèmes du structuralisme." Issue of *Les Temps Modernes* 246 (November 1966).

Putnam, Hilary. "A Philosopher looks at Quantum Mechanics." In *Beyond the Edge of Certainty: Essays in Contemporary Science and Philosophy*, edited by Robert G. Colodny, pp. 75–101. Englewood Cliffs, N.J.: Prentice-Hall, 1965.

Roy, James G., Jr. *Pierre Boulez*. New York: Broadcast Music, 1973.

Sachs, Mendel. "On the Mach Principle and General Relativity." *British Journal for the Philosophy of Science* 26 (March 1975): 49–51.

Salmon, J. H. M. Review of *Ecrits sur l'histoire*, by Fernand Braudel. *History and Theory* 10 (1971): 347–55.

Sartre, Jean-Paul. "Replies to Structuralism." Translated by Robert D'Amico. *Telos* 6 (Fall 1971): 110–16.

————. "Sartre répond." Interviewed by Bernard Pingaud. *La Quinzaine littéraire* 14 (15–31 October 1966): 4–5.

Schwitters, Roy F. "Fundamental Particles with Charm." *Scientific American* 237 (October 1977): 56–70.

Siegel, Martin. "Henri Berr's *Revue de synthèse historique*." *History and Theory* 9 (1970): 322–34.

Skinner, Quentin. "Hermeneutics and the Role of History." *New Literary*

History 7 (Autumn 1975): 209–32.

Starobinski, Jean. "The Meaning of Literary History." *New Literary History* 7 (Autumn 1975): 83–88.

Steinmann, Martin, Jr. "Cumulation, Revolution, and Progress." *New Literary History* 5 (Spring 1974): 477–90.

Stoianovich, Traian. "Theoretical Implications of Braudel's *Civilisation matérielle.*" *Journal of Modern History* 41 (1969): 68–81.

Teuber, Marianne L. "Sources of Ambiguity in the Prints of Maurits C. Escher." *Scientific American* 231 (July 1974): 90–104.

Treiman, S. B. "The Weak Interactions." *Scientific American* 200 (March 1959): 72–84.

Weimann, Robert. "French Structuralism and Literary History: Some Critiques and Reconsiderations." Translated by M. Goldberg and J. Zipes. *New Literary History* 4 (Spring 1973): 437–69.

White, Hayden. "The Absurdist Moment in Contemporary Literary Theory." *Contemporary Literature* 17 (Summer 1976): 378–403.

INDEX